DANGERS OF DETERRENCE

PHILOSOPHERS ON NUCLEAR STRATEGY

Edited by

Nigel Blake and *Kay Pole*

Routledge & Kegan Paul

London, Boston, Melbourne and Henley

First published in 1983
by Routledge & Kegan Paul plc
39 Store Street, London WC1E 7DD, England
9 Park Street, Boston, Mass. 02108, USA
464 St Kilda Road, Melbourne,
Victoria 3004, Australia and
Broadway House, Newtown Road,
Henley-on-Thames, Oxon RG9 1EN, England
Set in Press Roman by Columns, Reading
Printed in Great Britain by
T.J. Press, Padstow
© Routledge & Kegan Paul 1983

Library of Congress Cataloging in Publication Data

Dangers of deterrence.
Includes bibliographical references and index.
1. Deterrence Strategy – Addresses, essays, lectures.
2. Atomic warfare – Addresses, essays, lectures.
I. Blake, Nigel. II. Pole, Kay.
U162.6.D36   1983   355'.0217   83-13857

ISBN 0-7100-9885-5

Contents

Acknowledgments   vi

Notes on Contributors   vii

Introduction: A Sceptical Look at the Nuclear Debate   1
Nigel Blake and *Kay Pole*

Deterrence, Provocation and the Martian Temperament   19
Mary Midgley

Unilateralism: A Clausewitzian Reform?   41
Ken Booth

Nuclear Blackmail   84
Jeff McMahan

Proliferation and the Nature of Deterrence   112
Barrie Paskins

Games Theory and the Nuclear Arms Race   132
Nicholas Measor

Three Main Fallacies in Discussions of Nuclear Weapons   157
W.B. Gallie

Index   179

Acknowledgments

Many people, apart from ourselves and our families, have lived with this project for a long time, advising, encouraging and sustaining us. Chiefly, of course, we thank our contributors, whose work it is. They have borne our tight deadlines, heavy editorial requests and administrative efforts with generosity and responded to them with care. We thank, too, those other philosophers whom we approached in November 1981 and who, by their '100 per cent support but haven't the time' messages, underlined our own belief that an anthology such as this was a necessary addition to the debate on disarmament.

At the more practical level, we relied on the speed and efficiency of our secretary, Margie Talbot, as well as on that of the anonymous secretaries of our contributors. The Institute in which we work was generous to us with its research time, not to mention with the rather more mundane facilities such as photocopying. Other parts of the Open University, notably members of the course team preparing 'Conflict and Security in the Nuclear Age', have, by their interest and involvement in the same area of concern, been of immense help. We'd like to thank particularly Roger Harrison and Janet Radcliffe Richards in this respect.

For their timely comments and general support, often through difficult periods, we are also indebted to Peter Wright and Greg McLennan of the Open University and to Bob McGowan of the University of Leicester. Lastly, we too have an editor whom we'd like to thank — Stratford Caldecott of Routledge & Kegan Paul was unfailingly patient and we much appreciated his understanding and practical help.

Notes on Contributors

Ken Booth is Senior Lecturer, Department of International Politics, University College of Wales, Aberystwyth. In 1977 he was Scholar-in-Residence at the U.S. Naval War College, and from 1979 to 1981 was Senior Research Fellow in the Centre for Foreign Policy Studies, Dalhousie University, Canada. He is a member of the International Institute for Strategic Studies and the Royal United Service Institute for Defence Studies. Among his books are *Contemporary Strategy: Theories and Policies* (co-author), *Navies and Foreign Policy*, *American Thinking about Peace and War* (co-editor), and *Strategy and Ethnocentrism.*

W.B. Gallie is Emeritus Professor of Political Science at the University of Cambridge. His publications include *Pierce and Pragmatism* (1952), *Philosophy and the Historical Understanding* (1964) and *Philosophers of Peace and War* (1978).

Jeff McMahan is Research Fellow in Moral Philosophy at St John's College, Cambridge, and the author of *British Nuclear Weapons: For and Against* (1981). He has contributed articles to *Ethics, The Bulletin of the Atomic Scientists*, and the *London Review of Books*. He is a member of CND.

Nicholas Measor teaches Philosophy at the University of Leicester, having previously held posts at the Universities of Keele and Oxford. Although he has been engaged for some years in the teaching and study of 'Practical Ethics' this is his first published contribution to the nuclear weapons debate.

Mary Midgley was formerly Senior Lecturer in Philosophy at the

Notes on Contributors

University of Newcastle on Tyne. She is the author of *Beast and Man* (1978) and *Heart and Mind* (1981), and co-author with Judith Hughes of *Women's Choices, The Philosophical Problems of Feminism* (1983).

Barrie Paskins is Lecturer in War Studies at King's College London. His publications include *The Ethics of War* (with M.L. Dockrill, 1979) and several articles on deterrence. He is one of the authors of the Church of England report *The Church and the Bomb* (1982).

Nigel Blake is Research Fellow in the Institute of Educational Technology at the Open University. He is a philosopher by training and specializes in philosophy of education. **Kay Pole** is Lecturer in the same institute; her background is in psychology and she works with course teams in philosophy, as well as social sciences and education. Both are members of CND.

Introduction: A Sceptical Look at the Nuclear Debate

Nigel Blake and *Kay Pole*

It cannot be denied that the concept of nuclear deterrence abounds in illogicalities and paradoxes. At the heart of the problem is the dilemma that if one wishes to deter war by the fear that nuclear weapons will be used, one has to appear to be prepared to use them in certain circumstances. But if one does so and the enemy answers back, as he has the capability to do and has clearly said he would, one is very much worse off than if one had not done so, if indeed one is there at all. To pose an unacceptable risk to the enemy automatically poses the same risk to oneself. But to attempt to reduce the risk in order to make the threat more credible — through some form of limited nuclear war, territorially, or by types of target or means of delivery — begins to make that risk more acceptable and therefore less of a deterrent. The more acceptable nuclear war may appear to be to the governments and military men of the nuclear powers, the more likely it is that it will actually come about and, even if it is limited in some way, the effects on those who live in the countries, in or over which the nuclear weapons of both sides are exploded, will be catastrophic. To call the results defence or security is to make a mockery of the terms.

Field Marshal Lord Carver, *A Policy for Peace*[1]

I

Soldiers and philosophers share at least one deep-seated attitude, a loathing of confusion in the face of serious challenges. The contributors to this book share with Lord Carver a concern about radical confusions, precisely where they are most dangerous; our arrangements for

1

collective security.

In the passage quoted above, Lord Carver shows one major reason why philosophers should contribute to the nuclear debate, no less than scientists, strategists or politicians. Deterrence theory carries a heavy burden of illogicality, paradox and dilemma, and these are kinds of confusion that philosophers are used to studying. They present different kinds of problems from those that scientists and social scientists usually deal with, such as difficulties about the likely physical effects of the use of particular weapons or the military, political or economic consequences of their use. Such problems are solved by experiment or extrapolation from established scientific knowledge. Paradoxes, dilemmas and the rest are solved rather by careful analyses of concepts and of the arguments in which they're used; and these are philosophical activities, whether or not it's a philosopher who does them.

There are other reasons too why philosophical work is needed. Deterrence theory is concerned with the actions and reactions of supposedly rational people. Philosophers spend much of their time analysing the concept of rationality and have pertinent criticisms to make of the way in which it is treated in deterrence theory. Secondly, deterrence in practice involves careful interpretation of political situations, diplomatic signals, and deployments of weapons. The methodology of interpretation is in part a philosophical concern. Contributors to this volume argue that much current political interpretation is of a dangerously poor quality. Thirdly, national defence policy must be predicated on particular views of the West's real interests and the duties of allies to each other; questions about duties and real interests, and about what does or does not advance or fulfil them, are also philosophical questions.

Whatever kind of problem is being discussed, attention to the quality of argument is no less important than attention to facts. Intellectuals from many different backgrounds have done invaluable service unearthing falsehoods and inadequacies in official justifications of our deterrence policies — and in doing so, have exploded many bad and dangerous arguments. But in the areas just mentioned — resolution of paradoxes, analysis of rationality, political interpretation and discussion of duties and interests — unearthing new facts has little relevance. Deeper philosophical analysis is called for, and this has been noticeably lacking.

Of course, debate hasn't been wanting in these areas; on the contrary, dissension is frequent and vehement. But by ordinary intellectual

2

standards, the quality of public debate about issues in nuclear deterrence has been dangerously low. The philosophers contributing to this volume share a grave unease about this state of affairs. They also, however, share a particular opposition to current NATO policy in general, and to British nuclear policy in particular. Most, if not all, would call themselves unilateralists, and write partially out of sympathy — which is by no means blind sympathy — for that cause. Readers unsympathetic to that cause may remark that incoherence and irrationality are not unknown among unilateralists; and, of course, many philosophers oppose unilateralism. How, then, do we justify the commitment in this book to one particular side of the debate?

Both West and East are currently wedded to military doctrines which offer neither side any military protection from the other beyond attempts to deter attack. The destructive weight and power of the arsenals which are intended to service this purpose grow more fearsome every year, and the human cost of the failure of deterrence more grave. Yet the likelihood of continued success in keeping war at bay looks yearly more minute. The burden of justification surely lies with those who wish the two sides to continue in this way in default of multilateral disarmament, rather than with those who call for change. It is not enough to point to the allegedly dangerous consequences of unilaterally abandoning nuclear deterrence — such as political blackmail, conventional war, invasion, or even limited nuclear destruction — if they appear to so many people to be lesser evils than those which face us if nuclear deterrence fails. Anti-unilateralists have to show that unilateralism is more likely to lead to the same damage as the failure of deterrence, or equally likely to lead to worse. If neither can be shown, then moral considerations weigh decisively in favour of unilateralism.

The contributors to the present volume, however, argue a more urgent case against current policies than that they are morally defenceless. They contend that such policies — at the time of writing, those of the Thatcher government and the Reagan administration — are actually more likely to provoke war than a properly managed stance of unilateral nuclear disarmament in Western Europe. They further believe that the human, physical and indeed political costs of a war resulting from the present policies would vastly outweigh the cost of any war which might be fought if NATO were to adopt a non-nuclear stance in Europe. Those who place the political integrity of the West above any other human or economic cost and argue 'Better dead than

3

red', would do well to consider the arguments in this book; for if they are correct then unilateralism is also the best method for securing our political independence.

There are moral, political and prudential presumptions against the current policies. Sticking with them requires far more justification than abandoning them. Nevertheless, there are a number of objections which are believed by anti-unilateralists to hold against any form of unilateralism whatsoever. The task of this introduction is to address these sceptically and clear them away, so that the more detailed contributions may be better heard. First, there are a group of objections which allege that current policy is conservative and cautious, is grounded in proven expertise and is realistic; and that unilateralism is none of these things. We reject these claims.

Anti-unilateralists are prone to present unilateral nuclear disarmament as a leap into the dangerous unknown. Against this, it ought always to be remembered that no less a leap is involved in the new proposals for deterrence. The new 'deterrence' will not be just a new attempt at the same kind of strategic stance, but a radically new departure. At the concrete level, a NATO 'deterrence' policy built around the super-accurate Trident D5 and medium-range Euro-strategic missiles (such as the cruise Tomahawk (ground- and air-launched) and Pershing II) is *not* just a variant on one based on atomic shells, howitzers, depth-charges, Lance missiles, Pershing Ia and a few aged Polaris subs chugging around the North Sea.

NATO strategy has for years incorporated a risky threat to involve the Russian homeland in any war which might break out on a European battlefield, whether or not the Soviets have made strategic strikes on Western Europe. The installation of Euro-strategic missiles on land (cruise and Pershing II) and the introduction of Trident D5 into the British nuclear fleet exacerbate an already dangerous threat. It seems to signal a power and willingness to target at least a large number of Russian missile silos, and to move with unprecedented and possibly decisive speed to a level of attack just short of all-out strategic war. The essence of Soviet counter-deterrence measures is likely to be to ensure that once such a level of hostilities is reached, there will be no possibility of they themselves capitulating. They will ensure that they will have too much at stake. (It must be remembered that Russian military doctrine envisages situations in which it would be to Soviet advantage to engage in an all-out strategic nuclear war rather than to surrender.) Whether this will be clear to the Western leaders and whether they will in turn allow themselves to be deterred from the use of Euro-strategic weapons is highly questionable. Yet if they are not so deterred, the result could be unqualified catastrophe.

Those who claim this new departure to be safer than unilateral disarmament cannot make their case by appeal to the supposed success of the old deterrence, since the new 'deterrence' is different from the old in too many important respects. It is disingenuous to present it as essentially a conservative development.

Nonetheless, caution does seem to many people to enjoin an acceptance of much that is actually militarily radical. The myth of secrecy is potent here. Many people seem to find it impossible to entertain serious doubts about established defence policy. The supposition runs deep that the government and the defence establishment must possess both secret knowledge and special expertise, and that these render their judgments in some sense authoritative, while simultaneously creating the need for secrecy about the rationales of those judgments. If this were so, it would imply two damning criticisms of a book such as this. Firstly, any positive analysis and prescription would have to be seen as being grounded in ignorance and lack of understanding. Secondly, to show up the inadequacy of so much that is said in public defence of our deterrent policy could only have the effect of stimulating adverse criticism of the government concerning precisely those decisions where we least need it to be hindered.

These would be damning criticisms indeed. Obviously we reject them. Considerations of secrecy raise complex issues which we cannot go into at length, but briefly we are prepared to stand by the following points. Firstly, while much defence information is obviously and for good reason secret, the kind of information needed to assess the general validity of our deterrence policy is itself not secret. The gross technical characteristics of weapons are public knowledge by and large, if not all the details of their engineering. And in so far as our policies genuinely are deterrence policies, then they too have to be public rather than confidential. For a policy cannot be a deterrence policy unless one makes clear to the enemy himself just what retaliation will be visited on him for this, that or the other form of aggression. To imply darkly that something unspecified but dreadful would happen if he struck would not be a genuine deterrent. Most military confrontation involves some such threat. Merely to promise to fight back is to invite the enemy's suspicion that he could get away with it if he attacked.

Thus while the public certainly doesn't know everything about how the government actually implements its deterrence policy, it can learn all it needs to know to assess the policy itself. To the extent that strategic secrets were really important, to that extent our policy would not actually be one of deterrence but of nuclear war-fighting. That in itself would give strong grounds for valid public dissent. Thus any government which insists that its policies are indeed deterrence policies must allow that they are open to criticism from people outside government and defence circles.

The question of expertise is more straightforward. The implementation of a defence policy is not a purely strategic matter by any means. It also involves moral and political judgment. And it cannot be supposed in a democracy that either the government or the defence establishment have a monopoly of moral or political wisdom.

As well as claiming that their policies are cautiously conservative and grounded in governmental expertise, anti-unilateralists also allege that there is little to be hoped for from a nuclear disarmed world anyway, because nuclear weapons cannot be disinvented. Were hostilities to break out in a nuclear-disarmed world, there would almost immediately be, they claim, a race to reconstruct and use them or threaten to use them. Apologists for minimal deterrence draw the conclusion that there is little serious scope for anything more than minor redeployments of nuclear weapons and that a lowish level of nuclear deterrence is to be preferred to the instabilities of complete nuclear disarmament, whether this is to be achieved by unilateral or multilateral means. However rash and inexpert recent NATO policy may seem to have been, they will argue, what we really need is a good policy of minimal nuclear deterrence rather than total nuclear renunciation.

Perhaps a few sceptical comments can help loosen the grip of this idea. Firstly, while a move to minimal deterrence could well be safer than to continue with the situation we now have, or worse still that which presently awaits us, minimal deterrence would still be prey to instabilities that it would share with any form of nuclear deterrence at all. And if the risks of a low level of deterrence were real, it is not obvious that they would be less than the risks of complete nuclear disarmament, even if the latter were also real. And it is expecting a lot to suppose that a lowish level of deterrence could be kept low. Metaphorically, a gardener does not control a tenacious weed by allowing it to spread 'Thus far, no further', and hoping it won't put on a spurt of growth when the weather's fine. Rather, he roots it up whenever he can, even though he knows it will return. He hopes that eventually he will exhaust it before it overwhelms him. Similarly, a century of history during which the recrudescence of nuclear weapons was regularly put down might well eradicate hopes of their eventual usefulness; even if they were occasionally used on a small scale, as at Hiroshima. So the possible re-emergence of the bomb is no clear argument against disarmament.

Secondly, the 'realist' argument conflates invention and production. In a disarmed world, it may be impossible to forget how to produce these weapons but it would not be equally easy to produce them again, especially in the middle of an on-going war. (Remember the bombing of the Baghdad power station in the Iraq-Iranian war — a strike aimed precisely at pre-empting the production of such weapons.) Indeed one might reasonably assume that in a world where nuclear disarmament had been achieved, some degree of control of supplies and suppliers of radio-active materials would also be within the wit of man to devise.

Thirdly, it is not clear why the threat of the possibility of producing nuclear weapons should have much less or indeed any less secure a deterrent effect than actual possession of them.

Fourthly, while it must be admitted that one potential source of fear would be the possible covert peace-time development of such weapons, to say as much is only to point to long-recognized problems of policing. And to highlight a problem is not in any degree to show it to be insoluble. But attempts to work out credible solutions to the policing problems have not been widely canvassed.

A fifth point is widely overlooked. One could well point out, with a similar sense of world-weariness, that a moratorium on the development of further weapons is of little use since it would leave the technologists perfectly capable of developing later that which they have not yet developed already. Does it not then follow that the arms race can at best only be controlled in its course, rather than halted or reversed? To believe this, though, is to place enormous faith in arms control. It is to suppose that the superpowers can happily agree to control jointly precisely that race which is fuelled by their mutual mistrust. Yet to admit that this race is doomed never to die is to admit that adequate trust is the chimera of the idealist. It obliges us to accept the possibility that at any time one or even both superpowers might suddenly cut and run for superiority and dominance. (This is actually what many people believe the USA to be attempting to do right now. Nicholas Measor deals with the dangers of such situations in his contribution to this volume.) To propose this as less of a danger to the world than complete nuclear disarmament seems the very nadir of common sense.

Why does the intellectual inadequacy of such self-styled realism go unrecognized? We suspect that its subscribers commit two banal fallacies; firstly, that the idealistic cannot be realistic and secondly, that merely to oppose idealism is to guarantee one's own realism. It is mistakenly assumed that unilateralism is only an abstract, absolute and so idealistic moral stance, which one might admire but need not emulate since it's a counsel of saintliness. That it might be a source of sophisticated and realistic criticism of supposedly realistic policies seems not to occur to many people. And if unilateralists are taken to believe that nuclear weapons could be disinvented, the fact that this is impossible can be taken to discredit unilateralism.

But what is idealistic about unilateralism anyway? It must surely be obvious that its roots do not lie just in a fastidious concern for purity of soul. They lie in a vivid awareness of the ways in which nuclear deterrence is likely to fail. Reasons for expecting such failure are discussed by several of our contributors, but we may briefly mention two or three here.

Deterrence rests on three expectations; that the enemy will behave rationally, that the threat which daunts him now will continue to be the most daunting he could face, and that he will not find technical means by which he could counter-deter that threat. Now taking these in reverse order, there are reasons to believe that the USSR is actually finding ways to deter the launching of medium-range weapons at her from Western Europe. It is no mere political convenience which makes her keep her medium-range missiles in Soviet rather than Warsaw Pact territory, for it is this which signals her determination to retaliate at the highest level if those weapons are attacked.

Next, the arms race is arguably developing in a way that will eventually present the Soviets with a grave dilemma; to make an early preemptive strike at America or to wait for the Americans to strike first at them, or threaten to do so. Conservative Party contempt for fears about first-strike possibilities rests mainly on the assurance that the stationing of cruise and the installation of Trident will not amount to making a credible first-strike threat. Perhaps not; but further developments, possible and in some cases already planned and not necessarily involving Europe primarily (such as deployment of the MX missile), give no warrant for continuing complacency. If a first-strike threat is not yet imminent, neither is it in the indefinite and unpredictable future.

Thirdly, the NATO strategic stance of flexible response creates a situation of great uncertainty for both sides regarding the probable reactions of the other side. The Soviets could fail to take the most rational course of action, not out of an hysterical reaction to events but from sheer intellectual confusion. Barrie Paskins, in this book, points out that it would be irrational to embark on even a small-scale nuclear exchange if escalation were at all possible; but it might none the less seem easier to do so under those unclear circumstances than if escalation were quite certain. It is possible that taking a desperate chance could at some time look like a lesser evil than inaction to a leader of a nuclear power.

We leave it to our contributors to argue in more detail the instability of nuclear deterrence. Here we would only point out that there is no clear ideological concomitant to the view that deterrence is indeed unstable. There is no reason why a Liberal, a Social Democrat, nor yet a Conservative should be unimpressed by it. Further, if unilateralism were to be shown to be the best available means of increasing stability, then it is difficult to see what ideological claims any political party could oppose to it.

For reasons such as these we have included in this volume one article that is not by a philosopher, but by a strategic specialist, Ken Booth. Booth's is a form of unilateralism with which we the editors, and many of our contributors, are in sympathy – though of course Booth cannot be said to represent any kind of party line for us. Here he demonstrates the development of unilateralist arguments from hard-headed political and military considerations, and shows that unilateralism is not a doctrine for moral idealists alone.

Those who oppose unilateralism often make the important charge that unilateralism actually plays into Soviet hands, even if unintentionally – that a unilateralist Britain and a nuclear-disarmed Europe are precisely what the Russians want, and therefore that it would be folly to let them have things their own way.

But how might it be true to say that unilateralism plays into Soviet hands in a way that's genuinely dangerous to the West? It is, first of all, absurd to deny the Soviets *everything* they want if much of that is wanted by ourselves as well. It is difficult to suppose that the Soviet people are not bothered about whether they live on an inhabitable planet, would not be bothered at all if they lost a few million citizens again, are not bothered about whether their European satellites collapse into a state of post-nuclear chaos and so on. Surely the one thing they want is peace, even if for the furtherance of their own political ends. If it is to be taken seriously at all, the charge has to be that unilateralism would create conditions in which the Soviets could gain significant advantages *at the expense of the West* in conditions short of nuclear war. Secondly, and more importantly, the charge carries the implication that there is no way at all in which the West could prevent the Soviets from gaining such advantages if Britain, or more broadly Europe, renounced nuclear weapons unilaterally. And thirdly, the expense to the West would have to be *severe*, severe, that is, compared with the minimum risk involved in continuing with nuclear deterrence. If any one of these three conditions is implausible, then the charge of playing into Soviet hands is morally weightless.

Thus it would be infantile to cling to nuclear deterrence just to deny the Soviets those advantages which were not to our own disadvantage, and equally childish to do so if less risky means were available to achieve the same object. Several of the papers in this book argue that it is indeed possible to contain the Soviets by non-nuclear means within Europe. As to the severity of the risk, even the minimum risk from continuing indefinitely with nuclear deterrence is very high. Most things in this life have a price, as Mrs Thatcher and Mr Reagan are particularly well aware. If the price of peace is really that there is some advantage to the USSR at the expense of the West, then it may well be morally correct to pay it. We repeat, however, that we do not believe that this is the price, anyway.

Unilateralism is a constantly travestied position in the current debate. A paradigmatic example of such misrepresentation falls to hand as we write — namely a speech by James Callaghan to the Cardiff Fabian Society in the autumn of 1982.[2] Callaghan represents unilateralism as resting on the twin beliefs, (a) that a unilaterally disarmed Britain would be safe from nuclear attack and (b) that the moral example of British unilateral disarmament would be the beginning of the end of the nuclear arms race. He adds, 'By definition, (unilateralists) have no concern for the utility of negotiation and they weaken the concept of collective security, which the Labour Party has always stood for.' Yet several of our contributors explicitly deny the plausibility of both beliefs, as do we, the editors, and nobody in this volume bases their case for unilateralism on either of them.

It is not inconsistent, for example, to establish good grounds for unilateral disarmament, while admitting that a Britain which has unilaterally disarmed would still be a nuclear target. Firstly, it is arguable that the mere nuclear disarmament of Britain would lessen the actual risk of war. Secondly, it is arguable that Britain in such a state would present fewer and less dangerous targets. This is particularly relevant now, in the debate about cruise. Cruise's potential dispersal across virtually the whole of central and southern England turns the entire area into a prime target for pattern-bombing. The prospects of any significant numbers of survivors in the area are minute. To renounce cruise is to lengthen the odds on survival for the English very significantly.

As to negotiation, it is not the case that every initiative, or even the most important, is necessarily a proper matter for multilateral bargaining. Pershing II missiles are a case in point. They will be able to reach the Soviet Union from West Germany and strike at counter-force targets in five to ten minutes. Whether or not this amounts to first-strike capability, it certainly has an enormous destabilizing effect. Being prepared to accept such weapons in order to tempt the Russians into bargaining away their SS20s seems a remarkably dangerous game. For if such negotiations prove to fail, NATO will have little political option but to deploy the Pershings; to do that, however, will be to invite massive pre-emptive strikes in wartime against the territory from which they are deployed. In the present state of urgency, arguably we cannot afford to do everything by negotiation.

However, none of this amounts to disregarding the utility of negotiation, as Callaghan alleges. On the contrary, unilateralists insist that governments should distinguish between appropriate and inappropriate matters for negotiation. For instance, British unilateralism could, and probably should, recommend that Britain stays inside NATO, where a unilateralist voice might be heard to best purpose. (To suppose that Britain's voice would count for nothing within NATO once we had unilaterally disarmed is to suppose that Britain can only have a voice if that voice lends support to the current policies. Yet a voice which is only heard when it supports one particular position is not an independent voice at all. If membership of NATO effectively involves a passive acquiescence in whatever policies NATO tends to favour, then it is of no benefit but rather a danger to be avoided.) Bargaining is becoming a mere fetish; it should instead be just one among several ways to improve Western security.

This point sends us back to more positive criticism of the kind of position Callaghan represents. In his speech he emphasized problems of international relations and failed to consider seriously any of the strategic issues. Like many, he fears that the US would react to British unilateral disarmament by turning its back on Europe, thus weakening NATO and making a Soviet attack much more likely. Yet he also recognizes that 'in some quarters' (he means those closest to the President), the new NATO developments are viewed as an excellent opportunity to destabilize the European balance. But if these developments are as dangerous as unilateralists claim, then it is doubtful whether the perils associated with a collapse of NATO would be any worse than those associated with continued membership of it.

In any case, to expect such a collapse is the worst of political defeatism. Are we really to believe that the US, courting as it does some of the most desperate regimes of South America, Asia and Africa, is really likely to withdraw its support from its major trading partners and ideological allies? Further, even if that were the case, must we also believe that the Americans are beyond persuasion? In particular, if a unilateralist strategic posture for Britain were to lessen the risks of war, as the contributors to this volume argue, would this be of no interest to the US? Must we believe that it does not matter to them either way whether there be a limited war in Europe, providing they are not directly involved?

If all of this really is the case, then one can be forgiven for doubting the value of NATO membership; while if it is not so, then Britain and America should be conducting a more serious strategic discussion, one which does not arbitrarily preclude British unilateralism. To give diplomatic solidarity a higher priority than strategic security, or even to make it its principal component seems to us totally irresponsible. To suggest that a move to greater strategic security can only disrupt diplomatic solidarity and thus become self-defeating, is to despair of one's allies and of ever being able to influence them.

II

The concept of deterrence itself is one which is rarely analysed in specific discussion of nuclear deterrence. There are good grounds for doing so however. Many people share a fear that current policy is as likely to provoke the Soviet Union as to deter it from attacking us. Mary Midgley argues in the first of our papers that such fears are to be treated seriously, rather than dismissed as merely the special pleading of the appeaser. For deterrence and provocation are related to each other in one fundamental respect. Both involve the making of threats. It is important therefore to try to distinguish carefully between those threats which will indeed succeed in deterring and those which will actually provoke. Much depends, Mrs Midgley argues, on the interpretation of the threat, and this in turn will be influenced by whether the threatened party recognizes that he shares aims and interests with the party who threatens him. If he has absolutely nothing in common with the party who makes the threat, then it is unclear why he should react to the threat in the manner which suits the threatener best.

Both the drift of international relations in recent years and the increasing emphasis on war-fighting in nuclear strategic thinking have tended to minimize those aims and interests which East and West share. In international diplomacy we seem to have forgotten recently that deterrence is only one of many forms of international relationship which contribute to the maintenance of peace and stability. Similarly, our strategic stance runs the risk of confusing deterrence with reform and retribution, both of which are as likely to provoke a proud and self-reliant nation as to deter it. If we are serious when we proclaim that our main aim is simply the practical aim of deterring war, then it is high time that we look to these issues to try to ensure that our policy is less provocative than at present, not more so.

If our aim is to maximize deterrence whilst minimizing provocation, it is still not obvious that we in Britain should take the step of unilateral nuclear disarmament. There is certainly no ground for suggesting that we should simply neglect our national defence altogether. None the less, simply to commit ourselves to a policy of national self-defence is not to commit ourselves to any strategy whatsoever which may be urged on us as a means to achieving that aim. In the second of our essays, Ken Booth reminds us of Clausewitz's criteria for good military strategy. Good strategy is rational, national and instrumental; it should be carefully calculated, in other words, to further national political aims. Ken Booth's objection to the British nuclear deterrent is that it contributes nothing to any such aims. It goes without saying that our first priority is to try to prevent war breaking out at all. But that cannot possibly be treated as our only goal. If deterrence fails us, then we have other and further needs. We need a strategic stance which allows us to try to defend our people from destruction. We also need methods of fighting which afford the chance of securing a meaningful end to a war – an end

13

which leaves us with at least some of our national interests safeguarded, rather than the end of total national destruction.

Booth argues that there are indeed strategic stances which would give us the chance of accomplishing these ends, and that these are conventional rather than nuclear. Such stances would not simply allow British unilateral nuclear disarmament, they would require it. There would of course be costs – in particular an increase in defence spending and the re-introduction of conscription to form reserve forces. Politically, Britain would have to maintain her commitment to NATO, whilst campaigning for the adoption of a totally conventional NATO strategy for the defence of Europe. (If Europe were to decide to shoulder such costs, she could hardly be accused by the Americans of negligence in her own defence.)

Booth defends his proposals against several major objections, dismissing as idle the hopes of those who urge trust in multilateral disarmament talks and arms control negotiations. These are not the routes to a saner strategic posture, and those who wait for them to bear fruit are merely prolonging our current danger. Of course unilateral nuclear disarmament is a risky prospect, but so too is our current strategic posture – every bit as dangerous. As to effectiveness, it would be no more sensible to try to defend ourselves from nuclear attack by actual use of nuclear weapons than by appropriate conventional means.

Perhaps the most compelling argument against proposals such as Booth's is that we need a nuclear deterrent to defend ourselves from nuclear blackmail. Booth touches on this argument in his paper, and Jeff McMahan develops the topic in detail.

One cannot seriously discuss whether nuclear weapons are necessary to a country which aims to deter nuclear blackmail until one has a clear notion of what nuclear blackmail really is. But there are significant difficulties of definition with regard to this term. Jeff McMahan distinguishes nuclear blackmail first from nuclear deterrence – for it has long been commonly agreed that the Soviets have as much right to deter us as we have to deter them. It is not Soviet nuclear deterrence that we need to defend ourselves against, then. McMahan also distinguishes nuclear blackmail from what he calls 'coercive nuclear threats'. These he defines as threats made by one party against another in order to coerce them either to take action they are arguably obliged to take or to prevent them from doing things they have no right to do. (Clearly this idea makes sense only if one has recognized and agreed standards of international morality in mind.) It is not clear whether any party has a right to seek to defend itself against coercive nuclear threats.

McMahan proposes that we define nuclear blackmail threats as those which coerce a state either to do things which it has no international obligation to do or to refrain from actions it is morally at liberty to do. Defined thus, it is completely implausible to suppose that a nuclear country would ever attempt to blackmail a non-nuclear country during peace-time. The only point in retaining a nuclear deterrent as far as nuclear blackmail is concerned is to protect the state against nuclear blackmail in wartime.

But this does not 'sew up' the case for retaining a nuclear deterrent. There are other methods for attempting to prevent nuclear blackmail, and McMahan considers these in detail. He does indeed come to the conclusion that retention of a nuclear deterrent is the surest way to deter such threats. None the less, that is still not the end of the argument, for with the greater effectiveness of the deterrent go greater dangers too — dangers of deterrence sufficiently great to count against retention of the nuclear deterrent. The case against the deterrent is yet stronger if one considers the scale of sheer confusion which we can expect in any war in which nuclear weapons are likely to be used. In such circumstances, fears of nuclear blackmail are likely to be a minor worry. Thus the argument about nuclear blackmail is ultimately a minor one, not strong enough to count heavily in favour of nuclear deterrence in Europe.

Accusations of hypocrisy are common in the nuclear debate. One which is often made with regard to nuclear blackmail is this; it's hypocritical for a state like Britain to claim a need to defend itself from nuclear blackmail yet to be unwilling to grant other states the moral right to a nuclear deterrent for the same purpose. Barrie Paskins points out in the fourth of our papers that this is only part of a more general problem concerning nuclear deterrence and proliferation.

He sees a real danger that non-NATO states will become increasingly eager to model their own national defence policies on those of the NATO alliance. The very success of East-West deterrence enhances the likelihood of this. Yet at least five serious dangers threaten the world if Third World countries actually do imitate NATO. These dangers have hitherto been overlooked by deterrence theorists since they tend to use an unrealistically abstract model of international relations, emphasizing what nation-states have in common with each other. But it may be the differences which best explain their behaviour, however.

In particular, deterrence theorists do not admit that if East-West deterrence has succeeded to date, it's arguably due to a background of stability in Europe, largely congenial to deterrence's success. Such conditions of stability just do not exist in much of the Third World, and there are no grounds for assuming that the introduction of nuclear deterrence into those areas would create stability. If we in the West want to avoid the dangers that proliferation will surely bring – including that of being dragged into conflicts which have nothing to do with us – then we should remove nuclear deterrence from its misleadingly central place in East-West relations, and stop advertising it as a more useful thing than it is.

It is, of course, ironic that Third World states should be looking ever more enviously at East-West nuclear deterrence at just that time when it's becoming increasingly dangerous and counter-productive. This claim has been made several times in this introduction. Nicholas Measor makes out the claim in greater detail. Part of the interest of Measor's paper is that he makes his case by use of an intellectual tool which has traditionally been used in defence of deterrence; namely Games Theory.

In the past, Games Theory was often employed to show that unilateral nuclear disarmament was an irrational policy, for a superpower if not any nuclear power. It was also possible to use it to show why multilateral disarmament was bound to be difficult if not impossible – a less well-trumpeted upshot of Games Theory analysis. Measor shows that if there is indeed a new arms race in progress, whose goal is the achievement of a first-strike capability, then unilateral nuclear disarmament is rational *even* for a superpower. For if both sides should attain such a capability more less simultaneously, then all-out strategic nuclear war is highly likely. Yet if one side reaches this goal substantially earlier than the other, the latter would find itself at such disadvantage that it would be best advised to disarm; for in such a case its weapons would no longer deter but merely provoke, and sorely.

So what is to be done? In our final paper, W.B. Gallie argues that serious faults can be found with each of the three general tendencies of thought about disarmament – unilateralism, multilateralism and a general opposition to disarmament altogether. None the less, the nature of the faults he finds seem to point back to the kind of cautious and unsentimental unilateralism which the previous papers tend to point towards. Multilateralism, he argues, is a kind of Fool's Gold. The kind of concessions which multilateral disarmament talks enjoin on the participating parties are almost entirely negative in character. Yet a bargain well struck has to be a bargain worth the keeping. And a bargain in which the participants agree merely to constrain themselves with regard to aims which they actually believe to be legitimate is a bargain which begs to be broken. Bargainers need motives for keeping their word. Shared aims and purposes are all that could be relied on to provide such motives; for aims which are not shared can easily come to conflict in the future even if they don't conflict at present. The reader will, we hope, remember at this point that Mrs Midgley also accords a major role to shared aims and intentions, the role of sustaining deterrence itself. We trust too that the central papers of the volume will have left the reader with a clear sense of the ways in which aims and interests shared between the superpowers are being eroded.

If Measor's analysis of the arms race is on the right lines, then clearly disarmament cannot be abandoned as an ambition. To do so would be to resign ourselves to eventual catastrophe. Gallie asks himself why anti-disarmers are in fact tempted to give up this ambition. He believes that they assume that only the two superpowers are capable of controlling each other's behaviour. Hence they aim to ensure that 'our' superpower retains the whip hand. But the underlying assumption is false. Superpowers need allies and cannot function effectively without them. And this being so, minor powers need be neither neutral nor compliant. They have real chances for influencing and even partially controlling their senior partners' behaviour. Clearly Gallie is thinking of some form of unilateral action related to disarmament, though he does not say, nor need he say, that this would have to be a dramatic renunciation, a total and immediate rupture with deterrence.

For when it comes to point of action, unilateralists must none the less expect governments to proceed with caution. The apocalyptic style of some earlier forms of unilateralism induces a blindness of its own. It tends to concentrate minds on the worst case, the most dramatic scenario for the failure of deterrence. But there are also a number of comparatively undramatic ways in which the world could slide into a nuclear catastrophe, ways which themselves must not be neglected. And a programme of unilateral disarmament should be to edge away by cautious steps from the many pitfalls now possible, checking our position at each step we take.

Notes

1   Field Marshal Lord Carver, *A Policy for Peace*, London, Faber

& Faber, 1982, pp. 101-2.
2   James Callaghan, 'Why Britain must not go it alone', *Guardian*, 19 November 1982.

Deterrence, Provocation and the Martian Temperament

Mary Midgley

On avoiding controversial games

Many political problems look at first sight like direct clashes between prudence and principle. We ought, I think, always to suspect them of being more complicated, to assume that elements of both will be found on both sides. The effect of tackling these problems tribally, of signing up exclusively for one ideal or the other, with its corresponding style of dispute, is unlucky. Once this is done, both parties miss much of the force of opposing arguments because they simply do not take seriously what their opponents say. Debates then become alarmingly unreal. The disarmament debate has inevitably always suffered from this bifurcation, because the stakes are so high. Disarmers tend to find it inconceivable that anyone can endorse preparation for war, and sometimes refuse to argue fully against prudential arguments for it. Armers are equally at a loss to see how anyone can fail to grasp that this preparation is necessary and tend to write off disarmers instead as perverse, masochistic, self-deceiving and dangerous. Lately, however, the lines of this confrontation seem to have broken up somewhat, allowing some regrouping. Things are at present so alarming that prudence and principle are seen to converge. Many people who used to find it quite reasonable to rely on all existing armaments, and on those who furnish them, are now growing somewhat uneasy about the current tendencies of both and wondering whether better alternatives cannot be found. And many of those who formerly dwelt chiefly on the moral objections to this reliance are now as much or more impressed by its dangers. It seems possible therefore to avoid the doomed and typecast clash of supposed impractical idealist against supposed practical politician, and to start a more serious discussion of prudence, transcending party lines.

Idealists ought not, I think, to resist this as a debasement of the issue. Real corruption and stupidity apart, the difference between those who believe that current arms policies are the best way of keeping the peace and those who do not is a difference about means, not aims. The effectiveness of those means is not the only problem in sight, but it is a prime problem which needs to be discussed. This paper will proceed entirely within it.

This problem of effectiveness has become, to a remarkable extent, a psychological rather than a strategic or material or even an economic one. It seems to depend largely on gauging the reactions of expected opponents to actions which are meant to deter them. Modern weapons, though they are still described as constituting 'defence', cannot in general literally defend, in the sense of simply blocking attack before it reaches the general population. They exist primarily to deter, to prevent those attacks ever starting. Occasional exceptions such as the current attempts to find ways of destroying missiles before they are launched seem too slight a factor to alter this general balance. As modern technology works, then, the notion of defence has effectively melted away into that of deterrence, which bears a quite unprecedented weight. To understand what does and does not deter has become the main strategic consideration. For this we need, not just detailed Kremlinology, but a good interpretative scheme, a background understanding of those parts of human motivation which govern thought and behaviour under threat, not only in our possible opponents, but in ourselves as well, and also in the bystanders. Because civilized people are unwilling to think seriously about human agression, our culture does not, I believe, provide this scheme. The need to think harder about it is the main topic of this paper.

Past confusions

Understanding deterrence is a complex skill, not much like falling off a log. This emerges from every discussion of the arms problem today, and it is one faintly cheering feature of such discussions that they do now admit this complexity. Professor Laurence Martin's Reith Lectures were doubly cheering in this respect. Firstly, Professor Martin took the problem very seriously, admitting freely that he thought its difficulties crushing, and that it scared him still — a prime qualification, surely, for discussing the subject at all. Secondly, he pointed out how much of this difficulty was political and psychological, yet how crudely those aspects of it had been handled by the earlier architects of modern weaponry. He shows how casually, in the early years, it was assumed that atomic weapons should be designed for 'city busting', merely because no other use for them had yet occurred to anybody. 'There was' he remarks, 'certainly no psycho-political analysis of what it takes to deter.'[1] Larger and larger bombs were therefore provided, and this fairly unconsidered habit of mind was rationalized into the explicit policy of 'mutually assured destruction (MAD)', to be provided by building up the superpowers' capacity to demolish each other's cities instantly. This policy was cheerfully accepted as making a positive virtue of the weapons' destructiveness, and, as he explains, the West made deliberate efforts to convert the Russians to that idea, which they viewed with some alarm.

Inevitably, however, attempts were soon made to refine this hopelessly crude deterrent arrangement by technological advances. 'Flexible response' was developed and the supposedly simple, reliable deterrent balance was lost forever. 'The early architects of deterrence,' remarks Professor Martin, 'seem to have been so much preoccupied with staving off massive nuclear attack that they gave little thought to why it might occur.'[2] That is, they neglected the whole political context, and in particular the fact that most disputes are small. They provided no means of nutcracking except a steam-hammer. When the mass of nut-sized disputes on hand became obvious, they supplemented this with a variety of steam-powered nutcrackers, certain to smash the crockery and likely to set the steam-hammer itself going as well. Hence, at present, problems of appalling intricacy for which Professor Martin provided an impressive set of very subtle, but by no means confident, diagnoses. (His refusal to dogmatize is another of his virtues.) He concludes that, while it is a great pity that we ever got into this mess, and while we should do all that we can to bring about arms control, we probably do need for deterrence most of the weapons currently on hand or on offer, and a good few more conventional ones as well. If we say that we don't much like this, he replies (not offensively but sympathetically) in the words of Bruce Bairnsfather's Old Bill, 'Well, if you knows of a better 'ole, then go to it.'[3]

To say that I find this approach relatively cheering, and an improvement on some earlier ones, is obviously to start from a fairly depressed position. I have in mind two ways in particular in which reliance on weapons used to be defended. The first is the mindless, all-purpose

Empire-day patriotism which prevailed in my childhood, and which has lately been revived under the name of the Falklands Spirit. The second is the complacent certainty that — given the right aims — the current policies for implementing them must be right, the extraordinary confidence in military judgment about *means* which prevailed for some time after the Second World War. (It prevailed, in fact, at the very time when the mistakes which Professor Martin now nails were being made.) This is what has brought us to what he justly calls our present 'miserably dangerous situation'. That kind of complacency is scarcely possible now because the solid simple orthodoxy of belief in MAD has given way. In its place, those who are most expert and professional in these matters are now deeply divided, propounding a range of different ideas on how to deter. Among them are quite a few very distinguished people (such as ex-ambassador George Kennan and Field Marshal Lord Carver), who say that one thing we need badly is fewer nuclear weapons. Professor Martin himself makes an interesting point in noting that George Kennan himself, when he gave the Reith Lectures in 1957, poured scorn on this way of thinking. But the crucial thing is the direction of change. That was in the age of complacency.

Certainly we have to face realistically the problems of *how* to attempt reduction. If the angel Gabriel were to persuade all existing governments tomorrow that they had better get rid of the things, there would still be grave problems about how to do it. But that does not mean that these ideas should be sneezed away. Professor Martin, when he considers them, is discouraged to the point of despair by the difficulty of getting reliable agreements and inspection procedures. That is a psychological problem, concerning the motivation of all concerned. And to this general type of problem I now return, asking in a general way, firstly, what is deterrence?

The psychology of deterrence and provocation

The motivation of deterrence links the threatener's hardware to the motivation of the person threatened in a very simple way. It treats the threat merely as producing fear, and so discouraging action. Threats, however, do not only frighten; they can also provoke. The proportion of discouragement to provocation varies greatly in different situations, and always needs attention. This snag is well-known over deterrent punishment, which is the main sphere in which the idea of deterrence has so far been used outside warfare. The case of penal deterrence compares interestingly with international deterrence.

Someone who has been punished for one offence and is contemplating another does not necessarily see his former punishment, and the threat of a further one, simply as natural phenomena. He can see them also as hostile acts. He does not have to respond in a prudential manner, assessing the warning and the danger as he might when predicting renewed attacks of gout or indigestion. If he resents the punishment and the threat, he may see them instead as expressive gestures by which the punishing authority rejects him, and shows him that it is idle to try to come to terms with it – he will never be fully accepted by that authority. In this case, threats of stronger action will only intensify his defiance. The effectiveness of penal deterrence is limited by this tendency of punishment to turn many people into 'hardened criminals' – even if they have no particular views beforehand about the punishing authority. If they do – if they belong already to a group which feels alien to the authorities – it is even less effective. It is less so still where (as in Northern Ireland) long-standing political feuds underlie the rejection. In that sort of situation, even very heavy penalties fail to deter. This continually surprises judges, who often respond by giving heavier and heavier sentences in the hope that they can somehow get through to the next lot of offenders. But deterrence does not seem to work like this, in a way proportional to the expected penalty. It apparently depends far more on the community with which one identifies. It can even be counter-productive, causing bystanders to join the threatened community and reject the threatening one. Those of us who are thoroughly integrated into the communities which do the punishing are indeed easy to deter, because we mind about the disgrace of offending that community. Such disgrace seems to be far more feared than the mere pain or nuisance of punishment. (The fact that judges and legislators are usually members of this group, and offenders often are not, accounts for a good deal of mutual misunderstanding.) But for people who have no reputation to lose, or who belong to a distinct community in which punishment won't affect their reputation, this danger is removed. In this situation, the mere basic prudence which is adjusted to the size of the penalty is often extraordinarily weak. And judicial reproofs commonly cut no ice at all.

Without fellowship, communication fails

Penal deterrence depends, then, far more than seems to have been noticed, on the inclusion of deterrer and deterred within the same moral and emotional community. Where this fails, not only is the motivation presupposed by deterrence undermined, but its credibility also becomes much harder to establish. A normal law-abiding citizen tends to think that, if he offended, he would not get away with it. He expects on the whole that his fellow citizens would catch him and punish him, because on the whole he thinks they ought to, and thinks they will share this view. He sees them as an externalized extension of his own conscience. But to someone who feels detached from that community, things look quite different. For him, the question is one of objective probabilities, as it would be over dangers from disease or weather. And this calculation is often quite uncertain, because the data are scanty. It tends to appear as a gamble. He may well get away with it. And the less he grasps the reasoning of those who may punish him, the less certain will it seem whether they will actually do what they threaten. If he cannot see *why* they would be strong-willed, he will have less reason to be sure that they *will* be strong willed. Even heavy punishments, in such circumstances, tend to have little effect against a strong immediate motive for offending.

This is what made it possible for even quite prosperous eighteenth-century thieves to continue their business in spite of regularly seeing large numbers of their colleagues hanged for doing it. They took the physical risk, as fishermen risk drowning and car-drivers risk accidents, because it was occupational and they had indeed become hardened to it. They were not taking any emotional risk, because thieving was their tribal business, and they would have been despised for leaving it. All this is doubtless very imprudent. What it shows is that the human imagination is rather an unreliable device for producing prudence, because it has innumerable other functions to fulfill as well. And it is particularly unreliable in dealings with alien tribes. This is something which needs to be thought about whenever we are planning to rely on penal deterrence.

Now of course the penal situation is very different from the international one, and I am not trying to draw any simple parallel between them. But I think that the comparison can give us some light – the interesting thing is to see how far it will shine. In the first place I think there is really reason to suppose that between nations too, intelligible and useful deterrence can only work within the context of some sense of fellowship resting on shared basic aims, which – in spite of very wide local differences – makes it possible to understand and sympathize with the motives of one's opponent. Without it, effective deterrence becomes impossible, because the basis of reliable communication is undermined. We ill understand what others say if we fail to grasp why they are saying it. Complete aliens are in principle unintelligible, and therefore unpredictable. Consequently their threats lack credibility. In saying this, I am not being utopian about what a sense of shared aims can achieve, in any case. I am not ignoring the endless cases of successful international blackmail and oppression. Athens wipes out Melos. The Holy Roman Empire bullies its client states into suppressing the Protestant Reformation. And so on. But these are transactions between a dominant state and a much weaker one which is already well within its power. They do not help us to a model of deterrence between independent sovereign states of approximately equal standing.

Pursuing for a moment the case of equal and independent nations, we can put the question why, when they disagree, wars do not continually break out between them? (The question is an odd one, and I put it in this form only because it seems to be the question implicitly addressed by people who say that peace has been produced over the last few decades simply by the presence of nuclear weapons.) The most obvious way to answer this does not begin by listing the armies and the hardware, but by asking why it should. Nations have other ways of settling their disputes, and those disputes do not take place in a social vacuum. Nations are not sealed boxes, isolated from each other except for the conduct of disputes. Their boundaries are often arbitrary and inconvenient for current purposes; all sorts of activities go on across them. Unless deliberately prevented, citizens of different states tend strongly to travel and trade together, and to engage in all sorts of activities, ranging from sport to religion, which ignore political frontiers. Both personally and economically, much advantage is drawn from these habits. When therefore a cause of dispute arises, it has to be weighed against the drawbacks of breaking them. Even to threaten violently is something of a gamble; one may drive lasting friendship away elsewhere. Accordingly, though armed forces and the power to use them are a regular element in such disputes, the threat of using them forms only one part in a whole complex web of bonds, propositions, offers, half-offers, threats and promises, out of which, as a rule, some sort of tolerable understanding emerges. Other sorts of threat, for instance concerned with trade, are a much commoner coin, and probably more effective, because they are more credible.

Mary Midgley

Ambivalence does not destroy communication

Most forms of human intercourse both at the public and the personal level, are carried on in this sort of way, by a mixture of friendliness and opposition, with the possibility of real clashes always in the background. Not being social insects, we are never free from conflict in our dealings with each other. Ambivalence reigns. We are always conscious of conflicting wishes and aims. Yet, being also enterprising and sociable, we usually manage to communicate without actual disaster in spite of them. The mere presence of hostility is not of itself enough to prevent cooperation. Is it then necessary that we should find cooperation so hard at the international level? Professor Martin remarks that combining detente and defence is a wise suggestion but difficult to implement, 'rather — as Mr Dean Acheson once said to me — like asking a man to breathe in and out at the same time'.[4] Breathing, however, is usually done by turns. And a great deal of human intercourse is normally carried out on that principle, by alternating detente and defence in a regular and intelligible way. (That between parents and children is a prime example.) Indeed, the idea of adopting one of these modes alone seems rather like that of breathing out or in forever. If that were done, one party must either be absorbed into the other, or entirely distanced from him. For instance, unceasing defensiveness would seem to imply a lack of trust. What Mr Acheson meant, no doubt, was that one can hardly *increase* both modes simultaneously without being forced to choose between them. This is true. And it follows that if either is to be developed, the two must be shaped and thought about together. But it by no means follows that there is only one point at which a stable mixture is possible.

The symbolic use of threats

Within what we might call human relations — including political relations — the means of attack and defence do not make friendly cooperation impossible, because they have, most of the time, a purely symbolic function. Societies where swords are worn are not necessarily fierce and disorderly. The same is true of the means of amity. They need not be continually used to be bond-forming. People and organizations too can show friendship by offering each other help far more often than they actually need to provide it, and show hostility

26

by threatening interference far more often than they actually mean to interfere. Where a standardized ritual threat is normal it causes little alarm. This is why, during a great deal of human history, the fact that war was in principle possible has done little harm and a fair amount of good. The conventions governing ritual threats are usually well understood. Armies do a great deal of their work merely by existing and being properly trained. Accordingly, as much as the police, they tend to feel like keepers of order and public protectors. And this is reasonable enough.

Still, there does arise the difficulty that threats seem to lose their meaning unless they are sometimes cashed in reality. And here evolution has, I think, set us an awkward trap. We are a species naturally prone to make threats. But as creatures capable of reasoning, we are also under a certain pressure to assert our consistency and rationality by carrying them out. Anyone who finds the prevalence of threat-displays puzzling, should notice that they have an absolutely vital function in the life of social animals. They make it possible to settle disputes, and so to stabilize the social order, without physical injury. To do this effectively, they are often very alarming, and sensibility to them tends to be highly developed in such species. The displays give, and are adapted to give, the impression that a great deal of physical violence will follow. But this is misleading. The impressive display itself works *instead* of the violence. The animal still fears injury, and will keep actual fighting to a minimum. Since its opponent has the same views, there may easily be no contact at all, and, if there is, there may still be little or no injury. The display itself does most of the work. It is interesting that its effect is often so strong as to intimidate even members of other species. This is how it has come about that human beings have consistently exaggerated the pugnacity of the large apes and carnivores, and supposed them to be engaged in ceaseless mutual slaughter. Their disputes are in fact usually soon over, and far from leaving the ground strewn with corpses, commonly do no lasting damage at all. Now our own species clearly shares this equipment of threat and sensibility to threat. Among us, open anger does not just portend injury; it *is* injury – but manageable injury.

It is remarkable how promptly small children, who have never been ill-treated, respond with alarm and pain to even a slight irritation in those around them. The hostility is directly felt. Human anger, more-over, readily expresses itself in threats. But once you express them in speech, these threats get a literal meaning. And once you have the human power to envisage clearly the past and the future, that meaning can call on you to change your life. Someone who has brought an accusation or sworn vengeance in anger cannot easily just forget about it afterwards. The whole point of such utterances is to signal changes in behaviour to come. And someone against whom he has done so is not likely to forget it either.

Thus, threat for human beings is an inevitable institution, but a radically unstable one. The meaning of threats constantly shifts between a contained conventional one as social signals in their own right and a literal, predictive one, indicating the approaching use of force. And the hardware involved is itself capable of carrying both a purely ritual meaning and an alarming practical one. For threatened parties to make any mistake in interpretation here is disastrous. There is however only one way of preventing this. The whole signalling convention must be made clear. And it cannot be made clear on its own. It can only become so if it forms part of an enclosing 'language', a background of successful communication on a much wider range of subjects, belonging not just to the two disputants but to a wider community to which they both belong and which will help with their interpretation. To conceive one's opponent as nothing but an opponent is fatal. Intelligible communication is only possible where there is imaginative identification, sympathy in aims and interests between the protagonists. To refuse such identification with an opponent is to renounce any hope of understanding him.

The chronic tendency to misinterpret threats

This upsetting fact is clearly seen in the constant discrepancy, which would be entertaining if it were not rather serious, between the way in which we view the threats we make and those made against us. People at the receiving end are amazingly prone to over-interpret both the symbolic and the literal meaning – both the expressed hostility and the likely violence. And they also tend to take literally threats which are actually just symbolic. This is why some people, including disarmers, take pains to point out the offensive behaviour of their own governments – a practice which often puzzles their fellow-countrymen and gives rise to accusations of unpatriotic and masochistic perversity. Nations used to an imperial position are particularly prone to unthinking, rude and provocative behaviour. Now deliberate rudeness and provocation can of course sometimes be justified; they may be called for. But ignorance about how provocative one is being cannot. And if one is interested in prudence – as we are in this discussion – it seems specially important to be clear about this when one is dealing with an independent and powerful nation.

The dual function of armies

Increasingly in the last century it has been considered realistic to reduce warfare to simple material terms, as a weighing process between rival consignments of hardware (including, of course, manpower). The older, more civilized way of regarding it as primarily something to be threatened – a background of possibility, invoked rather rarely, and then as one transaction among others between members of a continuing community who have other dealings and must expect to coexist after it – has increasingly been dismissed as fanciful and childish. Threats have to a great extent been deprived of any but their literal meaning. The trouble about this is that the only way hardware can contribute to the *resolution* of a conflict is in being used. Thus a 'realistic' reliance on *nothing but* hardware inescapably entails a resort to war. Theoretical simulation is not a substitute, because the problem of estimating results is far too complex. As Vietnam showed, human behaviour upsets the calculations. At this point, the claim of this materialistic approach to superior realism becomes very doubtful; it may be discredited. (There is a general flaw in the notion that talking about physical objects is always more realistic than talking about thoughts and feelings. Human beings are indeed physical objects, but they are ones whose behaviour cannot be understood without taking their thoughts and feelings fully into account.)

In the attempt to meet this difficulty and to find a material and stable balance, strategists often place their faith in the notion of parity. This is an attractive 'solution' but it has two crippling flaws. The first is the tendency just noted for threats pointed at oneself to seem more serious, and to weigh more heavily than ones pointed the other way. Since this affects both sides, it is hard to see how a parity agreed on by both could ever remain stable. The other, perhaps the more serious, is that parity is not even what is needed. What is needed is merely enough to deter, which may be a lot less. When Tweedledum and Tweedledee were putting on their armour of fire-irons and pan lids, what each needed was not to equal the other's equipment, but merely to have enough for the kind of attack that was likely to be made on him. To assess this, what he needs is to understand the opponent's motivation. Once that is understood, few pan-lids may be needed and deflecting the attack by some other sort of démarche might be a much better response than any fire-irons at all.

Deterrence and retribution

The notion of parity has, however, a peculiar appeal of its own, which I suspect has nothing to do with efficiency, and quite a lot to do with justice. This seemed to be the key to understanding the recent episode when American spokesmen cited the suspected use of chemicals by the Russians in Afghanistan as a justification for reviving their own research into means of chemical warfare. The idea did not seem to be just that research might be needed to provide defence against such an attack, but that counter-attack in kind would now be called for. The point of this might be retributive; it could scarcely be deterrent. Here, too, I think that penal cases provide an interesting parallel. In criminal trials, both judges and the public are often uneasy about treating this as mere retribution, which they feel to be vindictive. They therefore tend to assume that heavier sentences are always better deterrents. From time to time, however, evidence surfaces that this is false, that beyond a certain point, the weight of sentences makes no difference. And in the train of this thought comes the still more disturbing one that deterrence itself may not always be the most effective means to the real end, which was, after all, not merely to frighten offenders but to prevent further offences. That, it seems, may sometimes be better done by other means than by punishment. Deterrent policies can be self-defeating, notably when they deprive the offender of any alternative to continuing in his offence, for instance, by making it impossible for him to make his living in any other way than by crime. If people find this notion unacceptable, even where the evidence about effectiveness is satisfactory, something interesting emerges about the concept of deterrence itself. It turns out to have two quite distinct elements — reform and retribution — whose connection may be accidental, and between which we sometimes have to choose. I do not at all want to deny here that retributive justice can be a proper aim. I think it can. It is essential, however, to distinguish it from reform and other practical ends, and not to let the two be blurred together under the name of deterrence. Historically, I think that they have always been so blurred, and that this has accounted for a great deal of confusion about punishment. There is unluckily no general law that the same penal action will achieve the aims of deterrence and retribution and reform, or that any of them is the best way to diminish crime. Quite often, realism demands that we choose between them.

In spite of the differences, I still think it will be helpful to look more closely at the parallels between penal and international cases more closely here. In both, those committed to purely deterrent policies may be asked to look at alternatives, on the practical ground that deterrence alone is not, and cannot be, effective in preventing further evil. In penal cases the suggested measures may include such things as lighter sentences, better prison conditions, more attention to retraining and better employment prospects after release and so forth, all with a view to reform. In the international ones, it is detente, which includes the provision of alternative solutions for conflict. Both these arguments ought, it seems, to be met and criticized on their own pragmatic ground, by investigating how far they actually do promise better results. Instead, both tend to be dismissed sharply, without attention to this issue, on the ground that those concerned are enemies or offenders and so do not deserve better treatment. In penal cases, the clash between justice and reform is a real one. I cannot discuss it further here, beyond remarking that people preferring reform ought not to be dismissed out of hand (as they often are) as necessarily imprudent and unrealistic. Whether their measures would work is a factual question, calling for investigation. In principle, their proposals are *more* prudent than those of people wedded to retributive justice, since that is an aim independent of our future communal advantage and quite capable of conflicting with it.

In international cases, however, it is much less obvious that there is any clash with justice at all. Neither nations nor their governments are solid, continuing responsible entities which can be blamed for past crimes in the same way as individuals. Policies of national retribution, such as that pursued by France after the First World War, seem to fall mostly on the innocent, the guilty having a depressing tendency to have made their pile and retired, died or gone off to South America. And Nuremburg Trials are rarely possible. But in any case, what is meant by 'enemy' here is certainly not just 'past offender, meriting punishment', nor even 'past opponent'. Most nations have

31

committed offences against, and been in opposition to others with which they are now on good terms. Japan, Germany and Italy are now in harmony with the West. Nor does 'enemy' just mean 'country oppressing its own citizens' or 'country following an alien political system', as is clear from many cases, notably China. An enemy nation is one to which we are now hostile, and which is now hostile to us.

What is an enemy?

What does this mean? It certainly cannot primarily mean 'one with which we intend to have a war one day' or 'whom our generals constantly use in their simulations'. The possibility of war arises from hostility; it is not the reason for hostility. It certainly does mean in part 'nation of which we strongly disapprove'. But there are many nations of which we have reason to disapprove no less strongly than the USSR. With most of them, we carry on some degree of more or less normal relations, varying the *less* or *more* with circumstances, on the general principle that it will be easier to influence their conduct by using this range of variation than by cutting ourselves off altogether. No doubt this is often done badly. But the principle seems right. It certainly cannot be proved wrong by the current habit of damning all such conduct as 'appeasement'. This word was indeed misused in defence of the encouragement given to Nazi Germany by the French and British governments during the 1930s. (It is extremely cheering to hear Professor Martin point out that 'properly considered the concept of appeasement is a good one; by properly I mean a due appreciation of the fact that others have security interests of their own which they are bound to defend'.[5])

Nazi Germany was a special and unusual case of a state whose government was dedicated by its basic policies not only to iniquity, but also to expansionist war, and depending for its internal support on the prospect which it held out of waging that war and winning it. Moreover, its government was initially weak, and was actually helped to power by the failure of other governments to protest at their successive iniquities — a failure due largely not to pacifism, but to regarding it as a useful ally against Russia. This was a case where immediate protest (short of war) was called for, and where, if it had come early enough and been made in the right way, it could probably have been effective by bringing down the new Nazi government. To use this strange case for a general condemnation of conciliation, and therefore as a general justification of hostility, including threats of war, towards any nation which one strongly fears or objects to is claptrap. The effect of this way of thinking became clear in the Suez adventure, which seems to have occurred because Eden was obsessed by the conviction that Nasser was another Hitler, and to have rejected as 'appeasement' all the objections to invading Egypt. In this case it is not clear that there was even any iniquity present of the kind and degree which could justify such a comparison. (The same, of course, is true of the recent Argentine case, whether or not one agrees that there was a case for the Falklands War.) But of course there often is iniquity. And it can present outside nations with frightful problems; how is effective protest to be made? Various methods are available, most of them inadequate and extremely frustrating. But since the suggestion of resorting to modern war to protect the victims of an oppressive foreign government is rather like that of blowing off someone's head to cure a cold, it cannot be reckoned among the possible ways of responding to this problem. There is no alternative but to think in terms of actions which will have some long-term effect towards changing the mind and policies of the iniquitous state. Among these, deterrent ones can only form one part, and often not the most promising one.

The notion of global imperialism

This seems to leave us with a meaning of *hostile* which is simple and familiar, namely, 'threatening us; intending to attack us'. And it is often suggested that the parallel with the Nazis does apply. Have we then here too an expansionist power, only waiting for its chance to achieve world domination? Is the occupation of Eastern Europe strictly comparable to the remilitarization of the Rhineland, and the invasion of Afghanistan to the seizure of the Sudetenland? Are these merely the first instalments of a global plan? It is certainly possible to look at things this way. But if we do, and if we assume (as we ought) that the Russians will use the same sort of spectacles, what are they supposed to make of the current American global quest for anti-Soviet alliances, the support given everywhere to the most varied warring factions, always chosen on this central principle? The idea of a world empire is on any thinking totally impractical, but makes no more sense this way round. If we find it totally absurd in the one case, there is no obvious reason why we should take it seriously in the other.

I am glad to find that Dr Barrie Paskins (who specializes, as God knows I do not, in the philosophy of military affairs) supports this point in a most interesting article on 'Unilateralism and the Nature of Deterrence' (*New Universities Quarterly*, Winter 1981-2). In general he argues that 'the new unilateralism' has an essential role to play in current debate, and 'should be pressing home radical questions about the very nature of deterrence'. His argument touches on two points in particular where the alarm which the USSR cannot possibly fail to feel at Western activities needs to be taken seriously. The first is the search which I have just mentioned of the American global military lobby for allies, which it seems to assess mainly as arsenals. Paskins dwells chiefly on the impracticality of this enterprise, in which one qualification, an anti-Soviet stance, seems to command attention at the expense, not only of all ideological considerations and the effect on the bystanders, but also of prospective stability. The point that I want to stress here, however, is the price paid for this flimsy article, namely that it leaves the Russians no choice but to conclude – as we would in their place – that a general attack threatens them, and that they cannot therefore allow any weakening of their bastions at home or in Eastern Europe.

Deterrence and flexible response

The second point is flexible response in Europe. Here, Paskins points out, the official western reasoning is that minor nuclear weapons are needed to deter the USSR from minor attacks, such as the seizure of West Berlin or Hamburg. The threat of major weapons is held not to be enough here because the West would think them too dangerous to use on such an occasion. But, Paskins points out, this calculation never could be safe, and the stakes are far too high to allow the East to gamble. He therefore asks:

> would it be rational for the USSR to risk an adventure of grave concern for the West so long as the likelihood of western retaliation is finite? Suppose, to take 'the worst' case, that Soviet planners reckon western retaliation is most unlikely. What they have to weigh up is whether something of grave concern to the West, say the loss of West Berlin or Hamburg, is all things considered worth the risk supposing

that reprisal is most unlikely. A part of their calculation must be that if that which is most unlikely eventuates then the result could well be World War III. Deterrence theory assumes that the powers are rational. It is far from self-evident that any rational being would risk a World War III which is adjudged most unlikely in order to secure any feasible objective however likely of attainment. In short, one might wonder whether the credibility problem is a problem in the first place.[6]

If it is, however (he goes on), it seems bound to remain so even with flexible response –

> *no-one denies* that the prospects of keeping war limited if it once breaks out are *poor*. The escalation ladder . . . is not designed to permit reliably limited war in Europe, for no-one claims that such a thing is possible . . . . Any President [of the US] concerned enough about his homeland to need flexible response [for the defence of his allies] is bound, if clear-headed, to realise that the escalation ladder is too likely to destroy what he values to be started upon.[7]

Therefore, it seems, he could not use his minor nuclear weapons. If credibility really is a problem, it is one which flexible response cannot solve, because escalation is always possible. Rational agents would not risk a nuclear war at all. If, on the other hand, we take those involved not to be rational, there is no possibility of predicting their reactions, and therefore no possibility of calculated deterrence.

Intransigence and fear

It is amazingly rarely mentioned that Russian intransigence has another very obvious possible cause besides expansionist intentions, namely fear. In the Second World War, Russia was deeply invaded without warning, suffering both casualties and damage on a scale which probably outweighs that of any other belligerent nation. The invader was a Western power which was at that time her ally. The other allies which she subsequently acquired were obviously not particularly friendly to her; the convergence of interests which briefly bound them to her could not be firmly expected to last. (At Yalta, therefore, she asked them to allow her a buffer sphere of influence in Eastern Europe, and they consented.) She was also invaded during the First World War, and again soon after that war by her recent allies, both times with considerable damage. Before that, she had been slightly invaded during the Crimean War and much more deeply — to an extent which included the capital — by Napoleon. In none of the cases was she the aggressor. To balance all this, Russian history contains plenty of heroic defence, but none of those ego-warming aggressive military successes with which other European nations like to raise their confidence. Her bitterness and distrust of outsiders are deep and reasonable.

Now it is known that experiences of this kind make nations touchy. The French were notoriously not quite themselves for a considerable time after the Franco-Prussian War; their obsession with the danger of a revived Germany bedevilled inter-war diplomacy and played a considerable part in the rise of Nazism. Similarly the Poles are not, and are not expected to be, balanced on the subject of either Germany or Russia. Those of us who have not been through this kind of experience do not understand its effects very well, and need to make a deliberate effort to grasp them, but we know them to be very strong. Might it not be reasonable to take this factor into account in interpreting Russian aggression, and to see a good deal of it as looking backwards rather than forwards? The invasion of Afghanistan itself was a somewhat panicked response to American activity in the Middle East rather than a calculated move in a game of world domination.

For some reason, suggestions like these usually seem to be taken as attempts to justify these aggressive moves. It is essential to stress that they are nothing of the kind. Fear is as common a source of crime as any, and crimes provoked by it are no more justifiable than those from any other motive. The difference lies in the diagnosis and prognosis to be made about the mood of those responsible, and the other behaviour to be expected from them. This difference is enormous, and it is just the sort of thing which is relevant to deterrence. Unscrupulousness due to alarm after past suffering can be expected to subside gradually if that alarm proves groundless, but to harden and increase if it is shown to be well-founded. Unscrupulousness which was really due to wild, adventurous, unbridled ambition would have a different meaning and call for different treatment. The use of threats can be expected to have diametrically opposite effects in the two cases, so that it seems fairly important to get one's diagnosis right.

The Martian hypothesis

Explanations of this kind do not very often appear in our papers. When they do, they tend to be met, not by counter-evidence but by derision. The Russians (it is generally held) never feel frightened, never dither, never look for reassurance, never over-estimate the dangers which threaten them, never continue with a policy simply because they are too scared and confused to think of a new one. Our own governments indeed do this sort of thing incessantly. But then the people in our own governments are human beings. And the Russians are not human beings. They are Martians.

Any actual Martian who happens to read these pages will, I feel sure, excuse me for using this word in its familiar sense which is purely negative. It means a highly intelligent being, physically almost invulnerable, not subject to human feelings, particularly human weaknesses like fear, and therefore not capable of undergoing conflict or confusion, since it has no motivation except the wish to increase its own power, and no doubts as to how this should be done. (There is no known social animal which is actually like this, but H.G. Wells's *War of the Worlds* supplies the model.) This view of the Russian character does not often get stated, but it continually gets assumed, and assuming it is in fact the only way to make sense of a great deal of current strategic calculation. In Professor Martin's sensitive and sophisticated pages, it stands out like a sore thumb. I cannot do better than quote from a letter to the *Listener* (from F. Kemble Williams) which pointed out one of the early examples —

> He (Prof. Martin) says: 'The Western democracies are naturally averse to war. Preparations for war, still more war itself, are ill-suited to societies preoccupied with material welfare and by no means all hankering for a military life.'
>
> The clear implication and whole point of this remark (in any case so palpably untrue as to resemble irony) is to exclude the Eastern Powers from such a pacific stance, and this innocent-looking sentence holds the key to Professor Martin's whole defence of the Western powers' ever-increasing nuclear arms program.
>
> But he then goes on to point out that 'war and armed force are far from out of fashion' . . . . The great powers are active there too . . . besides the two large wars in Korea and Vietnam, the US has exercised its military power in over 200 incidents since 1945,

while the Soviet Union has done the same on a little under 200 occasions.[8]

With the discrepancy of two large and several small wars summing the way it does, this seems fair criticism. The same strange view crops up all the time. And every time it weakens the argument. It comes out most fully, however, in the last lecture, where Prof. Martin faces directly the question of why the whole East-West rivalry is necessary. He writes —

I doubt whether one can have a relationship of trust with a power like the Soviet Union that combines a Bolshevik's dialectical view of politics with a Russian's experience of alternate vulnerability and self-aggrandisement. The fact that we can negotiate with the Soviet Union . . . doesn't alter a fundamentally antagonistic relationship — a relationship moreover, in which military power plays a fundamental part.

This is no mere Cold War judgment of my own. It is the consistently expressed view of the Soviet Union itself, made freely available to anyone who is not content to accept only the propaganda aimed at foreign audiences. Thus, in a fairly recent work . . . . Lenin himself is cited approvingly for having laid it down that 'no talks, no agreements, appeals or imprecations would stop the enemy if he was not faced with a substantial military force'. Following the same line, the editors conclude: 'The stronger we are, the stronger peace is.'[9]

Now what is so alarming about this? What Lenin and his exponent are saying here seems to differ in no syllable from what Western writers on strategy say all the time — namely that they feel threatened, and that you need military force if you are to be sure of preventing those who threaten you from carrying out their threats. It can scarcely be inflammatory to add, 'the stronger we are, the stronger peace is'. The suggestion of a dark secret here, on *Mein Kampf* lines, hidden from the uninstructed foreigner, seems out of place. If, with his wide knowledge of Soviet writings to choose from, the Reith lecturer comes up with nothing worse than this, we still seem to need evidence for that 'fundamental antagonism'.

Will the phrase about Bolshevik dialectics and Russian experience supply it? I do not find this bit clear at all. A history of 'alternate vulnerability and self-aggrandisement' is common to most powers, including certainly our own. (Switzerland may indeed be the only exception.) As for dialectics, it is not at all obvious why they should subvert the basis of trust. If, for instance, an incoming Russian government were to begin a 'thaw' — a policy of greatly reducing internal oppression — but still declared itself Marxist, would we still have to view it as fundamentally antagonistic? If we could not respond to such a move with an increase of trust and cordiality, half the point of opposing tyranny would surely be lost. Beyond this, the whole suggestion of a special, dialectical way of thinking peculiar to the Russians rings oddly in an age when many serious Marxists disavow any special connection with the USSR and view it as (since Stalin's time at least) just one oppressive state among others, using Marx's language to justify exploitation much as other States use Christ's. Whoever is right about this, however, there seems no reason to expect Russian dialectical thinking to affect deterrence. Since we all want to avoid suspicion of Romantic optimism, the dilemma had better be stated in dismal terms. We will suppose those in charge of Russian policy-making to be *either* devout fanatical Marxists *or* corrupt and cynical parasites, or somewhere on the scale in between. In the former case, their first priority must be to preserve the USSR at all costs, since they believe it to be (as just explained) the best or only hope for the future of socialism in the world. In the latter they must still preserve it at all costs, since it is the host on which they feed, and nobody is going to supply them with another.

Conclusion. Provocation vitiates deterrence

It is very hard, then, to find any realistic view of Russian motivation on which the accumulation of Western military hardware is not already so provocative as to be a serious danger, or on which further increases in it will not steadily make that danger worse. So far from this hardware's providing, as Professor Martin suggests, our only safe hole of refuge, it seems calculated rather to attract the hostility against which it cannot defend us.

What follows? Not, as I have mentioned, that we should throw the whole lot in the sea tomorrow. Not only would that be ecologically impossible, it would neglect the central point I have been making, which is that communication requires a context. A background of positive constructive military and diplomatic moves and proposals is needed to give a sense to the removal of weapons.

The difference between 'unilateralists' and 'multilateralists' is not that between the foolishly self-sacrificing and the prudent. It is that between those who are willing to take initiative in such moves and those who, apparently, think it makes sense to wait until both sides are suddenly inspired to attempt innovations simultaneously. The extreme improbability of this coincidence makes it a strange gamble for anyone interested in prudence. It is time, I think, for the claim that multilateralism is the more prudent and realistic policy to be properly explained.

Notes

1 Laurence Martin, *Listener*, 19 November 1981, p. 597.
2 Laurence Martin, *Listener*, 19 November 1981, p. 598.
3 Laurence Martin, *Listener*, 12 November 1981, p. 565.
4 Laurence Martin, *Listener*, 26 November 1981, p. 637.
5 Laurence Martin, *Listener*, 12 November 1981, p. 564.
6 Barrie Paskins, 'Unilateralism and the Nature of Deterrence', *New Universities Quarterly*, Winter 1981-2, p. 34.
7 Ibid.
8 Letter from F. Kemble Williams, *Listener*, 19 November 1981, p. 613.
9 Laurence Martin, *Listener*, 17 and 24 December 1981, p. 747. The articles by Laurence Martin may also be found in his book *TheTwo-Edged Sword*, London, Weidenfeld & Nicholson, 1982.

Unilateralism: A Clausewitzian Reform?

Ken Booth

Despite the scepticism and sometimes taunts of many of the supporters of Britain's existing pro-nuclear defence policy, it is not necessary for an advocate of a non-nuclear strategy to be either a dupe of the Kremlin or hopelessly naive about the world of affairs. The growing number of hard-headed critics of Britain's 'independent nuclear deterrent' attest to this, from Field Marshal Lord Carver (a former Chief of the Defence Staff) to Enoch Powell (an MP of notably unsentimental views). Indeed, it is possible to support nuclear renunciation while accepting most if not all the assumptions and aims of those who hitherto have dominated the defence debate in Britain. From this perspective 'unilateralism' (of one sort or another) is coming to be seen by a small but growing number of people merely as a sensible strategic option. It is not necessarily being advocated because of some overriding moral imperative, or because of any conviction that Britain does not face any serious military threat, or because of any belief that there is nothing to choose between the superpowers. Furthermore, among this group of relatively recent converts to nuclear renunciation — of whom the present author is one — there is no element of the common and understandable, but ultimately impossible desire to opt out of the deadly business of international politics altogether. Unfortunately, the problem of nuclear war will not go away even for those states which may renounce their own nuclear weapons, and try to stop thinking about them. War and the threat of war will remain a kind of tyranny. With this in mind, Michael Walzer brilliantly paraphrased Trotsky's aphorism about the dialectic: 'You may not be interested in war, but war is interested in you.'[1]

Since we have to try and live with the tyranny of war, if we are not to be destroyed by it, we are bound to think strategically. And

41

Ken Booth

this means offering prescriptions as well as analysis. The only good strategic thinking is that which works. It is not enough merely to provide a critique of the dangers and fallacies of existing deterrent policies: it is also necessary at some point to suggest desirable and feasible new directions. This essay will attempt both. It will point to some inadequacies in the current British defence posture and argue that 'unilateralism' offers our defence planners a neo-Clausewitzian alternative[2] to our deeply entrenched pro-nuclear strategy.[3]

The new risks of war

As the 1970s gave way to the 1980s, objective and subjective trends in the international arena seemed to be increasing the likelihood of major war. Indeed, a change of era appeared to be taking place which was as momentous as that which had occurred between the 1920s and 1930s.[4] In both cases a post-war era had come to an end, and we had entered an era in which wars and rumours of wars were back in season. At the start of the 1980s growing numbers of people had come to think and feel that nuclear war was becoming more likely. They had not come to live with, let alone love the bomb: they had in fact come to fear nuclear weapons more than the Soviet Union itself.

In the early 1980s we have a superstructure of nuclear deterrence between the superpowers resting upon an international political economy which contains ingredients which promise unprecedented brittleness. It is not necessary to be alarmist to recognize the following possibilities in the years ahead:

— a greater military confidence and capability on the part of the Soviet Union, but a greater sense of political insecurity on the part of its leaders as they confront the realization that history is not going their way;
— a 'new' (actually old) nationalism and ideological dogmatism on the part of the US leadership, which includes a determination after a period of introspection and uncomfortable passivity to lead the 'free world', to regain a position of military 'superiority' and, when called upon by events, to go out into the street and do what a superpower gotta do;
— increased competitiveness over non-renewable resources across the world, and growing pressure on renewable ones;
— a mood in a period of widespread economic hardship of 'every man

for himself';
- the likelihood of more nuclear powers, not least in regions of chronic instability;
- difficulties in 'North-South' relations, which may result in political strains and economic dislocation if the outstanding issues cannot be ameliorated, with a consequent rise in the atmosphere of tension in the world;
- the incapacity on the part of many states to meet their politico-economic challenges, with the result that breakdowns in order will occur which in turn will present openings for intervention by ambitious local powers, as well as the opportunist superpowers;
- a greater capability and probably greater will on the part of the superpowers to interfere and possibly intervene in the affairs of many countries, and a competitive determination to counter the activity of the other superpower;
- although the imperatives of the Monroe and Brezhnev doctrines will remain, political, social, and economic developments in Latin America and Eastern Europe will slowly turn these spheres of relative influence into spheres of relative impotence, with all the prospects for instability which that implies;
- the development of nuclear weapons and doctrines by the United States — following the traditional approach of the Soviet Union — which tend to blur the distinction between 'conventional' and 'nuclear' war, and which equate deterrence 'credibility' with the threat of military 'victory'; such doctrines offer no notion of sufficiency or stability in the arms race, and therefore the likelihood of more rather than less competitiveness and mutual suspicion;
- the erosion of the taboo[5] against the use of nuclear weapons in western strategic discourse, such that the prospect of a nuclear war is no longer the horrificly 'unthinkable' one it was for most of the post-1945 period; and, last but not least,
- the widespread fear, east and west, that nuclear war is increasingly likely, and the related fear that prophecies about human behaviour have a way of becoming self-fulfilling.

Given such ingredients, it is not surprising that the smell of war is back in the air. In the 1980s, like Stephen Spender in the 1930s, many of us feel increasingly 'hounded by external events'. We expect to face the sort of world in which crises will be more likely and more dangerous than in the 1970s. These will be crises in which the superpowers will be determined not to be outdone in displaying their interest and resolve. At the same time their ideological and national perspectives, their ethnocentric incomprehension, and their sheer uncertainty and rational suspicion will mean that they may make serious miscalculations about each other. If these serious miscalculations are in fact made, and shooting finally begins between Soviet and US troops, then slipping into a nuclear war will be quicker, easier, and more likely than has seemed possible since the height of Cold War I.

Cold War II, which dates from the death of detente in 1979-80, will be a grim period in international relations, and more complex than its predecessor. During this period nuclear weapons will remain a terrible threat and deterrent to any minimally sane national leadership, for the nuclear threat performs in international society the role which the leviathan of the state performs for private security. Neither are loved, but both are utilitarian. They are the beasts which force people, as individual and groups, to be prudent, if not actually good.[6] But even if the risks of nuclear war are still relatively low — how 'low' cannot be defined quantitatively[7] — the ingredients of world affairs in the early 1980s are such that the risks are 'higher' than they were. Growing numbers of people are less confident about the security offered by nuclear deterrence. Even within the strategic community itself, concern rather than complacency is now accepted as the only respectable position to adopt towards the theory and practice of nuclear deterrence. Nevertheless, official nuclear strategy remains wedded to the old beliefs, and particularly the belief that nuclear weapons have 'kept the peace' for nearly forty years, and that there is no better guarantee of peace in future.

Leaving aside the historical question of the extent to which it was nuclear weapons which have kept the peace in Europe, it is odd, to say the least, to hear self-professed 'realists', who pride themselves on their understanding of the aggressive side of human nature and the gloomy path of human history, expressing such desperate faith in our indefinite rationality, our indefinite ability to control our international destinies, and our indefinite luck. Strangely, these realists seem unwilling to accept that events could slip out of control, and seem incapable of imagining the horror of what would follow. But one day the nuclear deterrent might not deter. After all, deterrents have failed in the past, and the unpredictable and the cataclysmic have been rather commonplace in international relations. This suggests that we have an additional reason to worry about all crises and wars on our tiny planet, for they may spread to the powder keg of Europe. The process might be indirect and gradual, but events can have an iron logic of their own, and seem beyond human control. And we are no more skilled at handling human relations than our forefathers, nor can we expect to be granted any better luck. The history of war, if it teaches us anything, teaches us that plans do not always work and that the god of strategy is called Murphy.

The scenario for the Third World War cannot be forecast, nor can the chain of events which would lead from crisis to first explosion. But this should be no excuse for complacency, as it is with those who say, in effect, that since they cannot imagine how the Third World War would begin, it is therefore very unlikely. Such a *non sequitur*, and such a preoccupation with scenarios, invests undue significance in the 'immediate' as opposed to the 'underlying' causes of war. *How Wars Begin* is important, as A.J.P. Taylor has reminded us,[8] but even more significant are the underlying trends in the international system of the time. An over-concern with immediate causes inspired the winner of an inter-war newspaper competition, where the task was to think up the most original newspaper headline. The winner came forward with –

'ARCHDUKE FERDINAND FOUND ALIVE: THE GREAT WAR ALL A MISTAKE'

The assassination of the luckless Archduke – 'the scenario' – played its part in the events of the summer of 1914, of course, but the Great War did not just happen by accident. The scenario was simply the vehicle which moved a confrontation into a war. The same has been true of the outbreaks of many other wars, and might well be the case in future. McGeorge Bundy once expressed this problem with insight. Talking about the attack on the American base at Pleiku, which led to the US bombing of North Vietnam, Bundy said: 'Pleikus are street-cars. If you wait long enough, one will come along.'[9]

When the international milieu shifts from detente to confrontation, the escalatory potential of crises takes on additional significance. In this regard we can take some confidence – but not too much – from the fact that some crises have passed safely, as has been the case (so far) with Afghanistan, Poland, and the Gulf War in recent years.[10] In the nuclear age we cannot afford to let any streetcar get out of control; but we are unlikely ever to be able to predict which one might go wrong. Our most recent record of prediction and averting troubles is not impressive. Who could have predicted that the antics of some excited and excitable scrap-metal workers would have started the train of events which would lead to a war between such old associates as Britain and Argentina? Who could have predicted that an assassination attempt on the Israeli Ambassador in London would have led to Lebanese Christians massacring Lebanese Muslims and Palestinians in Beirut, and the landing of French, Italian, and US troops in the city? These violent outcomes were not 'accidents', given the history of the peoples concerned: nor were the 'scenarios' which turned peace into war predictable. Once more we were exposed as being just as much the playthings of our emotions, ambitions, and the dynamic of events as were our forefathers. Will the nuclear threat always protect us from nuclear war? It is doubtful, and the past is a poor guide, for less than forty years is only a moment in human history. The absence of a nuclear war in such a brief period offers little grounds for unlimited confidence about the indefinite future. The nuclear age is still in its infancy, and, in the long term, we should recognise that in the Argentinian scrap-metal workers in South Georgia, and in the wounded Israeli Ambassador in London, there lurked the ghost of Archduke Ferdinand.[11]

It is no more possible to dream up the scenario for the Third World War at the start of the 1980s than it would have been to dream up the scenario for the First World War in 1900 or 1910, or even on 28 June 1914. But it is possible to say at the start of the 1980s, as it was possible to say at the start of this century, that we are living in the sort of international situation in which nations are posturing, feeling edgy, and are determined to achieve their place in the sun; it is an era in which international crises are becoming more likely, and in which major war is again becoming thinkable. In the 1970s everybody would have been both very shocked and very surprised if major war had occurred: in the 1980s everybody would still be very shocked, but increasing numbers would only be *taken* by surprise.

British strategy: the need for change

If the argument of the preceding section is accepted, namely that the risks of war will be greater in the 1980s than they were in the 1970s, then it is imperative that the British, and others, begin to pay more attention to what should happen if the shooting does start. So far, in NATO, almost absolute reliance has been placed on nuclear deterrence.

This attitude has been particularly strong in Western Europe, and especially in West Germany, for if deterrence broke down theirs would be the territory on which the fighting would immediately take place. NATO thinking has traditionally been based on the idea that if the deterrent is used it has failed. At that point we have tended to throw up our hands in despair, both practically and conceptually. In contrast, Soviet thinking about nuclear weapons has never made the same sharp doctrinal distinction between 'deterrence' and 'defence'. Consequently Soviet defence planners have been better prepared to contemplate fighting a nuclear war.[12] This does not mean that they want to fight one, or that they see nuclear war as a preferred instrument of policy, but it has made for a coherence in Soviet planning for nuclear war which has generally been lacking in the West.[13]

Compared with the relative doctrinal certainty in Soviet planning, which largely arises out of the traditional belief that the best deterrent is the threat of an effective war-fighting capability, Western thinking about such matters falters on the question of what happens if deterrence fails, since 'deterrence' and 'defence' have been seen as conceptually different and, when it comes to weapons and strategies, their implications are sometimes seen to pull in different directions. Discussions within NATO about the role of tactical nuclear weapons normally expose the uncertainties about nuclear strategy in full light, while the problems of the political control of allied nuclear strategy were advertised at the highest level in October and November 1981 by the public disagreements between Alexander Haig, the US Secretary of State, and Casper Weinberger, the Secretary of Defense, on the subject of a possible 'demonstration' missile as a warning to the Soviet Union. During the presidencies of Jimmy Carter and Ronald Reagan many Europeans have become progressively disenchanted with the leadership being offered by the United States in world affairs, and anxious about the direction of US nuclear policy. Ironically, the more coherent US nuclear strategy has become under Reagan, the more anxiety it has produced among the allies.

If NATO's present nuclear posture is causing considerable concern to those it is designed to protect, several much-favoured alternative approaches to the problem of peace and security offer no greater, indeed less consolation. Multilateral disarmament and arms control, for example, are popular ideas among many sectors of Western society, but they presently hold out little prospect of success. In fact, both disarmament and arms control represent ideals in disarray. This was clearly demonstrated by the second session of the United Nations Special Session on Disarmament (UNSSOD II) in the summer of 1982, and by the ending of the negotiations on SALT II three years earlier. In neither case is there any reason to believe that it will be a case of third time lucky. Multilateral disarmament on any significant scale is an illusion. It is contrary to the nature of states. Consequently, multilateral disarmament policies must therefore be regarded as a cheat – a tactic in the business of arms competition.[14] Governments pursue such policies largely for propaganda purposes and, if successful, to enhance their own security in relation to a competitor. At present 'multilateralism' is more often than not a symbol by which the supporters of existing strategies are attempting to undermine the anti-nuclear momentum of the 'peace movement'. Multilateral disarmament negotiations are an exercise in which (a) it will be demonstrated that the adversary is unreasonable and uncooperative, and so the continuation of existing armaments policies will be justified, or (b) an attempt will be made to manouevre the adversary into accepting a disadvantageous agreement. Disarmament talks have little to do with *comprehensive* disarmament or *international* security.[15] It is not surprising therefore that so many people are so cynical.

The talks on Mutual Force Reductions at Vienna, which have been dragging on since 1973, are revealing of both the difficulty and political uses of 'multilateralism'. The talks have shown at tedious length the problems involved in defining a military 'balance' in a heavily-armed continent, the differing conceptions of what constitutes 'stability' between two contending alliances, and the pervasive mistrust and suspicion which exists between the representatives of countries with abundant reasons to fear each other. But the talks, even their lack of success, have been useful politically. They have proved useful on the NATO side as a tactic to discourage members from independently cutting their own troop levels.[16] Indeed, a prolongation of the talks will in some ways serve NATO's interests better than an agreement. This could well be the case if the MFR talks were ever to result in far-reaching cuts on the NATO side, since any further lowering of our conventional defences would only result in a further lowering of the nuclear threshold in the event of war. There is another danger, for it would be sensible for any Soviet regime bent on war to press first for a drastic MFR agreement, in order to build a false 'confidence' in the West and at the same time to reduce the density of NATO forces in position on the central front. Such a step would increase the Soviet chances of both achieving a surprise attack and a successful strategic breakthrough. As a tactic in the superpower confrontation there is more to multilateralism than meets the eye, but as an ideal, multilateralism – and certainly general and comprehensive disarmament – is in disarray, and represents a distraction from thinking about the real problems facing us.[17]

The theory and practice of arms control is in almost equal disarray. In the early 1960s the concept of arms control was exciting and promising, and some practical progress was made; but now the hopes of that period have almost entirely dissipated. SALT II was the turning point, for this protracted negotiating experience proved to be for arms controllers what the protracted Vietnam war was for limited war theorists. It was the day the heady strategic music of the 'golden age' of contemporary strategic theory died.[18] Arms control, in the era of SALT II, came to be synonymous with continuing (possibly accelerating) arms competition, the diversion of energy into qualitative improvements in weaponry, the erosion of the notion of easily definable 'strategic' arms, the hobbling of what some thought to be sensible defence measures, and the sacrifice of foreign policy interests on the altar of arms control. At the end of SALT II, for better or worse, no agreement was reached, and the prospects for START (Reagan's Strategic Arms Reduction Talks) are not better. Nevertheless, some cosmetic agreements might possibly be reached in future. These will have their domestic uses for the leaders of the superpowers, since arms control remains a popular idea, and they may be useful methods by which to change the atmosphere in international relations. But if arms control negotiations are again to become 'serious', they will almost inevitably slide into the deadlock caused by the need to compute complex balances and try to manage the problem of the awkward linkages which exist with military and political developments in the world outside the conference room. As long as the negotiating process remains lengthy, because of the complexities and the mutual desire to play safe, external developments will always threaten to subvert whatever is being negotiated. However, unlike disarmament theory, there is some scope for new thinking about arms control.[19] So, despite the present bleak prospects, there can be some hope that something might be done to stabilize the arms race. But arms control is not a trick, which can transform the superpower relationship. It is only a technique which can assist a stabilizing process to which both super-

49

Ken Booth

powers are already committed.

If we are justified in being concerned about the growing risk of war, and see no prospect of amelioration in either existing strategies of deterrence, disarmament, or arms control, then it is necessary to look for alternatives, especially if one also believes that history shows that no strategic sin is punished more implacably than a resistance to change.

Clausewitz and the British bomb

For Britain at the present time the least unsatisfactory of a variety of unsatisfactory defence options is that referred to as 'unilateralism'; this term, unfortunately, has become overloaded with a variety of unflattering connotations as a result of the hostility of its critics and some of the outlooks and weaknesses of some of its supporters. Nevertheless, we seem stuck with the word, and it is therefore imperative for those who wish to renounce Britain's independent nuclear deterrent to try to strengthen the strategic meaning of 'unilateralism', to get away from its exclusive and unhelpful association in the minds of many people simply with anti-bomb marches, degrees of unworldliness, and (rightly or wrongly) being 'soft on communism'. 'Unilateralism', if it is to become more than a slogan, has to be filled out as a sensible strategic option for a middle-rank power. Simply 'giving up the bomb' is not enough. Unilateralism has therefore to come to be seen as offering the prospects of a more rational, national and instrumental strategy for Britain – the Clausewitzian trinity.[20]

By reputation, Clausewitz is usually associated with *Realpolitik* and victory in war through fighting big battles.[21] But Clausewitz also has the reputation of being the founder of modern strategic thinking and the greatest philosopher of war. Today, above all, he is identified with the idea of the essential unity of war and politics, as is evident in his most-quoted dictum, the idea that 'War is nothing else than the continuation of state policy by different means.' In Clausewitz's view politics above all things modified war, and prevented real war from attaining the outburst of violence implied in his theoretical notion of 'absolute war', which was 'war on paper'. If one concentrates on Clausewitz as the man who insisted that war and strategy must be controlled by politics, and that war must be a rational and instrumental act, then it might be argued that had Clausewitz been British and alive today, he would have been a unilateralist: but not one of the sentimental kind (those who might be called 'soft' unilateralists) but rather one of the 'hard' unilateralists, who support a non-nuclear defence because it makes optimum strategic sense. Such a hard unilateralist posture, as was implied earlier, must involve not only the renunciation of nuclear weapons, but also the adoption of a package of measures designed to improve Britain's security, as well as simply demonstrate a commitment to 'peace'.

Strategy is concerned with the complex and frequently difficult relationship between military means and political ends. For most of the world, for most of the time, this means business as Clausewitzian usual when it comes to national security matters: but for those engaged in the central nuclear confrontation, the nuclear age presents a new and terrible dilemma. We still live in a Clausewitzian world as far as politics among nations is concerned, but we live in a post-Clausewitzian world when it comes to the potential destructiveness of our weaponry. Technologically we have something approaching the capacity to engage in the 'absolute war' which Clausewitz recognized as a theoretical construct, but did not imagine would be possible and could not conceive as an instrument of politics. In a Clausewitzian sense, therefore, a 'nuclear war strategy' is a contradiction in terms. This is especially so for such a vulnerable country as Britain: for Britain, nuclear war can only be conceived as a nightmare, and not as a continuation of politics. We should not even try to push the idea of nuclear war into the traditional Clausewitzian paradigm. But we do. And in large part we do it because there is a conceptual and semantic time-lag in the strategic community: we try to handle the problems of today and tomorrow when it comes to thinking about nuclear war with the Clausewitzian words and concepts of yesterday. We continue to use words such as 'war', 'strategy', and 'weapons' when technology at the most destructive level has deprived them of their former connotations with reasonable instrumentality. 'War', 'strategy', and 'weapons' all take on a drastically new meaning when the adjective 'nuclear' is placed in front of them: the adjective negates the Clausewitzian implications of the word which follows, and in so doing threatens the very future of state policy – the thing which Clausewitz's strategic ideas were intended to further.

Of course, no British strategist hopes that Britain's nuclear weapons will ever be fired against the Soviet Union. If this were to occur it would mean that they had failed in their primary function as a deterrent. Is then the threatening of nuclear war for deterrent purposes un-

Clausewitzian? The answer to this question is not as straightforward as the question of nuclear war, since it involves the central paradox of deterrent strategy, the fact that in order to deter effectively a nation must be able to persuade its adversary that it has both the capability and the will to carry out its threat if confronted by unacceptable behaviour. Because of this requirement, Britain has had to create an impressive standing nuclear threat to the Soviet Union. Perhaps, *in extremis*, no British government would implement its nuclear threat. But this is no consolation, for as well as 'enhancing' deterrence, Britain's standing nuclear threat also increases the importance of Britain as a potential target in the event of war; and hence its nuclear forces invite a decisive pre-emptive attack from any determined Soviet aggressor. Furthermore, the fact that Britain has the capability to meet a Soviet attack with nuclear weapons means that there would be a great compulsion to use them, particularly as that capability will presumably be in the hands of a cabinet whose members have always believed in the efficacy of a nuclear strategy. And the release of nuclear weapons might even be seen as an acceptable choice, given the array of unpleasant choices we would face when we were at what *The Times* called 'the very gates of Hell', with Europe fallen into a 'holocaust of suffering' as a result of Soviet attack.[22] At that point nobody could guarantee that Britain would not try to use its 'independent deterrent' as a means of defence.

Since we cannot guarantee that the nuclear leviathan will always deter, even if it usually will, then it is obvious that the un-Clausewitzian notion of nuclear war is integral to the idea of nuclear deterrence. It must therefore be concluded that nuclear deterrence is ultimately un-Clausewitzian. A strategy which has no reasonable answer to its breakdown, except inviting the prospect of 'absolute war', cannot be considered to be Clausewitzian in its inspiration, however remote the possibility of that breakdown.

In the light of the above remarks, it is necessary to revise Clausewitz's original paradigm as far as nuclear war is concerned. Once fighting approaches the notion of absolute war, politics – the purpose of war – goes out of the window. Because of the centrality of politics in Clausewitz's thinking about war, he would have accepted, as do all realists, East as well as West,[23] that the idea of 'victory' by decisive battle in nuclear war is meaningless. The concept of 'victory' in absolute war (general nuclear war) is as abstract an idea as was the idea of 'absolute war' to real war at the time when Clausewitz was writing.

'Victory' would merely be a mental construct: it could hardly represent a 'real' political success. The culmination of strategy can therefore no longer be considered to be the great battle, with the application of maximum force, since the great battle would now represent a negation of the idea of strategy. Instead, any national strategy now demands the avoidance of such a battle. This is especially the case for a small and overcrowded island such as Britain. As it happens, the limitation of war — fighting in limited ways for limited objectives — was something Clausewitz had planned to write more about, had he lived. In the nuclear context this would have led him — and this of course is highly speculative — to a drastic revision of his original argument. Instead of thinking about how to make war instrumental by achieving victory, his concern for the unity of war and politics would have led him to stress the necessity of avoiding nuclear war, but, if involvement became likely, he would have demanded that it be ended rationally, which is not the same as winning. Given Britain's peculiar nuclear vulnerability, ending rationally any war which breaks out should become the dominant feature of all future thinking about national strategy. This is a reversal of the traditional Clausewitzian approach, which equated victory with success and rationality with the search for that victory.

The theory of nuclear deterrence is impressive — some of its supporters even call it 'elegant' — but only until the shooting starts. Then it becomes messy, to say the least. Unhappily, the more attention has been directed towards tidying it up in recent years, the worse the problem has become, for most of the changes which have been made or are being thought about in US doctrine are in the wrong direction. They have been moving towards a lowering of the nuclear threshold by an erosion of the taboo on nuclear war. There has been movement away from the idea of nuclear war as 'unthinkable' towards such ideas as James Schlesinger's 'limited nuclear options' through to Colin Gray's 'theory of victory'.[24] Making this worse has been the relative inattention given to conventional forces by NATO over the years, which has led to an expectation of an early reliance on battlefield nuclear weapons in the event of war. Once such weapons are employed, however, the possibility that a nuclear war in central Europe could easily be kept 'limited' has been generally scorned, though in practice it is sensible that it be contemplated as long as nuclear weapons are in existence. But we are clearly on a slippery slope. The pro-nuclear tendency in thinking about Western defence means that it is becoming psychologically and practically easier to speed up the race to Armageddon, once a clash of arms takes place in Europe.

'We are all Clausewitzians now' is a sentiment which is not infrequently expressed within the strategic community. But the reality is somewhat different. From governments we frequently meet a disheartening accountant's approach to defence — knowing the price of everything but the value of nothing — while from civilian analysts we frequently get only a fascination with the techniques of strategy. Overall, we have more strategic talkers than strategic thinkers.[25] Surprisingly, in the last few years, it has been the British peace movement which has been providing a greater Clausewitzian inspiration than the strategic community in general, and the government in particular. The peace movement has continually been asking the question 'What is it all about?' — the question which Ferdinand Foch used always to ask, and which Bernard Brodie, the nonpareil of the nuclear theorists of the golden age, has described as 'the single most important idea in all strategy'.[26] This Clausewitzian question is not often asked within the strategic community, unless outsiders provoke it. Instead, we are sometimes offered fairy stories, but with a superficial smack of realism; these are made up of an equal but opposite amount of ridiculousness to the fairy stories which emanate from some of the more unworldly members of the peace movement. One popular fairy story by a respected strategist is General Sir John Hackett's *The Third World War: The Untold Story*, which is now in its second edition.[27] General Hackett was an impressive commander in the British Army, and is a sophisticated thinker and civilized man. His book, however, is both offensive and lacking in Clausewitzian sense. If it is to be taken seriously, which perhaps it should not be, it can be reported that *The Third World War* does not ask whether nuclear war can be a rational instrument of policy: it implicitly assumes it can be, for it shows there is a victor. It does not ask whether the risks of fighting a nuclear war are worth the potential costs: instead, its message subtly asserts that the risks are worth the costs, for the fairy story nuclear war which is described ends with the traditional happy ending, in this case the settling — to the West's favour — of Lenin's question as to which system will dominate, communism or capitalism. Finally, the book does not promote the message that the Third World War will be a nightmare beyond nightmares, but instead argues that if NATO takes remedial action quickly enough, the coming war with Soviet Russia can be *controlled* and *won*, if not actually deterred. Rather than regarding the book as a cautionary piece of future history — the intention of its author —

it should be seen as a knowledgeable, sophisticated and plausible attempt to think about tomorrow's wars with the mind-set of the last.

The inspiration of Clausewitz — especially the habit of asking 'What is it all about?' — is more alive and well within the peace movement than it is among at least a part of the strategic community. Nevertheless, it must be added that the British peace movement has serious problems of its own when it comes to translating its Clausewitzian inspiration into feasible and desirable policies. Traditionally, the level of strategic and international political expertise among supporters of the peace movement has not been impressive. Although it is improving, it still has a long way to go. Nevertheless, the strategic community — against its instincts — should cherish its critics, however unworldly they might appear, since they confront it with questions about first principles which the 'strategists' invariably ignore: is the Soviet Union our most worrying threat? should the values we cherish be protected by the threat of indiscriminate and massive slaughter? is the national interest enough? what is 'security', and should we only be concerned about our own? are there alternatives to those defences and alliances fashioned originally in the Cold War? Such questions are naturally open to debate in a democracy, but it has been the peace movement and concerned individual citizens who have largely been responsible for opening the present debate about war and the threat of war as a continuation of politics.

If Clausewitz's general emphasis on the unity of war and politics reinforces the central concerns of the critics of Britain's pro-nuclear defence policy, other aspects of his thinking should also give them encouragement. With his matter-of-fact attitude towards the role and persistence of war in the international system, he would surely have had little faith in the idea that any deterrent would always deter. With his ideas about 'friction' he would have had no faith in our ability to control nuclear what-are-called 'exchanges'. With his belief in the inherent strength of the strategic defensive he would have had more confidence in the defensive strength of NATO than some of the alliance's persistent alarmists.[28] And with his belief in the importance of numbers of men he would have stressed the benefits of having as many men in position as is possible.

Every War Must End was the title of an important book on war termination, but, as its author F.C. Iklé showed, it is far easier to become embroiled in war than to extract one's nation satisfactorily.[29]

This is a message of particular pertinence for Britain, which presently lacks a rational war-fighting and therefore war-terminating strategy. 'Flexible response', as Lord Carver and others have argued, is not a satisfactory war-fighting doctrine since it contains the inherent risk of transforming any clash into general nuclear war.[30] Furthermore, the catalytic or trigger rationale for Britain's independent nuclear weapons — the idea that British weapons would help ensure US involvement in any European outbreak[31] — is fundamentally irrational. Sparking off a general nuclear war by catalytic independent action makes no sense as either a war-fighting or war-terminating strategy. It sounds suspiciously like a strategy to save Britain by destroying it.

Since the prevailing pro-nuclear British defence strategy can be criticized for being both irrational and immoral, a non-nuclear option might appear to be a relatively attractive option. But we must not be misled by any wishful thinking, for a non-nuclear option also contains dreadful risks and heavy costs, and it is most unlikely that it would have all the beneficial outcomes so often suggested by its supporters. For example, it is doubtful whether any other state — least of all imperial Soviet Russia — would follow any British 'example' in giving up its nuclear force. Each country has its own reasons for wanting nuclear weapons, and the British example is not likely to be considered relevant to them. (But the corollary to this is important, namely that a Trident-hugging British government, which engages in a political campaign to stress the utility and relative cheapness of the possession of such an advanced system, is offering positive encouragement to horizontal nuclear proliferation.) Less seriously, it is not likely that Britain would save money for non-military purposes if it abandoned its pro-nuclear posture. Indeed, the 'conventional' strategy which will be suggested later will almost certainly cost more money than the present 5.4 per cent of the GNP. Furthermore, a non-nuclear strategy can never *guarantee* that Britain will not be involved in a nuclear war, or will not be the target of a nuclear threat: the critics of the unilateralist position would assert that giving up nuclear weapons only increases the prospects of such eventualities. These are serious arguments, and must be confronted rather than ignored by unilateralists.

Finally, it must also be admitted that a non-nuclear posture would not uncontroversially represent an improvement in the moral dimension of British strategy. Nuclear disarmament itself does not give its supporters clear control of what some strategists like to call the 'moral high ground', for once one leaves the certainties of absolute pacifism or assertive militarism, the ethics of different strategies are complicated and controversial.[32] Even so, moral considerations should be brought into strategic discussions:[33] but we should avoid moralizing, for what is striking is the extent to which men of good faith, and no faith, can be status quo or revisionist on the nuclear question. Nevertheless, strategy in a fully Clausewitzian sense cannot avoid moral questions, since national political objectives are pervaded by explicit and implicit moral choices and value preferences. But ultimately a stand has to be taken, and the unilateralist view is that there is no conceivable political problem between the United Kingdom and the Soviet Union — including the threat of invasion and occupation — which justifies the threat and possible use of nuclear weapons by Britain against millions of Soviet citizens. Even if the chances of the weapons ever being used are remote, and even if our lives would be riskier as a result of renunciation, it is believed that nuclear weapons represent a power of destruction which it is neither right or prudent to employ. And for what purpose, when the Soviet leader's reply to our nuclear behaviour might be to hasten on the end of British history?

Hard unilateralism

If a pro-nuclear posture for a small and overcrowded island is thought to be unsatisfactory, in terms both of long-term security and morality, it is necessary to propose an alternative which promises to be more rational, national, and instrumental. What is needed is a strategy which offers more than the sort of 'peace' which comes from rolling over and playing dead, or from paying off one's neighbourhood protection racketeer. A strategy is required which promises security and freedom, as well as merely peace. 'Hard unilateralism' is one possible alternative, though it must be accepted at the outset that it will not free us from political and moral problems, or the expenditure of fabulous costs, or difficulties with our allies, or uncertainties in our relations with the Soviet Union. It will not herald a bright new dawn in international relations: it will merely confront us with a different set of problems and risks.

The hard unilateralist alternative should be based on a posture of conventional continental defence and a strategy of expedients. Such a package might be called 'tediously reformist',[34] but in the defence field this might be thought of as a compliment rather than a criticism, since it implies realism as well as movement in a favourable direction. The package to be proposed has four elements: the beginning of a shift from a pro-nuclear to a conventional defence for Western Europe; the maintenance of the NATO framework but with a more explicit recognition of the separate interests of the European and North American sectors of it; the allocation of greater resources in Britain towards conventional forces, ultimately including some form of national military service; and, finally, the replacement of the escalatory strategy of flexible response with a doctrine based upon a 'strategy of expedients'.[35]

NATO should continue to provide the framework for British strategy. Unilateralists should not throw out our security baby with the dirty nuclear bathwater. The E.P. Thompson vision of a liberated Europe is appealing, but it is not a politically relevant proposition, and is unlikely to be, for at least a decade, if then.[36] In the meantime, Europe has to continue to live with the implications of the Cold War and the shadows of two determined superpowers.

In the actual circumstances we are faced with, we should be positive about NATO. For the foreseeable future Western Europe will be stronger collectively than individually; and Britain, as a relatively strong country, has some responsibilities to support the security of smaller western states. If divided, Western European states are more likely to defer to a militant Soviet Union than if they have the confidence which comes from a sense of collective defence. In practical matters, an integrated alliance offers the prospect of rationalizing the defence efforts of the states involved; and politically the alliance structure gives the Federal Republic of Germany a role and a limitation, and helps to create a sense of balance which offers whatever degree of hope there exists for arms control and detente. For Britain, it is prudent that national defence begins as far east as possible, and it remains important that the defence of Western Europe involves the United States. NATO continues to remain the only instrument for keeping the United States tied militarily to Western European defence, and as long as the United States remains directly committed, the Soviet Union is unlikely ever to attack. NATO therefore helps to draw those sharp lines which are so desirable for deterrence purposes: one of the problems of the 1930s was that nobody was sure where the lines were.

The issue of relations between the United States and Europe is a particularly knotty one at present, and from all points of view. Handling the Atlantic partnership will require consummate diplomatic skill in the years ahead, especially if Britain moves to a non-nuclear strategy. We are bound to recognize (a) that any Western European defence is stronger with US involvement; (b) that it is unrealistic to expect the United States to give up its nuclear weapons; and (c) that British 'unilateralism' is unpopular in some parts of the US foreign policy establishment. In such difficult circumstances it should be the aim of the advocates of a non-nuclear strategy for Britain to encourage the United States that it is in its own interests to freeze its own nuclear build up, and then move to a 'minimum deterrent' posture, deployed solely for deterring direct attacks on the US homeland. Whether or not this exercise is successful, the whole of NATO, including US forces, should begin making a slow adjustment to a conventional posture in Europe. While many Americans would be uneasy about depriving US forces overseas of a direct battlefield and theatre nuclear retaliatory capability, stability would be maintained by the presence of the distant US nuclear threat. The Soviet leaders would continue to appreciate that Western Europe remained a 'vital interest' for the United States, especially if the change in strategy were accompanied by consistent and clear political signals on the part of US leaders.

Some critics of unilateralism argue that such a posture, which leaves the United States as NATO's only nuclear power, would be 'hypocrisy' on Britain's part. This is an utterly misplaced criticism, as long as the British show that they are in fact 'serious' about defending themselves, albeit by a non-nuclear method.[37] At present we do not cry 'hypocrisy' at our nuclear-capable allies who have not taken up the option; indeed, we are rather relieved that they have not. To those who would cry 'hypocrisy' at a non-nuclear Britain which remained tied to a nuclear United States, and to those who would insist that the moral, economic, and political burdens of nuclear weapons should be 'shared',[38] it must be pointed out that consistency demands that they also argue that every member of the alliance which can afford nuclear weapons should therefore possess them. In this way we would have no 'hypocrites' or 'free-riders'. For some reason, those supporters of British nuclear weapons who purport to place so much emphasis on consistency of outlook do not make those arguments.

In order to meet some of the political problems alluded to above, the hard unilateralist position requires that Britain should adopt a form of national service (conscription). Such a course is equally urgent for military reasons: improving our conventional forces is a necessary reform for whatever strategy we adopt. National service would be a logical step for Britain both as the basis of a new commitment to continental defence and to raise the nuclear threshold, which even most nuclear deterrers admit is 'uncomfortably' low.[39]

The military rationale for having greater manpower is straightforward, and only conscription could reliably meet the needs.[40] The major considerations are as follows. Firstly, war is likely to come by surprise, however much warning time we are given, and this means that it is essential to have the maximum amount of manpower permanently in place. Secondly, NATO is greatly in need of conventional staying power, since attrition rates in war will be high; a system of military service would provide trained manpower over the years for active reserves, and a degree of UK territorial defence. Thirdly, the possession of greater numbers of men in a state of readiness will help the alliance cope with lesser contingencies, such as Soviet miscalculations or probes. Without greater effort, NATO will have to face the prospect of an early need to escalate, because of the forward position of NATO's battlefield nuclear weapons and the relatively low priority given to conventional defence. Finally, in a major war conscripts and reservists can release the professionals for more demanding tasks, as well as providing for a denser defence; they can thereby help to undermine any Soviet confidence in achieving a quick victory.[41] The military rationales for national service are powerful, and Britain's contribution would not be negligible. France, with a slightly smaller population, has 200,000 conscripts in its army alone.

In addition to the military benefits of national service, increased conventional efforts on Britain's part would also be a signal to our potential enemies, and also to any doubting friends, that we are indeed willing to make efforts to defend ourselves. And such efforts need to be made daily, in peacetime, and not left to the brink of war. As the Falklands War showed yet again, it is far cheaper, in all ways, to demonstrate that one intends to defend one's patch of territory than to leave potential aggressors with doubts. Restoring the *status quo ante* is always dreadfully more costly than an effective deterrent strategy. It is sensible, therefore, for Britain to make its sacrifices now, to help deterrence and contribute to the health of the alliance. The reintroduction of national military service can be considered as part of the price we should be willing to pay as a community in order to raise the nuclear threshold in the first instance and renounce nuclear weapons in the longer term. If we are not willing to make such efforts, can we complain if those who claim to know better insist that we have 'no choice' but to try to defend ourselves with nuclear weapons?

If national service were to be reintroduced, with some imagination, and if it were to be made broader than merely military service, then it should be possible to overcome the variety of social, economic, and political criticisms which would inevitably be levelled against such a step. National service, despite all its difficulties, should be accepted as a properly democratic duty: one man (or woman), one vote, one anti-tank guided weapon.

The third leg in the hard unilateralist continental defence posture would be a modern version of the Elder Moltke's 'strategy of expedients'.[42] This would replace the existing NATO strategy of 'flexible response', which has attracted much criticism for its escalatory potential. Over a century ago Moltke argued that a nation could only plan a war up to the first major encounter, and no plan could look with certainty beyond that: 'All consecutive acts of war are', he said, 'not executions of a premeditated plan, but spontaneous actions, directed by military tact'. Strategy, he claimed, 'is a system of *ad hoc* expedients; it is more than knowledge, it is the application of knowledge to practical life, the development of an original idea in accordance with continually changing circumstances. It is the art of action under the pressure of the most difficult conditions.'[43] In practice, Moltke refrained from issuing any but the most essential orders. He encouraged initiative and independence on the part of his commanders, high and low, but within the confines of a commonly understood strategic doctrine. This inspiration is appropriate for a future European battlefield, where chaos will reign and communication will be difficult. Such a strategic doctrine implies flexibility and mobility, dispersal and decentralized command; it implies good training, defence in depth, and heavy firepower packed in small bundles — all within a common 'seek and destroy' doctrine The details would need to be worked out by those skilled in tactics and logistics, but the essence of the doctrine is the attempt to frustrate and wear down the offence, while leaving the defence with flexibility and choice.

The prospects for conventional defence

Underlying all the reforms suggested above is the basic shift from a pro-nuclear to a basically non-nuclear defence; it is a shift which would obviously have profound implications for all aspects of NATO, political and military. Clearly, NATO is presently not ready to opt for such changes, and therefore it will be necessary to accept a time-scale of several years, at the very least. Some outsiders, in Britain and West Germany in particular, have been thinking about completely non-nuclear strategies, but NATO insiders have not, although some attention has been paid to methods of improving conventional defence. But the latter has been considered within the context of an overall pro-nuclear strategy. This shows great continuity on NATO's part, since from its earliest days its planning has been based on the threat of use of nuclear weapons. Changes in doctrine have come and gone, but usually what has been involved has been a change of label rather than a significant change in military facts. The reality, throughout NATO's history, has been that conventional and nuclear forces have been seen as complementary.

The NATO allies have always believed that conventional forces were necessary, but they have invariably been seen as contributing to a phase in a nuclear strategy rather than offering an alternative means of defence.[44] Under the 'Lisbon goals' of 1952, which looked towards the creation of ninety-six divisions, a figure which has never remotely been reached, it was expected that the conventional phase would be prolonged. But since that time both the size of NATO's conventional forces, and the length of time they might fight, have been reduced. As the 1950s progressed, NATO's conventional forces merely became a 'trip wire' or a 'plate glass window', to signify that the enemy had advanced further than he should have. At stronger moments these forces were meant to impose a 'pause', to give the enemy time to reflect upon the accident or miscalculation which had led him to advance; it would give him some time to withdraw before the nuclear sword was drawn. Only in Robert McNamara's conception of 'flexible response' in the early 1960s was the idea of fighting a fully conventional war in Europe seriously considered. But this idea was unpopular with the European governments of the time: it seemed to increase the chances of highly destructive wars in Europe; it was thought that it would weaken deterrence by limiting (geographically and in terms of destructive power) the horror of war; it was argued that it would 'de-couple' Europe from the US nuclear guarantee; it was seen to require the provision of greater resources, both men and money, than the Europeans of the time were willing to offer; and it seemed to be playing to Soviet strengths. In McNamara's doctrine of 'flexible response' nuclear weapons would inevitably remain in the background, but he hoped that the provisioning of large and effective conventional forces would increase the prospects of a US president being able to postpone the decision to escalate, and that in the time so bought the crisis managers would have the opportunity to resolve the conflict.

In the event, McNamara's doctrine of 'flexible response' was not adopted. Instead, the NATO members merely purloined his title. In 1967 a strategy of 'flexible response' was formally adopted, but it was a long way from McNamara's original idea. In the NATO version the conventional component was marginally improved, but NATO remained committed to an early reliance on the tactical nuclear weapons which had been piled up since the mid-1950s, and a general reliance on the strategic nuclear threat in the background. Psychologically there was a sense that things had improved, but what NATO had was what some have felicitously called 'flexible escalation' rather than pure 'flexible response'. Despite the apparent change of strategy, the expectation has remained that NATO would not fight a prolonged conventional war, but instead would probably have to escalate at each level, or risk defeat. As John Garnett has put it: 'the flexibility implied by the phrase "flexible response" does not relate to the decision of whether or not to escalate, but only to the timing of the escalation. The relevant question is not *whether* to escalate, but *when* to escalate.'[45] In 1969 the British Defence Secretary, Denis Healey, said that the pause between a Soviet attack and the need for escalation would be a matter of days not weeks. The dozen or so years since that comment was made do not appear to have changed the opinions of anyone closely involved.

Since NATO is committed to a pro-nuclear strategy, little immediately can be expected from within the organization by way of ideas about movement towards a basically non-nuclear strategy. However, there is a steady attention given to the tactics and weaponry necessary to strengthen the alliance's defensive potential, and a major initiative in this respect was the call in September 1982 by General Bernard Rogers, the Supreme Allied Commander, for a stronger conventional defence in order to reduce the alliance's reliance on nuclear weapons.[46] His public disclosure that more attention was being given to such matters was an indication of the need felt by insiders to respond to the concerns being expressed in the streets and elsewhere by outsiders, especially the peace movement. It also reflected a growing concern within the organization about its reliance on battlefield nuclear weapons, and the growing sense of uncertainty about nuclear strategy in general. Despite the efforts and concerns of such important individuals

63

as General Rogers, the strategy of the alliance remains heavily pro-
nuclear. However, one wonders what NATO planners could devise if
they were told that Western defence was to be both non-nuclear and
better funded at the end of five years. No doubt it would concentrate
wonderfully the minds of tacticians, logisticians, and weapon developers.

To a growing number of observers it appears that weapon development is assisting the prospects for non-nuclear defence. In this respect
NATO is at a potential advantage over the Warsaw Pact, since it is technologically superior, already has more men in the field, and could provide even more. The main characteristic of the conventional battlefield
in the years ahead seems to be the progressive vulnerability of the tanks
and aircraft on which any massive offensive would rely.[47] In the years
ahead tactical aircraft will become more vulnerable against sophisticated
air defences, and their costs will mean fewer such aircraft in national
inventories. Meanwhile, developments in area weapons such as minelets
could degrade the air threat by destroying the airfields on which they
depend. In addition, such weapons can help to canalize the movement
of tanks, and so enable the defence to bring indirect fire to bear. Without doubt, the development in conventional forces which has attracted
most attention in the past decade has been the progress of precision-
guided weapons – those which should reliably be able to hit a target,
if it can be seen. Such weapons should favour the relatively static defence
against oncoming tanks. Tanks will remain essential in the inventories
of any potential aggressors, but they have been losing some of their
former advantages, and can now be considered both clumsy and conspicuous. For the future, various types of anti-tank guided weapons
have much further evolutionary potential than their targets. Short of
some radical breakthrough, the prospects for adding more speed and
armour to tanks are very limited. Furthermore, the extensive use of the
latest anti-tank guided weapons, which improve the chances of infantry
being able to fight tanks, has only seriously been underway in NATO
since the late 1970s. Tactically, and in terms of training, there is clearly
much further to go. Through all the developments in tactics there is the
perennial problem of command and control. On a chaotic future battlefield the balance of advantage should favour the defender since he
should know where he is, he is in friendly country, and he has the
simpler task.

In conventional warfare present trends seem to be favouring the defence. Over twenty years ago B.H. Liddell Hart, the doyen of British
military thinking, said that this trend towards the defensive had been

evident since the time of Napoleon.[48] He noted that improvements in firepower, mobility, and communications meant that progressively fewer men were needed to hold a given piece of ground. Nevertheless, Liddell Hart warned that aberrations were possible, as had been the case with the German breakthrough in 1940. The aggressor would succeed, he said, if the defence was not properly manned, trained, and equipped, and if the defensive forces were organized around a dynamic strategic doctrine. This is an important warning to those who fondly hope that a conventional defence for Britain would necessarily be a cheap and easy alternative. It would not, and those who advocate a non-nuclear defence, such as the British Labour Party, should be aware of the costs and other implications of such a strategy if it is to be adopted seriously. Such a strategy requires, for example, a large and continuing commitment to research and development, for while it presently appears that techno-logical developments are assisting the defence, it is important to guard against the wish becoming father to the thought. The history of war shows a periodic swing in the pendulum of tactical advantage between the offence and the defence. Clearly, new vigour would be pumped into the conventional aspects of the arms race.

The non-nuclear option should not be embraced simply because it seems to offer some form of escapism from the horrors of nuclear war, for as a dozen campaigns have shown in recent years, modern 'conven-tional' war can be terrible. And obviously a major conventional war in central Europe between such heavily armed and technically proficient forces as those of NATO and the Warsaw Pact would be a bloody affair indeed. If it were to break out, the only consolation such a war might offer would be the thought that it would fall short of the nightmare of nuclear war, since the latter could wreak the damage of the Second World War in less time than it takes to read this essay. Advocates of a non-nuclear strategy for Britain must accept the potential horror of modern conventional war. For one thing, they must be able to convince their potential adversaries of this horror, so the latter will not imagine that any invasion on their part will be worth the costs. In this way a conven-tional defence will be transformed into an effective deterrent.

'Alternative defences'

The possibility of Britain becoming a heavily armed but non-nuclear member of NATO is only one of the options which have been discussed

65

recently by those who are not satisfied with the country's pro-nuclear defence posture. Among the other ideas which have been put forward are non-violent resistance, territorial defence, and guerrilla resistance.[49] None of these postures promises to be a serious option for Britain in the years ahead. Even if they were desirable, it is not likely that they would ever be considered feasible.

Non-violent resistance has a long history and is an interesting idea. However, it is not relevant as an option of state policy in the circumstances in which we believe we will find ourselves in the years ahead. Governments exist to provide security, and they cannot be expected to denude themselves of what they believe to be the instruments of that security, namely armed forces. And the British people will remain overwhelmingly behind their governments on this. They know, at least believe, that international politics is a nasty business in which it is necessary for a nation to demonstrate its willingness to defend its interests, if it is not to be pushed around. Non-violent resistance will therefore not be considered as a 'defence policy' for Britain, though it would be conceivable as a possible national reaction to some distant calamity.

A more serious military idea is that of territorial defence, the idea of militia forces preparing to resist in depth against any invasion. In some variants, this smacks too much of a 'Dad's Army' approach — amateurism, muddling through, and compromise. It represents the familiar British habit of willing the ends but not the means. If defence is to be pursued seriously, it requires a core of professional forces, a system of rigorous training, and as much 'defence in depth' as possible. Sensibly, the latter should begin at the frontier of East Germany, not on the shores of East Anglia. Territorial defence would have some utility for last-ditch resistance, but 'Little Englandism' is a poor choice for a nation which is and should be intimately involved with the affairs of the adjoining continent. The same argument is true for guerrilla resistance. Again, this is not an option which any conceivable British government is likely to embrace, short of an imminent or actual invasion. Some of those who have espoused this idea have probably not thought of its full implications. Sometimes, it seems that they do not like what we have and simply cannot think of anything better than guerrilla war. In other cases they seem to have an unjustifiably romantic view of guerrilla warfare; they are the last European children of Che.

One problem with all 'alternative defences', including the variant being proposed in this essay, is that what is needed is not simply an alternative *defence* policy, but rather an alternative *deterrent* strategy. Alternative defences might effectively deter some threats, notably that of invasion and occupation, but they do not deal satisfactorily in the minds of critics with the possibility of 'nuclear blackmail,' and other less extreme types of threat. In the pre-nuclear age a good defence was always a good deterrent. If A threatened B, and B called A's bluff, then A had to fight B in order to take what he wanted. Now, if he chose, A could fire missiles at the targets B cherished, notably his cities, and the best army in the world could not save B. In the era of the nuclear missile, deterrence and defence have become bifurcated. As a result, a good defence only promises to deter invasion, not 'blackmail'; and a conventional defence, however good, could not save a nation against a preventive nuclear attack. The existence of such possibilities implies the need in all defence policies for some retaliatory capability. Unfortunately, this logical strategic need counteracts one of the aims of many advocates of 'alternative defence', namely the desire to achieve a 'non-provocative' defence posture. By reducing or eliminating altogether the 'offensive' weapons in one's inventory, it is argued that it will be possible to reduce some of the pressure in the continuing arms competition between the blocs, which is a major cause of tension, as well as a symptom of their mutual mistrust.[50] Either some retaliatory capability has to be maintained, or additional risks have to be run when it comes to contemplating the prospect of nuclear blackmail. Unilateralists prefer to run these particular risks, in order to enhance their wider security.

In the event of war, a non-nuclear Britain would cease to be a prime target for a Soviet attack against Western Europe, although such an attack could obviously not be ruled out. However, in short-of-war scenarios a non-nuclear Britain would be just as vulnerable − some would say more vulnerable − to the risk of being the target of Soviet politico-military pressure, including blatant nuclear threats. Such threats might even be expected from other states which might acquire nuclear weapons in the years ahead. This is a major problem facing a non-nuclear strategy, but it is also one which is surrounded by great uncertainties: it is therefore one of the most urgent matters for attention, in theory as well as practice, on the part of the advocates of a non-nuclear Britain.[51]

When contemplating the problem of nuclear blackmail, the first point to stress is that it is likely to be rare, certainly as long as the United States remains in NATO. The Soviet leadership can be under no illusions about the importance of Western Europe for the Americans. Secondly, the practice of nuclear blackmail is very difficult: there is not much evidence to give the blackmailer any confidence that it can be achieved successfully. The Soviet leadership will be inhibited by its understanding of the relationship between ends and means, and by the frequent incredibility of such threats. Thirdly, if a nuclear threat were issued, then only the circumstances surrounding it would enable one to decide how it might be met. Sometimes a threat can be ignored; at other times a bluff can be called; sometimes it is necessary for a smaller power to give concessions. The British political establishment's phobia about 'Finlandization' is the last affectation of a former great power, since great powers are not accustomed to deferring. Fourthly, it is hoped (but not necessarily expected) that the de-nuclearization of the western half of Europe would contribute to more stability in the international relations of the continent, so that the occasions for nuclear threats would be few.

Whatever is done about British defence policy, some risks have to be run, and the supporters of a non-nuclear posture are willing to accept whatever is the increase in risk from nuclear blackmail because they believe that it will free the British people, somewhat, from the risk of being embroiled in nuclear war, and will wholly free any future British government from complicity in the indiscriminate slaughter of millions of people. Those who hold such views believe, with justification, that the danger from nuclear war is an ultimately greater one to the British national community than the danger from the Soviet Union, and that there is something abhorrent if not lunatic in trying to secure our cherished values and way of life by the simultaneous threat of quasi-genocide and quasi-national suicide.

A state without nuclear weapons will, in some circumstances, be at a strategic disadvantage in a confrontation with a determined nuclear state. One of the most persistent of the arguments used by the supporters of a pro-nuclear posture for Britain is based on the assumption that nuclear powers will not be attacked by other nuclear powers: the situation in the Far East in the summer of 1945 is usually brought forward to strengthen the point. It is argued that if Japan had possessed atomic weapons in 1945 then the United States would not have used its own atomic bombs to finish off the war. The conclusion drawn is that countries possessing nuclear weapons will never be attacked by nuclear weapons.

This is a false and highly dangerous conclusion. Firstly, if it is propounded with confidence, it is a certain recipe for unlimited nuclear proliferation, an outcome which few regard as enhancing international security. Secondly, it is based on an over-simple analysis of the 1945 scenario.

Without doubt, the debate in the White House in the summer of 1945 would have been different had the president and his advisers been certain that Japan possessed a number of atomic bombs. But at that stage in the war, given Pearl Harbour and all that had happened since, the president of the United States could not have decided to call the whole thing off, bring the boys back home, and forget what had happened. Instead, he may have been tempted into a pre-emptive strike, either to destroy Japan's atomic capability (if his intelligence was good enough) or to bring about a political collapse of Japan before it used its own bombs. Alternatively, the president might have sent signals to the Japanese government in order to try to secure a tacit agreement that neither side would use its atomic weapons. If this seemed to have been established, he could then have proceeded with a blockade to squeeze Japan into submission, and ultimately risk an invasion. But how would the Japanese have responded to such a course of events?

One plausible argument is that a Japan in desperate straits would have attacked the United States with what atomic weapons it possessed. Less than four years earlier an economically vulnerable Japan had attacked the most powerful country in the world, and in a most uncompromising way. It is entirely conceivable, therefore, that the same state, on the brink of a disastrous defeat, might have employed a kamikaze atomic strategy in order to try to make the war so costly for the Americans that they would decide to call off their invasion of the Japanese homeland. The Japanese leadership might have argued that demonstrative bombs on San Diego or Seattle, backed by suitable threats of more to come, would threaten to increase the costs of invasion far above any price the Americans would have been willing to pay. And what had the Japanese to lose? They had already been defeated on the battlefield and the Americans were on the point of invasion. Had the Japanese undertaken a kamikaze atomic strategy, the Americans would almost certainly have retaliated in kind, and followed this up by an invasion and a brutal occupation. Two Pearl Harbours — one of an atomic variety — could not have been tolerated.

Had the 1945 scenario evolved as suggested, then the 'lessons' which would have been learned would be far different from those of atomic stand-off which have been suggested by the supporters of an

Ken Booth

independent British nuclear deterrent. The lessons of the demonstration bombs on San Diego and Seattle, and the US retaliation against Hiroshima, Osaka, Nagoya, and Yokosuka would be three-fold. Firstly, nuclear weapons do not necessarily induce caution. In desperate circumstances anything goes. A 'pre-emptive' strike or a 'demonstration' explosion are both 'rational' nuclear strategies in such circumstances. The existence of weapons of mass destruction will not stop their possessors from using them even against other nuclear powers, where there seems no alternative but surrender. Secondly, once one weapon is used, restraints break down. And thirdly, once deterrence has failed, and fighting begins, nuclear weapons are not useful as instruments of national defence: they only increase the costs of war. In war, or on the brink of war, Britain's nuclear forces would represent a modern variant of the kamikaze atomic strategy just postulated for imperial Japan.

Problems of a non-nuclear defence

In addition to the problems of non-nuclear forces mentioned earlier, two others deserve particular mention: in peace the problem of the future of the alliance in the event of a radical shift in force posture by such an important member as Britain; and in war the problem of NATO fighting in a conventional mode against a nuclear power. There is no hiding away from either of them, and there is no easy answer to either of them. Difficult choices and compromises will have to be made, and loose ends will inevitably be left dangling; but these are familiar features of any attempt to relate strategy and policy in a complex situation. The theory and practice of independent nuclear deterrence is not without its difficulties, weaknesses and loose ends.

One of the major concerns expressed by the critics of unilateralism is the future of NATO. They fear that the alliance could not survive Britain becoming a non-nuclear power like all the other members with the exception of the United states itself. Undoubtedly, there would be convulsions among the allies, but what materialized would much depend on the diplomatic skill of the participants, the timing of proposals, and whether national and ideological emotions were allowed to cloud the sober calculation of the interests of the members. In the mid-1960s NATO survived – indeed was revivified – when a major nuclear ally, France, withdrew completely from the military structure of the alliance. It is not clear why the same could not be the result when another major ally, Britain, merely changed the balance of its force structure, especially if in so doing it increased its conventional contribution and also reaffirmed its commitment to continental defence. Clearly, if the process is conducted with skill, NATO should be able to survive such a transformation, and for the best possible reason, namely that NATO's survival is in the interests of all the members, including the United States.

It is imperative that any unilateralist British government should be positive about the change to a non-nuclear strategy. Our representatives should remind Americans that a former US Secretary of Defense, Robert McNamara, warned against the dangerous, costly, and obsolescent character of 'independent deterrents'. They should remind Americans that the present US Secretary of Defense, Caspar Weinberger, has praised Sweden's defence posture. They should remind Americans that adviser-to-presidents and SALT negotiator Paul Warnke has said that if he were a European the last thing he would want on his soil would be cruise missiles. They should remind Americans that there are some doubters about the wisdom of the cruise decision even in the Reagan administration itself.[52] They should stress the desirability of a shift to a conventional posture and make clear Britain's determination to uphold the continental commitment. And, finally, they should coach Americans, after a generation of doing the opposite, of the desirability of a degree of de-coupling in defence. Many Americans would like to hear such words, and Britain should help and encourage Americans to get what they want, but only within limits: the aim should be to secure the maintenance of the conventional US commitment, but a run-down in the US nuclear forces assigned to NATO. Some Americans would obviously fear that the denuclearization of NATO strategy would weaken deterrence and expose American forces in the event of war. Even if this is the case, the present posture, while strengthening deterrence, risks embroiling the whole of the US homeland in a war which breaks out, for any reason, in Europe. Most Americans would readily agree that such a possibility was not in their interest.

Inter-war isolationism and Cold War mega-commitment to Europe were both aberrations in US history. We need not expect to see either again in the foreseeable future. Recent years have seen the growth of differences in basic attitudes between Western Europeans and Americans. The alliance is under pressure, whatever, and change is to be expected. A mature long-term relationship between the United States and Western Europe will be close, but not as close as we have become

71

used to since the late 1940s. A degree of military commitment but nuclear de-coupling would seem to be an appropriate strategic component of such a relationship. Those who think that the alliance could not survive such a change might comfort themselves with the thought that as presently constituted the alliance is unlikely to survive the effort of trying to stay the same.

If the future of the alliance is the major political problem of unilateralism, the major military problem concerns the apparent irrationality of increasing the chances that we would lose in the event of war: who would like to command conventional forces against a nuclear-armed enemy? The answer, of course, is nobody, but this must be set against the belief that the use of nuclear weapons on our part would be an even more disastrous method by which to try to throw back a Warsaw Pact attack. The truth is that once war of any kind begins in central Europe, the choices are terrifying: who would like to command nuclear-equipped forces against a nuclear-equipped enemy? Fortunately, in the view of all serious analysts, the prospect of a massive Soviet attack against Western Europe is very low. While there will always be some risk – great powers being great powers – it will be remote as long as the costs of invasion and occupation appear to be high in relation to any possible gains. Soviet leaders appreciate the high costs which would have to be faced in any attempt to invade and occupy Western Europe against a well-armed NATO. Even if NATO in Europe went non-nuclear, the costs would remain high and there would still be the distant prospect of US nuclear weapons to consider. Afghanistan and Poland have been major setbacks for Soviet foreign policy: they are reminders of the costs rather than the benefits of empire.

Although the risks of a Soviet attack are low, the possibility must be faced. In the first instance we might assume that a Soviet attack against a non-nuclear NATO would begin with conventional forces, and there are several reasons why this might be the Kremlin's most sensible option. If this occurred, then NATO could take some satisfaction from the fact that over a number of years the members had strengthened their conventional forces. This would have increased NATO's chances of being able to wear the Warsaw Pact forces down. Already NATO's strength in this regard is probably much higher than the public imagines as a result of listening to cries of weakness reiterated over the years by establishment alarmists.[53] A major conventional war in Europe would be desperate, but at least a non-nuclear Britain would not face the temptation of using nuclear weapons in our 'defence', and so risk starting the process which might bring an end to British history.

If the postulated Soviet attack was an accident or miscalculation, our enhanced conventional capability should give their leaders all the more opportunity to pause and reconsider their mistake, and try to resolve it. If, on the other hand, the Soviet attack proved to be deliberate and determined, we would have to assess our interests in the light of the way the battle developed. If we found ourselves losing, our strategy having failed, then we should seek to negotiate – the advice General von Schlieffen evidently left to the German General Staff in the event of his great war plan breaking down. Such advice is not defeatist: it is obvious statesmanship, though clearly easier said than done in the fog and fury of war. And as the Schlieffen analogy suggests, even the worst conceivable cease-fire agreement at the point one's plan breaks down is likely to be preferable to the results of a race to a total war.

It is possible that NATO's conventional forces might actually find themselves winning, or at least holding any Soviet advance. If that were to happen the Soviet leaders might decide to employ nuclear and/or chemical weapons on the battlefield, or employ them selectively against military targets in the rear areas (including the United Kingdom) or indiscriminately (though the latter is not their style, hardly in their interest, and unlikely in view of the risks of escalation with a still nuclear-armed United States). If Soviet forces begin to use nuclear weapons on the battlefield, NATO would still be in a more hopeful position than would be the case today. The clash between a superpower using nuclear weapons and an alliance defending itself with conventional forces would be horrendous, but it would at least have some in-built restraints, unlike the existing pro-nuclear strategy of flexible escalation. The actual outcome of such a clash would depend upon many unpredictable circumstances: would communications be blacked out, leaving attacker and attacked to fight it out in a thousand local campaigns? would the Soviet commanders have the skill and initiative to take advantage of a chaotic situation? would Warsaw Pact troops remain loyal? Only one thing would seem certain: whatever happened, the overall destruction promises to be less than would be the case with a war fought under present pro-nuclear doctrines. This would also be the case if Soviet forces began their attack with nuclear and/or chemical weapons, which they might well do given their existing war-fighting doctrines and their advantages in these weapons over a non-nuclear NATO. Again, if the NATO forces found themselves in a losing position, then their governments might sue for peace. And any peace would surely be preferable to the outcome following a war in which both sides had outdone each other in demonstrating nuclear resolve.

There are obvious risks in any conventional strategy against a nuclear enemy, but they are not necessarily overwhelming. Deterrence by retaliation would obviously be weakened, but a powerful deterrent to invasion and occupation would remain, especially if the full package of measures indicated above was to be implemented. Even against a non-nuclear NATO, the Soviet Union would have to contemplate enormous costs before taking a decision to invade. A framework of deterrence would therefore remain, but it would be one which would be less provocative to the adversary. At the same time it offers NATO a more rational war-fighting capability. Who would win on the ensuing battlefield must remain an open question, but what is not an open question is that we would all risk losing everything in a theatre of warfare where both sides were competing in nuclear destructiveness. If some of the foregoing arguments appear weak, consider the weaknesses of the alternative. At the worst, a non-nuclear defence gives Britain some hope of losing rationally. But there are more positive advantages: a strategy which offers us some prospect of emerging from a war with our national community and cultural infrastructure intact enables us to face even an horrendous war with some confidence. In contrast, wars which promise mutual nuclear destruction will be politically pointless. A non-nuclear strategy cannot guarantee victory, any more than any other strategy, but it is the best hope Britain has of ensuring that war and the threat of war will remain a continuation of politics.

Conclusion

Hard unilateralism involves risks, political problems, and heavy costs. However, these are all characteristics of the existing pro-nuclear posture, and it has been argued that a non-nuclear option would be more rational and instrumental for Britain than the mega-logic of nuclear deterrence and 'flexible escalation'. The urgency behind the need for change is created by a number of immediate issues, notably the Trident decision in Britain, the prospective deployment of cruise missiles and Pershing IIs in several Western European states, and by a growing sense that there has been a perceptible increase in the likelihood of nuclear war in the years ahead. However, the proposed non-nuclear option is not merely an emergency measure. If in five years the world has come to look a safer place, the case for a non-nuclear strategy will remain equally valid.

Political problems never come conveniently, one at a time; and this is the case with British defence policy at present. For reformers, this inevitably means that in practice some issues will have to be fudged, others temporarily ignored, and compromises and inconsistencies accepted on others. It is a fact of life, to the chagrin of reformers, that defence policies cannot be bought off the shelf: they have, instead, to be cobbled together, with new ideas adapting and being adapted to existing capabilities and doctrines, often in face of entrenched bureaucratic positions and interests. The proposals below add up to a series of steps which, in the light of the earlier discussion, might be said to represent a convergence of the feasible and the desirable for those who believe that Britain should end its reliance on nuclear weapons, but should still play a part in Western defence commensurate with the country's size and interests. Some individuals will be happier with some steps rather than others, but what is important is agreement upon a sense of direction:

1 The first step should be to restore the recent cuts in Britain's conventional forces. A long-term commitment should be made to improve these forces to show that we are serious about security and are determined to push up the nuclear threshold. An important dimension of such a policy will be diplomatic rather than military. This will involve demonstrating a positive commitment to NATO, expressing a determination to free NATO from its reliance on nuclear weapons, underlining the importance of a Western European identity in defence, and, finally, stressing the desirability for US interests as well as our own, of keeping the United States involved militarily in European affairs.

2 Almost simultaneously, consultations should begin with our allies to encourage them to agree to a unilateral withdrawal of battlefield nuclear weapons, as far from the East-West frontier as can be agreed, since these are the most vulnerable and immediately dangerous of all nuclear systems. This would be the first active step in the progressive denuclearization of Western European NATO.

3 The modernization and deployment of theatre nuclear forces should be resisted. If these weapons are deployed, they will only provoke countervailing Soviet efforts. Within five years we will have no more security, but will merely have incurred greater costs, undergone

increased international tension, and committed European affairs even deeper in a pro-nuclear direction. The deployment should be resisted, and multilateral disarmament talks should be used as the tactic to get our governments off the hook. The cruise missile/Pershing II deployment scheme should be defused as a political issue by deflecting it into the boggy pathways of something like the Vienna talks on mutual force reductions. There, the issue could sink out of sight, and with it, perhaps, our pedantic insistence on 'balance' in all categories of weapons. Within a few years the issue would be forgotten and unlamented, like the earlier Multi-Lateral Force, another idea whose political disadvantages outweighed its possible military utility.

4 We should accept that no British government is likely to give up its nuclear weapons immediately. Consequently, the major task for supporters of a non-nuclear posture is to do whatever is possible to stop the next generation. Trident is therefore the main target. There is already a significant constituency against Trident, but as time goes on opposition will become more difficult because of the steady accumulation of costs and other commitments associated with its preliminary development. In the not-too-distant future a favourably-disposed government will be able to claim that the Trident decision is 'irrevocable'. There is therefore some urgency for its opponents. Trident should be opposed and a replacement decision should be postponed as long as possible. In order to scuttle the idea of Trident it may be necessary, politically, to exert positive pressure to extend the life of Polaris. This would be more acceptable to the majority of the British political establishment at present than simply 'banning the bomb'. This positive pressure would stress that Polaris is cheaper than Trident and is still capable of providing an effective deterrent: Britain does not need, or want, the capability to raze 700 Soviet cities.[54] If the option of extending Polaris is taken, it is possible that a British government might be able to decide to slip out of the nuclear business in the second half of the 1980s. Within a shorter time span, it is not likely that a British government will simply 'ban the bomb'.

5 While Britain denuclearizes its own defence policy, and supports the progressive denuclearization of that of NATO strategy in general, it is politically imperative that British governments show our allies and adversaries that we are serious about defence and are determined to do what we are best able to do in a military sense. As a result, at the time we announce the extension of Polaris and the rejection of Trident we should also announce that we intend to institute national

service within however long it takes to organize. Registration could begin at once.

If such a package of proposals could be put into place, we could hope by 1986 or so to have put in train a major re-orientation of our defence effort. The prognosis will be better, of course, if in the meantime we come to have more flexible and relaxed leaders in Britain and the United States – leaders who do not turn every political and military issue into a loyalty test, and whose views about strategy are not shaped by the standard Sovietology of the 1950s. If the proposed steps can be begun, and if we are lucky enough to avoid trouble, NATO as a whole and the British in particular might, within a few years, grow comfortable with the idea of national service and a non-nuclear emphasis. If this were to happen, it would seem less dangerous and less traumatic if we then said 'no' to the idea of extending our nuclear deterrent force beyond the life of the present Polaris system, or even earlier.

Conventional continental defence based on a strategy of expedients represents a change of direction for British defence policy, but the major features of our defence predicament would still remain: we cannot escape our geography, or the recent history of Europe. Furthermore, the changes being proposed will be costly and difficult, and if not handled properly they could provoke worrying instabilities. As with nuclear deterrence, the policy must be handled with care and attended by luck. One wonders whether 'unilateralists' would be the best suited to implement a unilateralist defence policy.

Looked at historically, it is evident that there is much less to the 'change of direction' being proposed above than might meet the eye. Firstly, if Britain had not slipped into the nuclear business originally – and it now seems to have been an extremely close decision[55] – then the Britain of 1982 would not be contemplating acquiring nuclear weapons. We would have adjusted, psychologically and otherwise, to a non-nuclear defence, like all our NATO partners except the United States. Instead of stressing the extent to which the massive increase in destructive power represented by Trident will improve our national security – the position of the present government – our leaders would instead be stressing the virtues of non-proliferation. Secondly, if we had not ended conscription twenty-five years ago, and instead had continued it like all our Western European partners in NATO, then the institution would not appear the impossible burden which it now seems to many people. What is being proposed in this essay is therefore not radical: in fact it is rather conservatve. It is based on the idea that British defence policy in the last thirty years has been an historical aberration, caused by the difficulties facing a former great power in adjusting to a new world in which its role, strength, and aspirations are much reduced. What hard unilateralism entails, therefore, is merely another stage in Britain's adjustment to a world which is very different from that in which most of its leaders had their formative years. We need, as a nation, to get back into historical tune with ourselves: this means putting behind us the imperial has-been's longing to have a seat at the top table, the traditional military great power's wish to possess the best (i.e. most destructive) weaponry, and an affluent society's hope that it can have defence on the cheap.

The hard unilateralist position which has been elaborated in this essay is clearly not inspired by any faith in the feasibility or even desirability of disarmament for its own sake. Nuclear pacifism is being advocated for a mixture of prudential and moral reasons, but as a part of a new NATO strategy based on Britain setting a lead in multilateral conventional rearmament. The latter, it has been argued, offers the best prospect of a rational, national, and instrumental strategy for Britain in the dangerous years ahead; in short, it offers the best prospect of making Clausewitz relevant. In so doing, the world would be made a little safer for international conflict, and strategic history would be given a nudge in the right direction.

Notes

1 Michael Walzer, *Just and Unjust Wars: A Moral Argument with Historical Illustrations*, Harmondsworth, Penguin Books, 1980, p. 29.
2 Anatol Rapaport coined the phrase 'neo-Clausewitzian' to describe those American strategic thinkers who embraced Clausewitz's political philosophy of war, and who tried to adapt it to the nuclear age. This essay attempts the same task. Anatol Rapoport (ed.), *Clausewitz on War*, Harmondsworth, Penguin Books, 1968, pp. 60-9.
3 'Unilateralism' comes in several varieties. In its simplest and original form it simply means 'unilateral nuclear disarmament', the giving up by Britain of its nuclear weapons without requiring a parallel move on the part of Britain's adversaries. It is one of the purposes of this essay to fill out and strengthen the strategic meaning of 'unilateralism'.

4 See Ken Booth, '1931 + 50: It's Later Than We Think', in David R. Jones (ed.), *Soviet Armed Forces Review Annual*, vol. 5 (1981), Gulf Breeze FL, Academic International Press, 1981, pp. 31-49.

5 'The taboo against nuclear weapons is the only protection we have.' Carl-Friedrich von Weiszacker, 'Can a Third World War Be Prevented?', *International Security*, Summer 1980, vol. 5 (1), pp. 198-205.

6 The idea of likening nuclear weapons to the leviathan of the state is John C. Garnett's.

7 It is statistically meaningless to argue, as do some CND supporters, that there is a 50 per cent (more or less) chance of nuclear war in the next twenty (more or less) years. Probabilities cannot be assigned to historically unique events. This does not mean that bets cannot be taken.

8 A.J.P. Taylor, *How Wars Begin*, London, Futura Books, 1979. Taylor argues that the immediate origins of war often bear little relation to the 'profound causes': p. 14-15.

9 Quoted in Townsend Hoopes, *The Limits of Intervention*, New York, McKay, 1969, p. 30.

10 None of these episodes, it must be pointed out, has yet run its course. It is difficult to see precisely how they might lead (have led) to a conflict between the superpowers, but they are representations of three favourite doomsday scenarios: escalation following superpower intervention in the Third World, an oil crisis following a war in the Gulf, and a chain reaction following an outburst of nationalism in Eastern Europe.

11 This is certainly not to suggest that the Falklands War might have led to a World War, though in contrast most analysts would agree that any war in the Middle East has escalatory potential. The point is merely a reminder that small and unpredictable 'happenings' can have very far-reaching and dangerous consequences.

12 See, for example, Peter H. Vigor, 'The Semantics of Deterrence And Defence' and Geoffrey Jukes, 'The Military Approach to Deterrence And Defence', chs 25 and 26 in Michael McGwire, Ken Booth, and John McDonnell (eds), *Soviet Naval Policy: Objectives and Constraints*, New York, Praeger, 1974; John Erickson, 'The Soviet View of Deterrence: A General Survey' in Frank Barnaby and Geoffrey Thomas, *The Nuclear Arms Race – Control or Catastrophe?*, London, Frances Pinter, 1981, ch. 5.

13 On Soviet attitudes to the rationality of nuclear war, see Robert L. Arnett, 'Soviet Attitudes Towards Nuclear War: Do they really think they can win?', *Journal of Strategic Studies*, vol. 2, no. 2, September 1979, pp. 172-91, and 'The Consequences of World War III: The Soviet Perspective' in Jones, op. cit., pp. 256-65.

14 The standard text on this is J.W. Spanier and J.L. Nogee, *The Politics of Disarmament: A Study in Soviet-American Gamesman-*

ship, New York, Praegar, 1962. Sceptical surveys of the state of disarmament theory and practice are Ken Booth, 'Disarmament and Arms Control', ch. 5 in John Baylis *et al.*, *Contemporary Strategy, Theories and Policies*, London, Croom Helm, 1975 (second edn, New York, Holmes and Meier, 1983, forthcoming) and John Garnett, 'Disarmament and Arms Control Since 1945', ch. 7 in Laurence Martin (ed.), *Strategic Thought in the Nuclear Age*, Baltimore, The Johns Hopkins University Press, 1979.

15   There is little new under the sun as far as thinking about multilateral disarmament is concerned. To understand its problems, see Salvador de Madriaga, *Disarmament*, Oxford, Oxford University Press, 1929; one is as well reading Madriaga as the very latest book to be published on the subject.

16   See Henry Stanhope, 'The arms talk show that never ends', *The Times*, 23 September 1982.

17   Note the attitude, for example, of Hedley Bull, 'Arms Control: A Stocktaking and Prospectus, *Adelphi Papers No. 55*, London, IISS, 1969.

18   Academic strategists often refer to the period between 1955 and 1965 as the 'golden age' of contemporary strategic theory. Its beginning was marked by works such as Henry Kissinger's *Nuclear Weapons and Foreign Policy*. The period was characterized by an extraordinary burst of productivity and creativity in the field of strategic studies: see Ken Booth, 'The Evolution of Strategic Thinking', ch. 2 in Baylis, op. cit., especially pp. 34-41.

19   An attempt in this direction was C. Bertram, 'Arms Control and Technological Change: Elements of a New Approach', *Adelphi Papers No. 146*, London, IISS, 1978.

20   See Rapoport, op. cit., p. 13. Rapoport characterizes Clausewitz as 'an outstanding proponent of the political philosophy of war'. It might be thought unhistorical to try to relate Clausewitz's ideas to current British defence policy. Some would argue that his ideas are only relevent to the context in which they were written. This is not so. Some writers, and Clausewitz is one of them, have something to say to every generation; hence we should engage in time-transcending dialogues. Whether one concludes that Clausewitz would or would not have been a unilateralist is, in the end, immaterial. What matters is whether the dialogue illuminates our predicaments and leads to ways ahead.

21   The standard modern edition of Clausewitz's *On War* is edited by Michael Howard and Peter Paret, Princeton, Princeton University Press, 1977.

22   *The Times*, editorial, 19 October 1982.

23   On the Soviet view, see note 13 above. Some of those who would call themselves 'realists' in the West are presently among our least realistic when it comes to thinking about nuclear war: see, for example, Robert Scheer's interview with Thomas K. Jones, Deputy Under Secretary of Defense for Research and Engineering,

Strategic and Nuclear Forces, *Guardian*, 6 November 1982.

24 See Colin Gray's major contribution to the strategic debate: 'Nuclear Strategy: the Case for a Theory of Victory', *International Security*, Summer 1979, vol. 4 (1), pp. 54-87.

25 This nicely cynical distinction was first made by Hugh Nott: quoted in Ken Booth, *Strategy and Ethnocentrism*, London, Croom Helm, 1979, p. 138.

26 Bernard Brodie, *War and Politics*, London, Collins, 1973, p. 1.

27 Sir John Hackett, *The Third World War: The Untold Story*, London, Sidgwick & Jackson, 1982 (first edn, 1978).

28 For an authoritative but relatively relaxed view of the state of the Soviet war-fighting threat to NATO, see John J. Mearsheimer, 'Why the Soviets Can't Win Quickly in Central Europe', *International Security*, Summer 1982, vol. 7 (1), pp. 3-39.

29 Fred Charles Iklé, *Every War Must End*, New York, Columbia University Press, 1971.

30 Field Marshal Lord Carver, *A Policy for Peace*, London, Faber & Faber, 1982.

31 This rationale is discussed, for example, in Jeff McMahan, *British Nuclear Weapons, For and Against*, London, Junction Books, 1981, pp. 29-32.

32 This has been most recently brought out by the controversy within the Church of England surrounding the publication of *The Church and the Bomb: Nuclear Weapons and Christian Conscience*, the report of a working party under the chairmanship of the Bishop of Salisbury, London, Hodder/CIO Publishing, 1982.

33 This is the essence of Walzer's argument, op. cit. See also Booth, *Strategy and Ethnocentrism*, p. 9: 'Ultimately strategy is a continuation of philosophy with an admixture of firepower.'

34 The phrase is used by Adam Roberts, 'The alternative non-nuclear way to defend ourselves', *New Society*, 4 February 1982, p. 176.

35 The military aspects of this posture are discussed in more detail in Ken Booth, 'Strategy and Conscription' in J. B. Baylis (ed.), *Alternative Approaches to British Defence Policy*, London, Macmillan, forthcoming.

36 E.P. Thompson's arguments are collected in his *Zero Option*, London, The Merlin Press, 1982. See also his 'Peace in search of Eastern allies', *Guardian*, 25 October 1982.

37 The Reagan administration has little or no authority if and when it comes to lecturing Britain about 'hypocrisy'. Compare the administration's different attitudes to Western European sales of technology to the Soviet Union as part of the pipeline deal, and its attitude to its own grain sales to the Soviet Union; compare its attitudes to human rights violations in South America, and those in Eastern Europe and the Soviet Union; and compare its attitude to martial law in Poland, and to martial law in Turkey. In a 'fallen World', it is better, on the whole, if allies forget the word 'hypocrisy'.

38 Among its other weaknesses, this argument greatly exaggerates the clout which the British have on nuclear matters within the alliance.
39 Kenneth Hunt, 'Alternative Conventional Force Postures', ch. 8 in Kenneth A. Myers (ed.), *NATO: the next thirty years: the changing political, economic, and military setting*, Boulder, Westview, 1980.
40 For details of this, see Booth, 'Strategy and Conscription', op. cit.
41 There are signs that this is already on the wane: see Mearsheimer, op. cit., and especially his references in notes 26, 44, 65, and 75.
42 For an introduction to the thinking and life of this most intelligent of soldiers, see Hajo Holborn, 'Moltke and Schlieffen: The Prussian-German School', ch. 8 in Edward Mead Earle, *Makers of Modern Strategy*, Princeton, Princeton University Press, 1961.
43 Ibid., pp. 178-80.
44 Hunt, op. cit.; for a useful brief survey of the development of NATO doctrine, see John C. Garnett, 'Limited "Conventional" War In the Nuclear Age', ch. 5 in Michael Howard (ed.), *Restraints on War*, Oxford, Oxford University Press, 1979.
45 Garnett, op. cit., p. 91.
46 In September 1982 General Bernard Rogers announced that Western Europe could be defended against a Soviet conventional attack without using nuclear weapons if NATO members agreed to quite modest improvements in their own conventional forces. He disclosed that a plan to fight a non-nuclear war had already been developed at NATO headquarters. To meet the needs of such a plan he believed that it was necessary for an overall annual increase in defence spending in real terms of 4 per cent (compared with the 3 per cent agreed in 1978). He estimated that this would mean only an additional £6 a head to the populations of the NATO members. See *Guardian*, 29 September 1982; *The Times*, 29 September 1982; and *Time*, 25 October 1982. Shortly afterwards President Reagan's chief disarmament adviser, Mr Eugene Rostow, made it clear that a commitment by NATO members to increase their spending on conventional arms would not affect the deployment of cruise or Pershing II missiles. Furthermore, other 'US sources' stressed that while higher conventional efforts might make it possible to scrap 'some obsolete tactical nuclear weapons', the United States would proceed with plans for the MX system. John Palmer, 'Reagan sticks to missile base plan despite NATO proposal', *Guardian*, 19 October 1982.
47 For a useful introduction to the developing 'state of the art', see Kenneth Hunt, 'The Development of Concepts for Conventional Warfare in the 1970s and 1980s', ch. 12 in Robert O'Neill and D.M. Horner (eds), *New Directions in Strategic Thinking*, London, George Allen & Unwin, 1981.

48   B.H. Liddell Hart, 'The Ratio of Troops to Space', *RUSI Journal*, vol. CV, no. 618, May 1960, pp. 201-12. For a sceptical position, arguing that the tactical balance of advantage 'may be moving markedly in favour of sudden and heavy offensive action', see Neville Brown, 'The Changing Face of Non-nuclear War', *Survival*, September/October 1982, vol. XXIV, no. 5, pp. 211-19.

49   These approaches are summarized by Michael Randle, 'Defence Without The Bomb', *AUDI Report*, vol. 3, no. 1, January/February 1981, pp. 4-7.

50   Achieving a 'non-aggressive' or 'non-provocative' defence posture is one of the major objectives of most thinkers about 'alternative defences'. This implies depriving oneself of the ability to retaliate with long-range weapons, or sometimes even of the ability to carry the war back into the enemy's territory in a counter-attack. An example of such an approach is Johan Galtung, 'Europe's balance of selfishness', *New Society*, 19 November 1981, pp.327-8.

51   Note the arguments of McMahan, op. cit., pp. 40-7, 83-5, 140-3; and Robert Neild, *How To Make Up Your Mind About The Bomb*, London, André Deutsch, 1981, pp. 117-20.

52   John Palmer, 'Why NATO's battle for cruise is far from won', *Guardian*, 4 October 1982.

53   Significantly, as the opponents of NATO's pro-nuclear policy have increased in strength and knowledge, proponents of existing policies have come to admit that the balance of conventional forces between NATO and the Warsaw Pact is not as unfavourable as has commonly been thought. Note the disclosures of General Rogers, n. 46 above, and *The Economist*'s survey of non-nuclear defence, 31 July 1982. The latter's leader-writers found the results of their survey 'surprisingly cheerful'.

54   On Britain's options, see Peter Nailor and Jonathan Alford, 'The Future of Britain's Deterrent Force', *Adelphi Papers No. 156*, London, IISS, 1980; Lawrence Freedman, *Britain and Nuclear Weapons*, London, Macmillan, 1980. Trident-2, together with Tornado, could theoretically give Britain a 724 target capability by the 1990s: *The Economist*, 18 September 1982, p. 31.

55   According to one eye-witness, it was only Ernest Bevin's intervention in a cabinet on 25 October 1946 which ensured that the British programme proceeded to its conclusion; and as it happened, Bevin almost missed the meeting. Peter Hennessy, 'How Bevin saved Britain's Bomb', *The Times*, 30 September 1982.

Nuclear Blackmail

Jeff McMahan

The notion of nuclear blackmail

Military planners at the Pentagon have decided that the US must develop the ability to fight and 'prevail' in a 'protracted' nuclear war. They reckon that, to meet this requirement, the US should pursue the development of anti-ballistic missile systems, space-based weapons, including anti-satellite weapons, and more advanced systems of 'command, control, and communications' — among other things. When asked to justify these goals, Caspar Weinberger, the American Secretary of Defense, replied that they are all necessary to deter the Soviet Union from engaging in nuclear blackmail.[1]

Weinberger's views about the threat of nuclear blackmail are apparently shared by his former British counterpart, John Nott. In a parliamentary debate on 29 March 1982, Mr Nott twice referred to the threat of nuclear blackmail in an attempt to defend his view that Britain must maintain an independent strategic nuclear force. His particular aim on this occasion was to justify the government's decision to purchase the Trident D5 missile system.[2] He failed to say whether he thought that Britain too needs the ability to fight and win a protracted nuclear war with the Soviet Union.

More recently, the head of the US Arms Control and Disarmament Agency, Mr Eugene Rostow, stressed at a press conference that NATO governments must persevere in their plan to deploy cruise and Pershing II missiles in Europe. Otherwise, he claimed, the Soviet Union would 'retain its potential for nuclear blackmail'.[3]

In putting forward their arguments, none of these NATO officials bothered to explain what they meant by 'nuclear blackmail'. This is not unusual. References to nuclear blackmail are ubiquitous in the current debate about nuclear weapons, but the term has never been carefully defined or analysed. Perhaps it is for this very reason that government spokesmen find it so useful to invoke the spectre of nuclear blackmail in defence of their policies. Everyone is bound to agree that we must prevent the Russians from blackmailing us. But it is difficult to challenge the various claims about what will be necessary to deter nuclear blackmail — partly because no one seems to have a clear idea what nuclear blackmail consists in.

The aim of this paper is to clarify the notion of nuclear blackmail, and then to explore various ways in which a country might attempt to prevent nuclear blackmail from being used against it.

Blackmail and deterrence

What, then, is nuclear blackmail, and how does it differ from other coercive uses of nuclear weapons — for example, nuclear deterrence? One thing seems clear, and that is that it will not be helpful to pursue a comparison between nuclear blackmail and ordinary blackmail, in the hope that the essential features of ordinary blackmail will also characterize nuclear blackmail. The two types of blackmail are in fact very different. The nuclear blackmailer attempts to coerce his victim through the threat of nuclear destruction. But cases in which one agent attempts to coerce another through the threat of physical violence are not normally classified as blackmail. The typical blackmail threat is the threat to expose publicly something which the victim would prefer to keep concealed. (This is true in spite of the etymology of the term. 'Blackmail' originally referred to the payment which was extracted by freebooting chiefs on the Scottish border for immunity from pillage.) Moreover, the fact that the standard blackmail threat is the threat of public exposure implies that the victims of blackmail are often exposed to it by having been guilty of some past crime or folly. But this is never a condition of susceptibility to nuclear blackmail.

One suggestion might be that, while nuclear deterrence aims to coerce an adversary to *refrain* from acting, nuclear blackmail aims to coerce the adversary to *act* (for example, to surrender). In other words, it might be claimed that the goal of deterrence is to prevent action, while the goal of blackmail is to compel it. This suggestion is correct on one point: namely, that it is an essential feature of deterrence that it attempts to prevent action. But otherwise the suggestion is wrong. One problem is that all coercive uses of nuclear weapons could be trivially redescribed as instances of deterrence. For example, an attempt to coerce an adversary to surrender could be redescribed as an attempt to deter him from fighting, or from continuing to fight. A second problem is that there are cases which seem to be instances of nuclear blackmail, but which can only be described as cases in which the victim is coerced to *refrain* from acting. Suppose, to take a fanciful example, that sometime in the future Yugoslavia declares an intention to join NATO, and to allow the establishment of American forward bases on its soil, and that the Russians then secretly issue a veiled threat to attack Yugoslavia with nuclear weapons if it carries out its intention. This would seem to be a case of nuclear blackmail, but it is one in which the blackmailer aims to prevent the victim from acting rather than to compel him to act.

This example shows that nuclear deterrence and nuclear blackmail cannot be contrasted in the way suggested. Indeed, if we define deterrence broadly, so that any nuclear threat which aims to deter action rather than compel it counts as nuclear deterrence, then the categories of nuclear deterrence and nuclear blackmail will overlap.

Our inclination, however, is to suppose that nuclear blackmail *contrasts* with nuclear deterrence. It seems wrong to say that a threat to bomb Yugoslavia if it were to allow NATO bases on its soil would be an instance of nuclear deterrence. So perhaps we should adopt a more restrictive definition of nuclear deterrence. Let us say that nuclear deterrence consists in the attempt to prevent an unprovoked attack on one's homeland by threatening potential attackers with nuclear retaliation. An 'unprovoked' attack is defined here simply as an attack which is not itself a counterattack. Thus the definition excludes as an instance of nuclear deterrence a nuclear threat which aims to deter a *retaliatory* attack — that is, an attack provoked by an initial attack by the threatener. This definition of nuclear deterrence is restrictive in its stipulation that a coercive nuclear threat will count as an attempt at nuclear deterrence only if it aims to deter unprovoked attacks on the threatener's homeland and nothing more. Attempts to deter other types of action by means of nuclear threats do not, according to this definition, count as instances of nuclear deterrence. The definition does not, however, impose restrictions on the types of attack which might be prevented by nuclear deterrence. Thus nuclear deterrence could be used to deter either conventional or nuclear attacks. Finally, the definition as stated does not cover nuclear threats aimed at deterring unprovoked attacks on the homelands of the threatener's allies. But we may wish to extend our definition so that it covers these threats as well. It would then encompass what is known as 'extended deterrence'.

Having advanced this stipulative definition, can we now say that nuclear blackmail contrasts with nuclear deterrence in this restricted sense? It might be suggested that the categories of nuclear blackmail and nuclear deterrence (so defined) are mutually exclusive and together encompass all the possible coercive uses of nuclear weapons, or, rather, of nuclear threats. According to this understanding, all coercive nuclear threats would count as nuclear blackmail except for those intended to deter unprovoked attacks on oneself or one's allies.

This definition has a certain initial plausibility. But it raises a number of important questions – in particular, questions about the various nuclear threats which successive US governments have made since 1945. Starting, perhaps, with Hiroshima, US governments have apparently made use of nuclear threats on several occasions in pursuit of goals other than the deterrence of attacks on the American homeland or the homelands of the US's allies.[4] By our provisional definition, these would all be instances of nuclear blackmail. Consider first the nuclear bombings of Japan in 1945. Whether or not these are to be classified as a case of nuclear blackmail depends on how we understand the intention behind them. If the intention was only to create chaos and weaken morale among the Japanese, then perhaps the bombings can be regarded simply as instances of nuclear terror bombing. But it is possible that they were also intended to convey an implicit threat of further bombings unless the Japanese surrendered. Thus it is not surprising to find a reference by the defence correspondent for the *Guardian* to 'the kind of blackmail to which Japan was successsfully subjected in 1945'.[5]

One well-documented instance in which the US used the threat of nuclear war to achieve foreign policy aims other than the deterrence of attacks on its own territory or the territory of an ally occurred during the Arab-Israeli war in 1973.[6] In the course of that conflict, Henry Kissinger, then the American Secretary of State, persuaded the Israelis to accept a cease-fire agreement which he had negotiated in consultation with the Russians. The Israelis, however, subsequently continued and completed their encirclement of the Egyptian Third Army, thereby violating the cease-fire. Apparently suspecting that Kissinger had tricked them, the Russians made known their support for President Sadat's request that a joint US-Soviet peace-keeping force be interposed between the Israeli and Egyptian armies. At the same time they began to make preparations for intervention. When the US rejected the proposal for joint intervention, Brezhnev sent a message to Nixon which reportedly urged the US to reconsider the possibility of joint intervention, and warned that, if the US refused to participate, the Soviet Union might be forced to intervene unilaterally.

As the Soviet preparations for intervention in Egypt continued, the US replied to Brezhnev's note by placing all of its forces, including its nuclear forces, on a higher level of alert. Later a written message which twice referred to the *'incalculable consequences'*[7] of Soviet intervention was sent to the Soviet ambassador. Finally, Kissinger gave a press conference at which he gravely emphasized the dangers of nuclear war inherent in the crisis. It seems undeniable that these various gestures together constituted a clear and unmistakable nuclear threat. (As Blechman and Hart have stressed, the threat was not a crude and implausible threat to initiate a nuclear war the minute the Russian forces landed in Egypt. It was not that specific. It was simply a threat to confront the Russians militarily, but one which emphasized the likelihood of escalation to nuclear war.) The threat seemed to work, for the Russians refrained from intervening and the crisis was soon defused.

Was the US practising nuclear blackmail in this case? Is the coercion to which the Soviet Union was subjected an example of what Messrs Weinberger and Nott want to deter the Russians from doing to us? Most people in the West would reject the suggestion that the US subjected the Russians to nuclear blackmail in 1973. This is partly because many feel that the US action was legitimate, and the notion of nuclear blackmail seems to imply illegitimacy.[8] Since people in the West generally approve of the aim of restricting Soviet influence and Soviet activities, they are inclined to resist the charge that nuclear threats in support of that aim count as nuclear blackmail. Perhaps Flora Lewis is right when she refers to 'what Amercans call deterrence when speaking of their own policy and nuclear blackmail when speaking of the Soviet Union's policy'.[9]

Let us imagine a series of events which parallels this incident in the 1973 war except that the roles are reversed. Suppose that Egypt is still a Soviet client and is at war with Israel. The Egyptian army has advanced into Israeli territory. The Soviet foreign minister flies to Washington to negotiate the terms of a cease-fire agreement which he subsequently gets the Egyptians to accept. The Egyptians, however, continue their military activities during the period of the cease-fire, thereby managing to complete the encirclement of an Israeli army. Suspecting that the cease-fire violation was planned by the Russians and the Egyptians in collusion, the US announces to the Russians its support for an Israeli appeal for the establishment of a joint Soviet-American peace-keeping force. The Russians promptly reject this proposal. The US then writes back urging the Russians to reconsider and warning them that the US may feel compelled to intervene in Israel unilaterally to prevent the destruction of the Israeli army. Ever since the cease-fire violation, American forces have been mobilizing in preparation for intervention. When the Russians receive the American message, they immediately place their forces, including their nuclear forces, on a higher level of alert. They later send the American president a note containing ominous references to the 'incalculable consequences' of American intervention, and the Soviet foreign minister then appears at a televized press conference making threatening references to the danger of nuclear war. Fearing nuclear war, the US backs down and refrains from intervening.

Does *this* seem like an instance of nuclear blackmail? (Would it have made a difference if one had not known that the Soviet action in this hypothetical scenario exactly parallels the American action in 1973?) It is not mere cynicism to suppose that many people in the West would regard this hypothetical example as a case of nuclear blackmail, while at the same time thinking that the American action in 1973 was not. This is because whether or not we classify a certain coercive nuclear threat as an instance of nuclear blackmail seems to depend on our moral evaluation of the end which the threat is intended to achieve. And many people feel that, while it would have been wrong for the Russians to have intervened in Egypt in 1973, it would not be wrong, in our hypothetical example, for the US to intervene on behalf of Israel. The goals of Soviet foreign policy are generally regarded in the West as pernicious, since it is thought that, among other things, they tend to advance the spread of communism on the Soviet model. Accordingly, the end of preventing Soviet intervention in Egypt is generally held to have been legitimate. On the other hand, few would question the right of the US to intervene in Israel in order to prevent the defeat of the Israeli army. So the aim of preventing American intervention would generally be held to be illegitimate.

These reflections suggest that the second proposed account of nuclear blackmail is unsatisfactory. It is not the case that all coercive nuclear threats which are not instances of nuclear deterrence (as defined earlier) must therefore be instances of nuclear blackmail. Nuclear blackmail must be more narrowly defined. The account which is suggested by the foregoing discussion is that a coercive nuclear threat counts as nuclear blackmail if it aims to prevent a country from doing what it has a right to do, or if it aims to compel a country to do what it has a right not to do. The phrase 'has a right' in this context means only 'has a liberty-right'. A liberty-right is the weakest type of right. A liberty-right to do X entails only the absence of a duty not to do X. So an alternative way of stating our definition would be to say that a coercive nuclear threat counts as nuclear blackmail if it aims to prevent a country from doing what it is morally at liberty to do, or if it aims to compel a country to do what it is morally at liberty not to do.

According to this account of nuclear blackmail, whether or not we classify a particular nuclear threat as an instance of nuclear blackmail depends on whether we regard the behaviour deterred or compelled as morally permitted, required, or forbidden. Thus how we classify certain coercive nuclear threats will depend on our views about the moral rights and privileges of states, and about morality in war. An important consequence of this fact is that in practice there will be little agreement about which particular threats count as nuclear blackmail. Often the threatener and the victim of coercion will disagree about the morality of the action which the threatener aims to deter or compel. (Of course, they will *always publicly* disagree about this.) The victim will regard himself as acting within his rights; so he will perceive a nuclear threat which aims to coerce him to act differently as an instance of nuclear blackmail. But the threatener will see the victim's intended behaviour in a different light, and so will not regard himself as guilty of nuclear blackmail. In many cases there may be no generally agreed criteria for determining which assessment of the victim's intended action is correct. In these cases there may be no right answer to the question whether the coercion to which the victim is subjected counts as nuclear blackmail.

Consider again the nuclear bombing of Japan at the end of the Second World War. The two bombings, and the implicit threat of further attacks, were intended to coerce the Japanese to surrender unconditionally. Were the Japanese morally bound to surrender unconditionally? If so, then the bombings presumably did not constitute blackmail. But suppose we believe it was morally permissible for the

Japanese to seek favourable terms of surrender. In that case, according to our proposed account, the American bombings were an instance of nuclear blackmail.

Now it might be objected that, even if the Japanese were not morally required to surrender unconditionally, the American threat did not involve blackmail because the US was *entitled* to demand unconditional surrender.[10] This suggests a slightly different account of what constitutes nuclear blackmail. According to this alternative account, a coercive nuclear threat is an instance of nuclear blackmail if what is demanded is something that the threatener has no right to demand. This proposal will differ from the account I have given if one country can be entitled to demand that another should act in a way in which the other is not morally required to act. That this is possible is suggested by the situation of the Japanese in 1945. We may believe that the US had the right to demand unconditional surrender, but not that the Japanese were obliged to surrender unconditionally. If this is our view, then it makes a difference which of the two proposed accounts of nuclear blackmail we accept. If we accept the original account, then the US was guilty of nuclear blackmail; but, if we accept this alternative account, then, whatever else it may have been, the American action against Japan was not blackmail.

I will not attempt to determine which of these two proposals is preferable. It is normally true that, if A is entitled to demand that B do X, then B has a duty to do X. It may even be the case, though I doubt it, that A's entitlement entails B's duty. In any case, since the two accounts will normally coincide, I will henceforth not bother to distinguish between them, and will focus exclusively on the original proposal.

Assuming that the original proposal is plausible, we can now distinguish three categories into which nuclear threats can be divided. There is first the category of nuclear deterrence. Nuclear deterrence has been defined as the attempt to deter unprovoked attacks on one's homeland or the homelands of one's allies by threatening a potential attacker with nuclear retaliation. Next there is the category of nuclear blackmail. Nuclear blackmail consists in using a nuclear threat to coerce a country to do something which it is morally at liberty not to do, or not to do something which it is morally at liberty to do. In the case of nuclear blackmail, the nuclear threat may be more subtle than the simple threat of nuclear attack. It might, for example, instead be a threat to do something which the threatener and the victim both know will dramatically increase the risk of nuclear war. Thus defined, the categories of nuclear deterrence and nuclear blackmail overlap only slightly, if at all. This is because countries seldom if ever have the right to conduct unprovoked attacks on other countries ('unprovoked' in the narrow sense stipulated earlier).

The third category I shall refer to simply as the category of 'nuclear coercion'. Nuclear coercion consists in the use of nuclear threats to compel a country to do something which it ought to do, or to deter a country from doing something which it ought not to do. It is *this* category, and not that of nuclear deterrence, which is defined by contrast with nuclear blackmail. Nuclear coercion, in other words, includes all nuclear threats other than blackmail threats. If we believe that countries seldom if ever have the right to launch unprovoked attacks on other countries, then nuclear coercion will encompass much or all of the category of nuclear deterrence. But the category of nuclear coercion is broader. Most if not all nuclear deterrent threats are instances of nuclear coercion, but not all instances of nuclear coercion are also instances of nuclear deterrence. The category of nuclear coercion also includes certain nuclear threats aimed at deterring counter-attacks. Consider, for example, a case involving two states, A and B, each of which possesses crude nuclear forces which are insufficiently accurate to be used against any targets except cities. Suppose that A attacks one of B's cities and threatens to attack others if B retaliates by attacking any of A's cities. A's threat cannot be classified as an instance of nuclear deterrence, since it is not aimed at deterring an unprovoked attack. The attack it aims to deter is instead a counter-attack. Yet if we believe, as I in fact do, that B has no right to retaliate by attacking A's cities, then neither can we classify A's threat as an instance of nuclear blackmail. It is instead a simple case of nuclear coercion.

It should be emphasized that to say that A's threat is not a blackmail threat is not to say that it is legitimate, or that A has a right to threaten B in this way. It might be thought that, because the classification of a threat as an instance of nuclear blackmail implies a belief that the threat is wrong, and because nuclear coercion contrasts with nuclear blackmail, it then follows that the classification of a threat as an instance of nuclear coercion implies a belief that the threat is not wrong. But this is a mistake. It is true that the classification of a threat as an instance of nuclear coercion involves a moral evaluation. But the evaluation is not of the threat itself, but of the action which the threat is intended to deter or compel. The classification of a threat as an instance of nuclear coercion, or, more narrowly, as an instance of nuclear deterrence, implies nothing about the morality of the threat itself. The definition leaves it an open question whether or not it is morally permissible to engage in nuclear coercion.

Another point which should be emphasized here is that these definitions — of nuclear deterrence, nuclear blackmail, and nuclear coercion — are all to some extent stipulative. They are intended to reflect as much as possible our intuitions about the way the terms should be used, but our linguistic intuitions are in these cases neither clear nor firm. The terms 'nuclear deterrence' and 'nuclear blackmail' have only recently become part of the language, and it is partly as a result of this that they do not have very firmly established uses. 'Nuclear coercion', of course, has no established use, since it is a technical term introduced here for the first time. Moreover, many of the various nuclear threats which we need to classify are fortunately only hypothetical, and thus there are no precedents to which we can appeal in deciding how to classify them. For these and other reasons our linguistic intuitions cannot be expected to provide reliable guidance in the classification of marginal cases. In short, we cannot simply consult our linguistic intuitions in determining how to apply the terms. We must to some extent *decide* how we are going to use them. The definitions offered here attempt to accommodate those linguistic intuitions which we have, but they also constitute *proposals* for how the terms should be used which move beyond what can be inferred from our intuitions.

Nuclear blackmail in times of war and peace

Thus far I have attempted to establish a definition of nuclear blackmail. Later I will be addressing the question how a country might attempt to prevent itself from being subjected to nuclear blackmail. The scope of that inquiry will, however, be restricted: for I will be considering the problem only as it applies to currently non-nuclear countries. Precisely what a nuclear-armed country requires in order to be able to deter nuclear blackmail is too large a question to be dealt with here. Consider, for example, Weinberger's claim that, in order to deter the Soviet Union from blackmailing the US, the US must have the capability to fight and win a nuclear war with the Soviet Union. Presumably what he is worried about is the possibility that the

Soviet Union may use nuclear threats in order to push the US around — that is, in order to gain political concessions which the US would be morally entitled not to make. His reasoning may be that, if the Russians know that the US has the ability to defeat them in a nuclear war, they will then be deterred from threatening to initiate such a war.[11] This, however, raises the question why Weinberger thinks the Russians might *not* be deterred by the simple threat of 'assured destruction', which was the basis of the American policy of nuclear deterrence in the past. In order to assess Weinberger's claim we would need to determine whether the threat to *defeat* a country in a nuclear war would be a more effective deterrent than the threat to *destroy* it. This would lead us into a highly complicated and controversial strategic debate. So it seems preferable to restrict the inquiry so that it does not embroil us in that debate.

Focusing the discussion on the threat to non-nuclear countries will not, however, significantly restrict the scope of the inquiry, since nuclear-armed countries seem considerably less vulnerable to nuclear threats — especially direct threats of attack — than non-nuclear countries. Perhaps the most alarming scenario for nuclear blackmail which also seems to some extent realistic is one in which an aggressive nuclear-armed country uses the direct threat of nuclear attack in order to coerce the surrender of a non-nuclear country's conventional forces. This scenario suggests that the possibility of nuclear blackmail potentially undermines the idea of conventional defence against a nuclear-armed adversary. Because of this, the threat of nuclear blackmail constitutes a serious obstacle both to nuclear disarmament and to stopping nuclear proliferation. The discussion in the second major section of this paper will be concerned primarily with this worst-case scenario. There I will examine a number of possible steps which a non-nuclear country might take to prevent itself from being forced by nuclear blackmail to surrender to an aggressive power.

This worst-case scenario is essentially a wartime threat. Yet nuclear blackmail is generally thought of as a peacetime threat. Fear of nuclear blackmail seems essentially to be the fear that nuclear-armed countries might in times of peace use the threat of nuclear attack to coerce concessions from non-nuclear countries which the non-nuclear countries would not be morally obliged to make. Is this worry well-founded? It seems difficult to imagine a realistic and plausible case in which the threat of nuclear attack might be used in a time of peace to try to coerce a non-nuclear country to make concessions which it would be morally at liberty not to make.[12] Earlier we considered a hypothetical case in which the Soviet Union threatens to attack Yugoslavia with nuclear weapons if Yugoslavia allows the establishment of American bases on its soil. This case is as close as one is likely to come to a plausible scenario of peacetime nuclear blackmail, and even it has a definite air of fantasy about it. The problem with cases of this sort is that the benefits which the blackmailer might derive if his threat were successful would seem to be outweighed by the political penalties he would suffer if he were actually to carry out his threat. Since the victim would be aware of this, he would have good reason for calling the blackmailer's bluff. And, foreseeing this, the blackmailer would have good reason not to issue the threat in the first place.

The political penalties which a country would be likely to suffer if it were to launch an unprovoked nuclear strike against a city or even a military installation in a non-nuclear country would be enormous. The blackmailer would almost certainly incur the odium of the entire world. Trade sanctions on an unprecedented scale might be imposed against it. It could, in effect, be ostracized by the world community, and excluded from most political and economic relations among nations.

The blackmailer could incur many of these penalties even if the blackmail threat were successful and never had to be fulfilled. The victim is unlikely to have strong incentives to conceal the fact that he has been intimidated (unless, of course, the blackmailer's demands include concealing the blackmail, in which case it would be even more difficult for him to fulfil his threat if his demands are not met). If the victim reveals that he has been successfully subjected to nuclear blackmail, the other nations of the world could combine to implement sanctions against the blackmailer, demand reparation for the victim, and so on.

But would the victim even wait to expose the blackmail threat until after he had yielded to it? He could instead expose it beforehand. By alerting the rest of the world that the threat had been made, he could hope to gain the support of other countries, perhaps including at least one nuclear-armed country. Mere exposure might prompt the blackmailer to back down and deny that he had ever issued a threat. So the possibility of exposure could itself serve as a strong deterrent to nuclear blackmail in times of peace.

Thus far the idea that nuclear blackmail is a serious threat in peacetime seems pretty implausible. There is, however, one way in which nuclear weapons might enable their possessor to intimidate a non-nuclear country in peacetime. If nuclear weapons would provide a decisive advantage in war, then the nuclear-armed country might coerce concessions from the non-nuclear country simply by threatening to go to war. The threat might be implicit or explicit. It might, for example, be similar in character to that issued by the US in 1973.

The assumption that the blackmailer's nuclear weapons would provide him with a decisive advantage in war is open to doubt if what one has in mind is *tactical* advantage. But the advantage might instead be thought to lie in the nuclear power's ability to coerce the surrender of its adversary's conventional forces by threatening punitive nuclear strikes. In this case the blackmail threat in peacetime would be a threat to bring about the conditions (namely war) in which a threat of direct nuclear attack would be more credible. The idea is perhaps far-fetched, but what it suggests is that, if there is a serious threat of nuclear blackmail in peacetime, it is parasitic upon the threat of nuclear blackmail in wartime.

The reason why the threat of nuclear blackmail is largely unreal except perhaps in times of war is that it is normally only then that the stakes might be sufficiently high to justify the potential costs involved in resorting to blackmail. In the one type of case in which nuclear blackmail in peacetime seems a realistic possibility, the stakes would also have to be high – high enough at least to justify a greatly increased probability of having to go to war, and of having to accept the consequences of using nuclear weapons against a non-nuclear country.

Even in times of open military conflict, nuclear threats against non-nuclear countries may not be a serious option for nuclear-armed countries. There is no evidence, for example, that in the recent Falklands War the British considered threatening Argentina with nuclear bombardment, or that Argentina was in any way intimidated by the fact that Britain had nuclear weapons at its disposal. Indeed, Britain was so mindful of world opinion, so fearful of losing support for its case, that it even refrained from bombing mainland Argentinian airbases with conventional weapons, even though this would have greatly reduced the threat to the British fleet. Of course, the case of the Falklands has special features, and conclusions about that war cannot necessarily be extrapolated to other possible cases. But the evidence it provides is relevant none the less.

All things considered, it seems unlikely not only that a country would in peacetime threaten an unprovoked nuclear attack on a non-nuclear country, but also that a nuclear-armed country would begin an aggressive war expecting to be able to use nuclear threats to intimidate a non-nuclear adversary. If people's worries about nuclear blackmail have been focused on cases like these, then the threat of nuclear blackmail has been exaggerated. The most realistic scenario for nuclear blackmail would seem to be one in which a nuclear-armed country has already embarked on an aggressive war against a non-nuclear country, perhaps anticipating an easy victory at the conventional level. If the aggressor then gets bogged down and is unable to achieve the expected victory, he may, in desperation, resort to nuclear threats in an attempt to cut his losses and gain a favorable settlement. This seems the most realistic version of our earlier worst-case scenario. It too may seem unlikely. But it is a possibility which non-nuclear countries would be unwise to ignore altogether.

Options for preventing nuclear blackmail

What steps might a non-nuclear country take to ensure that it will not be subjected to nuclear blackmail should it ever find itself at war with a nuclear-armed country?

Developing an independent nuclear force

The most obvious option for a non-nuclear country is to 'go nuclear'. By maintaining an independent nuclear force, a country might hope to deter a potential nuclear blackmailer by threatening him with retaliation. Even a relatively small force might be sufficient. Suppose that a potential blackmail victim acquires such a force. If there were then a blackmail threat against him, it would not seem to be irrational for him to risk losing a city by refusing to surrender. (This risk would be significantly smaller than it would be if he were without means of retaliation, for then there would be less reason to suspect that the blackmailer is bluffing.) Nor would it be obviously irrational to risk losing another city by retaliating if the blackmailer were to fulfil his initial threat. As long as the potential victim has a force sufficiently large to allow him to counter-attack several times, then his threat to retaliate in the first instance could be reasonably credible, and the potential blackmailer could expect resistance rather than capitulation. In most instances this expectation would probably be sufficient to deter him.

At present an independent nuclear force is not a feasible option for most countries. It is beyond their material, technological, and economic resources. In the future, however, a large number of countries may acquire the wherewithal to develop a minimal 'deterrent'. Such a force might be adequate to deter nuclear blackmail by regional nuclear powers. But it might not be a sufficient guarantee against blackmail by a more advanced nuclear power. In the near future the superpowers may each have the ability to destroy a relatively small nuclear force pre-emptively, regardless of whether the force is primarily land-, sea-, or air-based. They may also be able to develop anti-ballistic missile systems which, together with air defence systems, would be capable of defending them against an attack by a relatively small nuclear force. If either of these projections turns out to be correct, then a small nuclear force may not provide an effective deterrent to blackmail by one of the superpowers. Indeed, the possession of an independent force might even be on balance a liability, in that the acquisition of such a force could be regarded as a serious threat by other nuclear powers, and might, in extreme circumstances, even provoke a pre-emptive strike. So the development of an independent force might decrease the risk of nuclear blackmail at the cost of creating an even greater danger of pre-emptive attack. A further point is that the nuclear powers might be less inhibited about using nuclear weapons against a country which itself relied on the threat to use them. Simple non-nuclear status may itself provide some degree of immunity from the threat of nuclear attack.

The fact that this first option is at present not widely available is, of course, something for which we should be profoundly thankful. It is generally recognized that the danger of nuclear war increases with the number of countries which possess nuclear weapons. This is true for a number of reasons. Nuclear proliferation makes regional nuclear wars possible, and increases the probability that local crises will escalate to global nuclear war. It can destabilize existing deterrence relations by increasing the threat to one side without increasing the threat to the other. By pressuring the superpowers to explore new technologies for neutralizing the threat from small, independent nuclear forces, proliferation could lead to the development of technologies which will have a further destabilizing effect on superpower deterrence. Furthermore, proliferation increases the probability that nuclear weapons will fall into the hands of an irrational or insane national leader; it increases the risk of nuclear accidents, increases the risk of accidental nuclear war, and aggravates the threat of nuclear terrorism. Finally, it makes disarmament negotiations more difficult by increasing the number of participants with conflicting interests and divergent points of view.

Thus an independent nuclear force not only brings new dangers for the country which acquires it, but also increases the general risk of nuclear catastrophe. For these reasons, the development of such a force seems a highly undesirable response to the threat of nuclear blackmail. Moreover, it seems irresponsible for countries, like Britain, which already maintain an independent nuclear force, to attempt to justify the continued possession of the force on the ground that it is needed to deter nuclear blackmail. For this reasoning implicitly sanctions proliferation. There is an element of hypocrisy in the view, common among apologists for the British force, that, while it would be bad if other countries – even Britain's allies – were to acquire nuclear weapons, nevertheless Britain must have them in order (among other things) to deter nuclear blackmail.

Britain's position within the NATO alliance is rather anomalous. Except for the US it is the only country within the NATO military structure which maintains an independent nuclear force. Despite disclaimers by the present government, it seems clear that the nuclear force is maintained at the expense of Britain's conventional forces. If the other countries within NATO were to follow Britain's example, this would not only magnify the dangers associated with proliferation, but it would also emasculate NATO's conventional defences. NATO's conventional forces could become so depleted that, in the event of war, there would be little alternative but to resort to the early use of nuclear weapons, possibly in a strategic role. This hardly seems desirable. So there is an additional reason for hoping that none of the other NATO countries will aspire to possess an independent nuclear force.

Alliances and extended deterrence

At present the non-nuclear members of NATO rely on an implicit guarantee from the US for the deterrence of nuclear blackmail. The US is committed to assist in the defence of any part of NATO territory which might be attacked, and implicitly at least this commitment extends to retaliating on behalf of any NATO member which is attacked with nuclear weapons. This solution to the problem might be generalized.

Non-nuclear countries could form alliances with existing nuclear powers and rely on their arsenals for the deterrence of nuclear blackmail. This solution has been encouraged by the US. In the past the US has re- garded the extension of its 'nuclear umbrella' as an important means of preventing proliferation. Fred Iklé, who is now the American Under Secretary of Defense for Policy, once wrote that, 'for many nations, protection through a stable alliance is now the only alternative to a desperate search for security by getting their own nuclear bombs. . . . The alliances protecting most of these potential nuclear countries and which will make them willing to forgo nuclear weapons would not survive without continuing American support.'[13]

The primary advantage of this policy is that it avoids many of the dangers which would accompany the spread of nuclear weapons to more and more countries. This advantage is illustrated by the case of NATO. If West Germany had not enjoyed the protection of the Ameri- can nuclear guarantee, it might by now have decided to develop its own independent nuclear force – an act which might, to borrow Kissinger's euphemism, have had 'incalculable consequences'. Moreover, as we have seen, renouncing the option of an independent force has allowed most NATO countries to devote more of their resources to conventional forces, thereby making it less likely that NATO would have to resort to the first use of nuclear weapons in the event of a war.

If Britain sees its options as restricted to the two I have so far mentioned, then it ought to follow the lead of its European allies. The US already possesses in abundance the means of deterring nuclear blackmail in Europe. McGeorge Bundy has recently stated that, 'like the Soviet Union, we have long-range weapons in numbers grossly beyond any basic deterrent need; we can assign a few of them to NATO missions. . . .'[14] It seems irrational for Britain to duplicate a capability which the US already has – especially when it can do so only at the expense of its conventional forces.

In the same speech in which he twice referred to the threat of nuclear blackmail, Mr Nott rejected the option of relying entirely on the American nuclear guarantee. After piously expressing his faith in the reliability of that guarantee, he nevertheless went on to claim that, 'in the last resort, Great Britain must be responsible for her own defence. She could not shuffle that off onto another nuclear power.' But, if 'in the last resort' it is improper for Britain to rely on the American guarantee, then how can it be proper for West Germany to do so? Would Mr Nott propose that West Germany too 'must be responsible for its own defence', and develop an independent nuclear force? Again we see the inconsistency in the view that, while the American guarantee is fine for other countries, Britain must have its own nuclear force.

One objection to relying for one's defence against nuclear blackmail on the guarantee of a nuclear-armed ally is that the ally's threat to retaliate on one's behalf will never be as credible to a potential blackmailer as one's own threat would be. In the case of NATO, however, there are several reasons for thinking that the American guarantee is credible. One is that the US has 350,000 troops stationed in Europe which would, in the event of a war, fight alongside the troops from the various European NATO countries. Thus it would be difficult for the Russians to demand the surrender of the European forces without demanding the surrender of the American forces as well. So it would be difficult for them to blackmail a European country without indirectly blackmailing the US as well. Since a successful blackmail threat against one or more of the European NATO countries would be likely to lead to the defeat or surrender of the American forces fighting in Europe, the US would have good reason to prevent the threat from succeeding.

Certainly there would be major doubts about the reliability of the American commitment if the US were expected to retaliate by attacking Soviet cities in the event of a Soviet attack on West European cities. For that would entail too great a risk of retaliation against American cities. But to deter nuclear blackmail in Europe it would not be necessary for the US to threaten to attack Soviet cities. It could instead threaten to attack the cities of the Soviet Union's Warsaw Pact allies. This threat would be intelligible (in a way that, say, a threat to attack Havana would not be), for the Soviet Union's Warsaw Pact allies would also be involved in the war which would be in progress. It would also be more credible, since attacks on the cities of the Soviet Union's allies would be less likely to lead to retaliation against American cities than attacks on Soviet cities would. Finally, while attacks on East European cities would be undeniably immoral, they would be no more immoral than attacks on Soviet cities would be. Ordinary Soviet and East European citizens are equally innocent of responsibility for the acts of the Soviet leaders. Thus the threat to attack East European cities would raise no moral questions which would not also be raised by the threat to attack Soviet cities.

While the option of relying on a guarantee from an existing nuclear power has many advantages, it also faces certain objections. It is of course ruled out if one objects to any form of nuclear deterrence on moral grounds, but I will not explore that objection here.[15] In the case of Britain, the strongest objection may be political. Given the attitudes of the current American administration, Britain's unilateral abandonment of its independent force might alienate and offend the US and turn it more isolationist, thereby undermining the credibility of the guarantee which Britain would be seeking. While this danger is certainly real, there are reasons for thinking it could be overcome. What mainly annoys the US at present is the seeming unwillingness of some of its allies to contribute to the common defence on a scale which, relative to their levels of national wealth, is proportional to the American contribution. Thus if British nuclear disarmament were accompanied by a clear demonstration of willingness to make sacrifices for the common defence, this might serve not only to strengthen NATO's overall defensive capabilities, but also to stem any incipient hostility from the US. Britain could, for example, rechannel the money it would have spent on the nuclear force into strengthening its non-nuclear forces — indeed it might feel compelled to overcompensate for the loss of the nuclear force by increasing defence spending overall. Or it might consider the reintroduction of national service.

If Britain were to abandon its nuclear force and instead devote its resources to building up its conventional forces, this would in fact be *better* for the US in two respects. Firstly, it would raise the nuclear threshold in Europe, making it less likely that any conflict in Europe would escalate to all-out nuclear war between the US and the Soviet Union. And, secondly, it would mean that the US would be the only country within the NATO military alliance capable of initiating strategic war with the Soviet Union. It would mean, in other words, that the US alone would retain the prerogative of crossing the nuclear threshold, and of controlling the level of NATO's strategic nuclear action once the threshold had been crossed. Britain would no longer have the ability to threaten American interests by acting independently.

It would be instructive for both Americans and Britons to recall that during much of the 1960s it was the US which stressed the importance of increased reliance on conventional defences in Europe, and opposed the acquisition of independent nuclear forces by other NATO countries. In each case the American position was influenced by a concern for American interests. The European countries, on the other hand, generally wanted to keep the nuclear threshold low, thereby ensuring that any war in Europe would quickly escalate to all-out nuclear war between the superpowers. This, it was thought, would deter nuclear war, and also eliminate the possibility of fighting another prolonged conventional war in Europe. If Europeans now change their minds, and would like to implement the policy which they earlier forced the US to abandon, then American leaders ought not to complain.

While the option of relying on a guarantee from an existing nuclear power may seem attractive in the case of the NATO countries, there are various reasons why it will be much less satisfactory elsewhere. In the case of NATO there are, as I have mentioned, special circumstances which make the American guarantee seem sufficiently credible. But these circumstances may be absent in the case of other possible alliances. The nuclear-armed member of the alliance might not have troops committed to the defence of each non-nuclear member's territory. Thus an aggressor could blackmail any of the non-nuclear members without thereby blackmailing the nuclear guarantor – even indirectly. Also, the blackmailer might engage in aggression without the assistance of allies, in which case the nuclear guarantor would have to threaten to retaliate directly against the blackmailer. Since this would entail enormous risks for the guarantor, his guarantee might not be sufficiently credible. On the other hand, if the blackmailer were a regional nuclear power whose forces were so crude that they could not deliver nuclear bombs against the territory of the guarantor, then the guarantor's threat to retaliate would be entirely credible.

A second reason why countries may find the option of forming an alliance with a nuclear-armed state unappealing is that the nuclear guarantor would certainly demand concessions in return for his protection. Non-nuclear countries would have to accept a position of perpetual indebtedness, or even subservience, to their protector. To some extent this might involve an abdication of national autonomy. Certainly the widespread acceptance of this option would tend to reinforce and perpetuate the political advantages which the nuclear powers already enjoy over most non-nuclear countries. It would therefore be naive to expect non-nuclear countries to embrace this option with enthusiasm.

A further problem is that a country which allies itself with a nuclear power thereby risks becoming embroiled in any war in which its protector becomes involved. But an even more serious objection is that the establishment of a network of alliances would mean that the nuclear powers could more easily become drawn into local quarrels, with the consequence that regional conflicts would be more likely to escalate into global nuclear war. Within any given alliance it would be difficult for the nuclear-armed member to restrict its commitments simply to the deterrence of nuclear blackmail, and perhaps to the deterrence of one or two other extremely grave and well-defined threats. Rather, its assistance would probably be requested in dealing with a host of lesser threats, and it might itself be tempted to use its alliance obligations as an excuse for unwarranted interference in the foreign policy affairs of its allies. With the nuclear powers thus more deeply entangled in the affairs of their allies, what would otherwise have been isolated conflicts between non-nuclear countries would become occasions for confrontations between rival nuclear powers. The number of possible flashpoints for the outbreak of nuclear war would be greatly increased.

As a global solution to the problem of nuclear blackmail, the establishment of alliances between nuclear and non-nuclear countries seems therefore to be unsatisfactory. While reliance on the American guarantee has certain advantages for the non-nuclear members of NATO, it also involves many dangers, not least of which is the fact that it sets an undesirable precedent for other areas.

Defence in depth

It is often assumed that the only way to dissuade a potential nuclear blackmailer from attempting this form of coercion is through threatening him with nuclear retaliation. There are, however, other means. One is to make it difficult for the blackmailer to carry out his threat without thereby harming himself. Of course, a blackmailer will always harm himself to the extent that his act invites widespread condemnation. But, as I have suggested, the prospect of this penalty may be insufficient to deter the use of blackmail in a desperate wartime situation. In this case, the harm which the blackmailer would inflict on himself must be more direct and more severe.

One way of attempting to ensure that a blackmailer's threat would rebound against him would be for the potential victim to deploy his conventional forces in depth. Defence in depth involves dispersing a country's defending forces throughout its territory, and abandoning as the primary aim of defence the attempt to fend off an invading force at the country's frontiers. There are various forms of defence in depth. Each allows the enemy to penetrate the defending country's territory. One theory then calls for attacking him from prepared positions throughout the country, another for manoeuvering around him and attacking his vulnerable points, while yet another calls for harrassing him at every turn in guerrilla fashion. For the purpose of preventing nuclear blackmail, it is desirable to allow the invader to penetrate as much of the defender's territory as possible before the country's defences are brought into operation. For, once the invader's forces are dispersed throughout the defender's territory, it will then be difficult for the invader to fulfil a blackmail threat without thereby harming his own forces. For this reason, territorial defence is probably the best form of defence in depth for the purpose of preventing nuclear blackmail. Since it involves arming a major portion of the civilian population, territorial defence allows the invader to be ushered well into the defender's territory before he begins to meet with widespread and determined resistance.

There are at least two objections to the idea that defence in depth can provide a solution to the problem of nuclear blackmail. One is that a resourceful blackmailer could probably find ways of overcoming the obstacle which defence in depth presents. He might, for example, attempt to take the country piecemeal, capturing and occupying only one portion of the country at a time. This would constitute a new variant of the old 'salami tactics'. The blackmail threat could be that, unless the defenders in each area surrendered when it was time for their area to be taken, a city in some other area would be bombed. Once an area had been taken its defenders would be disarmed, and this would preclude the possibility of further armed resistance once the country had been fully occupied.

The second objection simply calls attention to a major limitation of this proposed solution, which is that it is not an option which is available to countries fighting together as an alliance. It is implicit in the notion of a military alliance that the forces of one country may be called upon to fight in defence of an country's territory. But when this happens, and the fighting is occurring away from one ally's homeland, that country's forces may be blackmailed by threats against *their* homeland. Since the blackmailer's troops would not be fighting on the victim's territory, they would not be harmed by attacks on the victim's cities.

Making success unlikely

A second means of dissuasion which does not rely on the threat of nuclear retaliation is to try to convince a potential blackmailer that any

Jeff McMahan

attempt at blackmail would not succeed. One possibility would be to try to convince the potential blackmailer that the potential victim's national priorities are such that the people would prefer to see their country destroyed than to have it fall under the blackmailer's domination. West European countries, for example, could try to demonstrate to the Soviet Union that they believe that it would be 'better to be dead than "red"'.

The idea that the open espousal of the view that it would be better to be dead than red could serve as an alternative to nuclear deterrence stands a familiar argument on its head. For it is often held that the rationality of nuclear deterrence may depend on the belief that it would be better to be dead than red. For example, it is sometimes claimed that the British prime minister must espouse this belief in order to shore up the credibility of Britain's nuclear force. For the sake of illustration, suppose that Britain is threatened with an invasion by Soviet forces which cannot be repelled by conventional forces, and that the prime minister threatens to destroy a Soviet city if the invasion occurs. For the threat to be credible the Russians must believe that the prime minister really would prefer a high probability of the nuclear destruction of Britain to the acceptance of defeat.

Of course, in this case the threat need not be fully credible in order to serve the purpose of deterrence. For, even if the Russians suspect that the prime minister is bluffing, the price they would have to pay for being wrong would be all out of proportion to the gains they would hope to make by calling his bluff. On the other hand, when a non-nuclear country faced with the threat of nuclear blackmail professes to believe that it would be better to be dead than red, the profession had better be wholly convincing. For in this case the blackmailer has less to lose in testing to see whether the profession is sincere.

It is doubtful whether such a profession could be sufficiently persuasive to convince a determined aggressor of the utter futility of attempting nuclear blackmail. But, if the victim could maintain his determination even after an initial nuclear attack, then this tactic of simple resistance — based on the conviction, whether genuine or feigned, that annihilation would be preferable to capitulation — might hold some promise of eventual (albeit limited) success. For, after one unsuccessful attempt to break the victim's will, the blackmailer would be unlikely to continue to bomb the country into oblivion. That would not only defeat his original aims in wanting to take the country, but would also invite the harshest political penalties that other countries could impose.

A second way of trying to convince a potential aggressor that any attempt at nuclear blackmail would be unsuccessful is provided by territorial defence. Territorial defence involves the active participation of the civilian population in the defence of the country. With the means of defence in the hands of the people — for example, factories might be supplied with anti-tank weapons, and workers might be trained in their use — an invader could expect to continue to meet with armed resistance on a large scale even if the government had officially surrendered. This would be especially true if the people were trained in guerrilla warfare tactics. Thus even 'successful' nuclear blackmail could not entirely eliminate armed opposition.

It is fairly clear what constitutes the surrender of a country with a professional army. If a blackmailer demands surrender, there are clear criteria for determining whether his demand has been complied with. Since there are direct channels of command from a nation's leaders to its professional fighting forces, and since these forces are trained to be obedient to authority, the failure of these forces to lay down their arms would be seen as an indication that the country had not yet surrendered. And since the armed services know that their action will be seen as a manifestation of the will of the political authorities, they will realize that it would be dangerous and imprudent to act contrary to the directions of these authorities. For these reasons, it is unlikely that a professional army would continue to fight once it had received orders to surrender.

Things are different in the case of a territorial army. Territorial units could enjoy a considerable degree of autonomy, and their actions could not be seen as direct reflections of the will of the political authorities. If a blackmailer were to demand surrender and then meet with resistance from, say, a group of workers in a factory, he would be unlikely to interpret this as a decisive indication that the country had not surrendered. He would not fulfil his threat to destroy a city simply because some workers had continued to fire at his tanks. Nor would two instances of resistance from workers be sufficient provocation. Indeed, it would be difficult for the blackmailer to say what would count as sufficient provocation. This will affect his ability to make a credible threat in the first place. When faced with a country defended by a territorial army, a potential blackmailer may find it difficult to make a threat sufficiently precise that the victim would be unable to exploit its ambiguity.

Jeff McMahan

Bluffing

The final two options I shall consider can be dealt with briefly. The first is a realistic option only for an ex-nuclear power or a country with a suspected nuclear capability. Such a country, when faced with a blackmail threat, could simply bluff. It could claim to have a clandestine stock of nuclear weapons which it could use in retaliation if the blackmailer decides to carry out his threat. Moreover, if a country senses that it is about to be subjected to nuclear blackmail, it could drop hints within hearing of the potential blackmailer that it has concealed stocks, and this could be sufficient to deter the attempt – especially since abandoning the attempt at this stage would involve no loss of face for the potential blackmailer. A bluff threat would of course have little credibility, but, because the threatened destruction would be so great, even a largely incredible threat might give a blackmailer pause.

The option of bluffing – even for those countries with a credible capacity for bluffing – obviously cannot be regarded as an acceptable solution to the problem of nuclear blackmail. A world in which countries would have the capacity to bluff would be a world in which proliferation could not be controlled, and in which apparent instances of nuclear disarmament could be fraudulent. If a country has the ability convincingly to pretend to have a clandestine stock, then it could easily *have* a clandestine stock. Secure controls over proliferation and adequate verification of disarmament would largely preclude the possibility of bluffing.

Nevertheless, there could be future occasions on which a non-nuclear country might find it useful to bluff. If it could satisfy its deterrent requirements through bluffing, that would be better for all concerned than if it felt compelled to develop an actual retaliatory capability.

Treaties

Finally, it might be possible to reduce the risk of nuclear blackmail through the negotiation of certain treaties or agreements. For example, nuclear and non-nuclear countries could negotiate agreements in which the non-nuclear countries would be guaranteed immunity from nuclear attack in return for a pledge never to develop or operate nuclear weapons, or to allow nuclear weapons to be stationed on their soil. Such an

108

agreement would be difficult or impossible to enforce, but there would be a penalty of sorts attached to the violation of the agreement by a nuclear power. The violator would be branded untrustworthy, and his ability to make advantageous agreements in the future would be damaged. An agreement of this sort would thus provide additional sanctions against nuclear blackmail. It could be used to supplement and reinforce other measures, such as the creation of a territorial army.

In Europe, where various countries operate nuclear weapons, or allow them to be deployed on their territory, this sort of agreement may be unlikely. There is, however, another possibility, which is for the two alliances to negotiate what has come to be known as a 'no-first-use' treaty. Each side would pledge never to be the first to use nuclear weapons.

The main obstacle to the negotiation of such a treaty has always been the nuclear bias within NATO's force planning. Partly for financial reasons, NATO long ago decided to try to compensate for weaknesses in its conventional defences by relying rather heavily on the threat to use tactical nuclear weapons. This nuclear bias originated at a time when the US enjoyed a considerable advantage over the Soviet Union in the deployment of tactical nuclear weapons. This advantage has subsequently been eroded. Nevertheless, faced with what it sees as the Warsaw Pact's superiority in conventional forces, NATO believes that it must reserve the right to initiate the use of nuclear weapons if it is unable to hold its own at the conventional level.

If NATO were to devote its resources to strengthening conventional defences, so that it could then feel confident about being able to stop a Warsaw Pact advance by conventional means, then the major inhibition against negotiating a no-first-use treaty would be removed. (It would be important to prevent the NATO force improvements from being offensively oriented; otherwise the Warsaw Pact might feel that it would need to reserve the right of first use.) Once in force, a no-first-use treaty could increase Soviet incentives to refrain from nuclear blackmail, for roughly the same reasons that a pledge not to use nuclear weapons against non-nuclear powers would. At the very least it would make nuclear blackmail in peacetime even more unlikely than it is at present.

Conclusion

This review of some of the various ways of trying to prevent nuclear blackmail, or of dealing with a blackmail threat once it has been made, is not reassuring. The most effective ways of preventing nuclear blackmail — namely, developing an independent nuclear force or forming an alliance with a nuclear power — bring with them dangers which are perhaps greater than the danger of nuclear blackmail itself. The other options do not involve equivalent risks, but even in combination they would not provide as effective a means of preventing blackmail as, say, an independent nuclear force. So we seem to be faced with a choice between risks.

What *is* reassuring is that the risk of nuclear blackmail seems to have been greatly exaggerated — especially by politicians anxious to sell us ever more and 'better' nuclear weapons. Of course, it is difficult to reach conclusions about the likelihood of nuclear blackmail in the absence of more historical information about those nuclear threats which have been made. A number of questions need to be asked about each of these threats. What was the nature of the threat? For example, was it a direct threat of nuclear attack, or was it less explicit? Was it made in peacetime, or was it directed against a belligerent in a time of war? Was it directed against a non-nuclear or a nuclear-armed country? Was the concession sought one that the victim was morally at liberty not to make? Did the threat succeed? If so, why?; and if not, why not? One thing which emerges very clearly from this discussion is the need for a historical study which addresses these questions. Until such a study is made, the claim that the possibility of nuclear blackmail poses a serious threat to non-nuclear countries should be treated with scepticism.[16]

Notes

1 For details of the Pentagon's five-year defence guidance plan, see the article by Richard Halloran in *The New York Times*, 30 May 1982. Weinberger's defence of the plan as a deterrent to nuclear blackmail is reported in *The Times*, 5 June 1982, the *International Herald Tribune*, 7 June 1982, and again in the *International Herald Tribune* on 23 July 1982. Also see Weinberger's letter in the *Guardian*, 25 August 1982.
2 *The Times*, 30 March, 1982.
3 *Guardian*, 19 October 1982.
4 For one survey of American nuclear threats, see 'Nuclear Armaments: An Interview with Dr Daniel Ellsberg', Berkeley, The Conservation Press, 1980, pp. 3-6, but especially p. 4.
5 *Guardian*, 26 November 1981.

6   This case is not mentioned by Ellsberg. It is discussed in detail by B.M. Blechman and D.M. Hart in their paper, 'The Political Utility of Nuclear Weapons: The 1973 Middle East Crisis', *International Security*, vol. 7, no. 1, 1982, pp. 132-56.

7   Quoted in Blechman and Hart, ibid., p. 141. Emphasis in the original.

8   In presenting the American justification for the alert, Blechman and Hart note that, among the American decision-makers, 'there was agreement that such a move [that is, Soviet intervention in Egypt] left unopposed would have had a major adverse impact, not only on the American position in the Middle East but, given then-recent history (particularly in Southeast Asia), on the US position worldwide'. (Ibid., p. 145). To prevent this adverse effect on the 'American position', the American government deliberately aggravated the threat of all-out nuclear war, thereby putting at greater risk not only the lives of people the world over but also the very existence of future generations. The arrogant parochialism of this assessment of the importance of the American position is astonishing.

9   The *International Herald Tribune*, 6 April 1982.

10 It does not, of course, follow from the assumption that the US was entitled to demand unconditional surrender that it was also entitled to back this demand with the threat of nuclear attack (or, in this case, to support the demand by conducting actual attacks).

11 Weinberger's worry is thus that, as long as the Russians enjoy strategic parity or strategic superiority (so that the US cannot credibly threaten to defeat them), they will be tempted to use nuclear threats to advance their own foreign policy goals and thwart those of the US. But the idea that the threat of force is more likely to succeed if the strategic balance favours the threatener is not supported by recent evidence. See B.M. Blechman and S.S. Kaplan, *Force Without War: US Armed Forces as a Political Instrument*, Washington, Brookings Institution, 1978, esp. pp. 127-9.

12 There are no instances of nuclear blackmail against non-nuclear countries in times of peace listed in Ellsberg's catalogue of American nuclear threats. Indeed, there are no instances of *any* peacetime nuclear threats against non-nuclear countries.

13 Quoted in an interview with Iklé by William F. Buckley, 'Where Are We Headed with Disarmament?', *Firing Line*, 6 August 1975, pp. 2-3.

14 'America in the 1980s: Reframing our Relations with our Friends and Among our Allies', *Survival*, vol. xxiv, no. 1, 1982, p. 26.

15 One type of moral objection to nuclear deterrence is very forcefully stated by Michael Dummett in his contribution to *Objections to Nuclear Defence*, Routledge & Kegan Paul, forthcoming.

16 I am grateful to Nigel Blake, Robert Neild, and Bernard Williams for helpful comments on an earlier draft of this paper.

Proliferation and the Nature of Deterrence

Barrie Paskins

One of the great dangers of deterrence is to be found in the continued spread of nuclear weapons. In this essay I hope to clarify the nature of this danger and to draw out the implications that it has for our under- standing of what deterrence is. I begin by contrasting two forms of deterrence. One, which I call 'the East-West deterrence system', has developed since 1945 and is the main subject of current debate. The other, which I call 'the proliferated world', is what I believe deterrence will be like if the bomb continues to spread. The long-term choice, I shall argue, is between drifting inexorably into the proliferated world and altering beyond recognition the East-West deterrence system.

I

The East-West deterrence system embraces all five of the self-proclaimed nuclear weapons states: the US, USSR, UK, France and China. The US and USSR have far larger arsenals and an immense technological lead on the other three. The UK and France are, gladly or reluctantly, firmly en- meshed in the Atlantic alliance. China is an independent third centre of decision-making. Three political problems have been of cardinal impor- tance in the inter-relationships among these five powers which have shap- ed the East-West deterrence system and the way these problems have been solved must be understood if we are to grasp the form deterrence has taken since 1945. The three problems are: the European question, great power competition in the Third World, and the China question.

The European question
In the late 1940s great power rivalry was focused primarily on Europe.

Much of the continent was very unstable politically. In regions occupied by the Red Army, non-communist regimes were subject to intense pressure which soon destroyed them; in much of Western Europe, communist parties loyal to Moscow were very strong, not least because of their good record against Nazism. The state in Germany, France and Italy had been destroyed. Economic problems were crippling. But against this grim picture of political instability one must set resilient social cohesion. The peoples of Europe had long been subject to nation-building and were to a very large extent clear about their national identities. It was clear what would have to be done for the peaceful reconstruction of Europe. Eastern Europe would have to develop under the tutelage of the USSR, militarily dominant in the area but struggling at home with the calamitous aftermath of the Nazi invasion. Western Europe could develop in cooperation with a dominant American partner, a partner unscathed by war, sharing basic political values with West European democrats, and, as by far the most important component of the world economy, well-equipped to support democratic reconstruction. Such a division of Europe would involve the permanent division of Germany, but Germany could hardly complain, having imposed calamitous war on Europe.

To solve the European question by dividing the continent into two spheres of influence was far from palatable. It involved, from the Western viewpoint, surrendering free peoples to the dead hand of Stalinist dictatorship. For Germans living in the sectors occupied by Western armies it involved the permanent subjugation of their compatriots and in many cases the sundering of families. West Berlin, surrounded and indefensible, lay deep inside the enemy's sphere of influence. And in the back of some minds was the residual dream of what came to be called 'rollback', of driving back communist domination and ultimately of freeing the world from the scourge of totalitarian socialism. For the Kremlin, genuine acceptance of the division of Europe was contrary to the ideological assurance of the ultimate triumph of communism. A strong Western Europe in alliance with the US was ominous to Russian leaders fearful of encirclement. West Berlin, a prosperous bolt-hole to freedom, lay deep inside the Soviet sphere of influence, giving the lie to Soviet claims of popular support by the one-way traffic of refugees pouring through it.

From the outset the European question admitted of a simple solution − peace by division − and the main obstacle to the implementation of this solution lay in political objections such as those I have just mentioned. Western 'failure' to support the Hungarian rebellion of 1956, the erection of the Berlin wall and the *Ostpolitik* of Willy Brandt are three of the very important pieces of evidence that the obstacles are being overcome and the solution implemented.

The point about post-war European history which is vital for grasping the form of deterrence that has developed since 1945 is this: whatever contribution nuclear weapons may have made to keeping the peace in this area during this period has been made against the background of a political problem whose solution was relatively simple. Nuclear weapons may well have played a constructive part, e.g. in preserving West Berlin from irresistible invasion but equally ensuring that the West made no moves in support of East European efforts at liberation which the Kremlin would have been bound to resist with all the force at its disposal. But even if this is so, its implications for the future are very limited. It is a guide only to the possible utility of nuclear weapons in concentrating minds and overcoming obstacles where the underlying political problems admit of relatively simple solution. It doesn't validate nuclear deterrence as a recipe for 'stabilizing' every conflict.

Great power competition in the Third World

Contrary to the expectations of more or less everyone in 1945, the European empires collapsed very rapidly and were replaced by a huge number of successor states, almost all fiercely nationalistic, inheriting from the imperialists boundaries which are a fecund source of intractable disputes. In Europe the nation-building process took centuries and furnished the European states system with an underpinning of social loyalties which was nevertheless insufficient to avert either the disasters of the First World War or survive the fragmenting peace settlement that followed. Third World states find themselves reliving the passions of European nationalism among populations many of whom have no national identity, others of whom have national identifications that cut across state frontiers and are a heady source of the kinds of conflict that readily engender war and civil war.

The problems facing Third World states are colossal and perplexing, a fact of great importance when we consider the proliferated world. But for the moment what concerns me is the way in which the great powers have coped with the Third World's weakness and complexity. They have competed aggressively and belligerently for power but, a vital point, they have been at pains to avoid overt fighting between their own nationals lest this draw them into war against one another. This avoidance policy has been possible for them because only relatively marginal interests have been at stake. The American involvement in Vietnam is a clear example of this. The official explanation of why America had to fight in that far-off country relied on domino theories. The correctness or incorrectness of these theories is beside the point. What matters is that Vietnam connected with American vital interests only through a line of dominoes: only if all of them fell would vital issues be at stake. If Vietnam was well chosen as a place to fight, this was because it was prudent to avoid the endangering of vital interests further down the line. When Vietnam fell, several dominoes remained between America and real danger.

Some great power disputes over Third World countries have been concerned with the defining of spheres of influence. In the Cuban missile crisis President Kennedy imposed limits on the extent to which the Cuban revolution would be permitted to threaten American hegemony in the Western hemisphere. In Afghanistan the Kremlin has replaced one tottering client regime with another. In such cases the vital interests of one or the other superpower may sometimes have been directly at stake, but never for both at the same time. The two spheres of influence do not overlap so that the world has been spared a spheres-of-influence crisis in which the vital interests of both superpowers have been at stake.

As in Europe so also in the Third World. Any contribution which nuclear weapons may have made to the prevention of war between the great powers has strictly limited implications. It is a guide at most to the possible utility of nuclear weapons in persuading the great powers to avoid direct military confrontation. Even in this role evidence of its effectiveness is confined to circumstances in which either the vital interests of the great powers were not at stake, or the vital interests of one were plainly at stake and this induced moderation in the other. To derive more general lessons as to the utility of deterrence from Third World experience to date would be fallacious.

The China question

The rise of China has been a sore trial to both of the superpowers: for the US, to have seen by far the largest of the world's populations fall under the domination of what the West believed to be a puppet government of Moscow; for the USSR, to have found its claims to ideological primacy in the socialist world challenged by a hostile neighbour of worldwide importance that did not shrink from lethal, if mainly symbolic, border skirmishing. China's alienation from Moscow prompted such discussion among Western deterrence theorists of 'the end of bipolarity'. The idea was that China altered the nature of deterrence in a way that Britain and France did not. For all President de Gaulle's protestations of independence, it was thought, the two West European possessors of nuclear weapons were basically members of the Western alliance, complications in a system whose basic logic was still dictated by Soviet-American dominance. China, on the other hand, was thought to have the potential to be a genuinely and thoroughly independent third member of the nuclear club with all the complications this would involve, e.g. for targeting plans and crisis management.

These fears have not been realized so far. To a greater extent than was realized in Washington and Moscow, China is in many ways an impoverished and backward country, preoccupied with dizzying internal problems exacerbated by factional struggles in and between the party and the army. In its present condition China has no incentive or ability to seek to emulate the superpowers' tendency to project their power by military means wherever they can throughout the world. China has shown itself mainly a regional power so far as military affairs are concerned and has not sought anything remotely resembling nuclear or military parity with the superpowers. The complicated military involvements of the US and USSR in Europe and throughout the Third World find no parallel in the Chinese case. Conditions in China have thus been such as to encourage a minimally disruptive role for Chinese nuclear weapons. The political reasons for seeking a complex nuclear deterrent have been absent because China has not sought or been able to compete for military power far beyond its borders and has no buffer zone analogous to Russia's in Eastern Europe or alliance commitments comparable to America's in Western Europe. China's independence and, to a lesser extent, her nuclear weapons have doubtless complicated Moscow's calculations by fuelling the fear of war on two fronts. This makes arms control more difficult because it puts the West in a dilemma (one of many): if Russia is allowed all it reckons it needs against China then much military muscle is legitimized which could be used against the West in time of Sino-Soviet rapprochement; if the Chinese dimension in Soviet planning is ignored then Western negotiating positions become unrealistic. Such complications fall far short of ending bipolarity: they complicate but do not radically alter the tense, crisis-torn struggle for power throughout the world in which the two principal nuclear weapons states confront one another.

In this simplified account of the three main issues dividing the nuclear weapons states I have sought to emphasize something that is all too little discussed in the technical literature on deterrence: the forces of history underlying the East-West deterrence system have so far been conducive to the avoidance of war between the great powers. Whatever the contribution that nuclear weapons have made to the preservation of peace, the underlying political factors have been such as to permit relatively simple solutions to the problems. These have been amenable to divisions and concessions which, however unpalatable, have not involved a direct clash of vital interests. I have not attempted to deny (or affirm) that nuclear weapons have played a constructive part in the East-West deterrence system but rather to emphasize that the lessons to be learned from any successes are of very limited scope. Notice, too, that my aim has not been to belittle the problems dividing East and West or to deny the reality of the resulting tensions. To have brought Europe to its current level of prosperity and stability seems to me an astonishing achievement of peoples and leaders when one considers the desperate plight of the continent in 1945. My point is not that the problems have been negligible but that underlying political factors have been conducive to peaceful progress and that these indicate that experience to date is no recipe for regulating every kind of conflict.

To see the main differences between the East-West deterrence system and the proliferated world we must consider strategy as well as politics. Strategic questions are central to current debates whose byzantine complexity cannot be reviewed in this essay. I can do no more here than to state briefly what seems to me to be the most reasonable view of strategy, especially Western strategy.

Western strategists are torn, I believe, between two conflicting notions of deterrence. I have not been able to find the distinctions I wish to emphasize spelled out in the technical literature and therefore discuss them in homespun terminology of my own. The basic conflict is between a strategy of Atlanticist deterrence and a strategy of Overall Strength. Much of what is most confusing and to Europeans most alarming about recent developments in American strategy is to be explained in terms of a shift in Washington away from Atlanticist deterrence towards Overall Strength.

Atlanticist deterrence and Overall Strength are different developments of the same fundamental idea, the idea of containment. Containment has been the underlying notion of Western security policy ever since the late 1940s. It holds that the Soviet Union is an expansionist power whose efforts to gain influence and territory must be checked at all points throughout the world. The first author of containment theory, George Kennan, wished to emphasize the desirability of containing Soviet power by diplomatic and economic means. These have never been entirely neglected but from the outset very heavy emphasis has been placed upon military containment. Atlanticist deterrence and Overall Strength are different ideas of military containment.

Thought about Atlanticist deterrence is primarily concerned with a definite political objective, namely, to safeguard the territorial integrity and political independence of the states signatory to the North Atlantic Treaty. It is arguable that this objective is relatively easy to attain because the states to be protected are stable internally and the borders to be safeguarded represent a separation of spheres of influence which the USSR benefits from and will not challenge short of some catastrophic change of policy.

Thought about Overall Strength is preoccupied above all with means. The idea behind it is that the military balance yields political advantages to the power whose forces are superior or to an aggressive power whose opponent has equal forces but a more defensive foreign policy. A strategy of Overall Strength requires that we maintain equivalent forces in so far as it is superiority that would benefit the opponent. It requires that we seek superiority insofar as the more aggressive policy attributed to the opponent gives him political advantages, advantages which cannot be offset by us at the political level. These objectives are manifestly difficult to secure on any but a short-term basis against an opponent who also believes in Overall Strength and has sufficient economic resources and political will to behave accordingly. Two opposing powers both committed to Overall Strength are bound to be in a state of perpetual insecurity as each struggles to obviate any perceived superiority on the part of the other. A strategy of Overall Strength is bound to be especially taxing for the US because containment requires that Soviet power be countered throughout the world, so that Overall Strength must be maintained at all significant levels of military capability in all theatres.

The military means to either Atlanticist deterrence or Overall Strength have two main parts: invulnerable second-strike capability, and flexible response capability. As we shall see, the two strategies differ profoundly in the gloss they put on the notion of flexible response.

In the present state of anti-submarine warfare, submarines armed with nuclear weapons are the main instrument of the West's invulnerable second-strike capability. This is because they are at present invulnerable to attack so that even if an aggressor subjects the West to massive nuclear bombardment, the submarines remain available for a retaliatory strike of such catastrophic proportions that the aggression will not seem worthwhile in the first place.

Why is an invulnerable second strike capability insufficient as a deterrent? Why must other systems be deployed in addition to it? The ideas of Atlanticist deterrence and Overall Strength answer these questions differently. The submarines alone are inadequate for Atlanticist deterrence basically because of the requirement for protection of allies as well as the American homeland. The strategic problem posed by allies can be formulated in various ways of which I shall mention two. One formulation emphasizes the credibility problem. Suppose that invulnerable second strike capability suffices to deter aggression against the American homeland. It by no means follows that the opponent will be deterred from aggression against, say, West Berlin. For he might reckon that an American president would never dare to invoke the ultimate deterrent, bringing destruction upon American society, for the sake of a foreign city. If the aggressor does calculate in this way he might well think himself able to make limited territorial gains at the expense of the NATO countries. Those who believe in domino theories add that over a period the opponent could nibble us to death, one limited gain after another.

A second way of formulating the strategic problem posed by allies is to concentrate on the fears of American public opinion rather than on the perceptions of Soviet decision-makers. However generous the American voter may be feeling towards his European allies, it is asking rather much of him to require that he face the constant peril of having his life, family and nation destroyed for the sake of foreigners. The spectre of a retreat into isolationism by the US is a nagging preoccupation of foreign policy elites in Washington. It is natural that they should seek to guard against it by developing a strategic doctrine which will assure the American people that the president has other options than suicide or surrender when dealing with threats to allies.

In this Atlanticist context the fundamental purpose of flexible response is *political*: to show the opponent that the US is deeply committed to the security of its allies while at the same time assuring public opinion at home that Washington is seeking alternatives to suicide or surrender. Theoretically, flexible response requires the deployment of forces sufficient to permit one to resist a military aggression at many levels of intensity of combat short of all-out nuclear war, a formidable demand. In practice, force levels far lower than theory requires may well suffice to demonstrate will and reassure public opinion. So long as the aim is Atlanticist deterrence, nice details of the military balance may be unimportant.

In the context of Overall Strength, flexible response has a very different meaning. If military capability brings with it accretions of political power that are damaging to us and which we must constantly strive to redress, then the military balance is crucial. The confrontation is worldwide because our policy is one of global containment. The number of levels of combat intensity for which we must prepare is large because the opponent's forces are very complex and can be used in many ways. We require conventional forces, chemical weaponry with which the opponent is well equipped, battlefield and theatre nuclear weapons to give at least a chance of preventing even a nuclear war from engulfing the American homeland, and limited strike strategic nuclear forces to permit a limited continental exchange if that is what the opponent can be coerced into accepting if a nuclear war degenerates so far. If the opponent is prepared to talk of 'winning' a nuclear war then so must we be prepared to talk of it, and to acquire the appropriate weaponry, lest his toughness provide him with usable political advantage.

The contrast between Atlanticist deterrence and Overall Strength can, I think, be summed up in four points. Firstly, Atlanticist deterrence has the relatively modest political ambition of safeguarding the territorial integrity and political independence of certain well-defined, internally stable states that fall within a sphere of influence about which they are at least acquiescent, if not enthusiastic. Overall Strength has no finite political ambition and can only reinforce the tendency of containment theory to draw the US into the role of universal policeman in which it is hopelessly over-extended. Secondly, in Atlanticist deterrence the function of military power is negative: to confirm a stalemate. The idea of Overall Strength involves no such repudiation of the idea of war as an instrument of policy. On the contrary, its insistence that political advantage can flow from the military balance suggests strongly that war can be an effective instrument of foreign policy. Thirdly, the scope of Atlanticist deterrence is strictly defined: NATO is not allowed to become involved in Third World conflicts. The idea of Overall Strength encourages one to reject regional limitations and one important contention of its proponents is that NATO should develop an out-of-area capability, that is, the ability to intervene in regions adjacent to the NATO zone. Fourthly, Atlanticist deterrence can be relatively reassuring about the state of the world: Europe is not an endangered region but one of the stablest parts of the world. So long as the alliance can be maintained and dangerously destabilizing technologies can be controlled, Europe can be a case study of successful deterrence. Overall Strength inherently aggravates the sense of insecurity by pinning our safety to the minutest of shifts in the military balance. Even if for a time we get ahead, there is no security in this in the long term since the opponent may always recover lost ground and threaten our superiority.

I have dwelt at length on the dialectic between Atlanticist deterrence and Overall Strength for two reasons. Firstly, it is widely believed among opponents of deterrence that both of the superpowers are seeking what is called a war-fighting capability, are coming to believe more and more that a nuclear war can be fought and won, and will sooner or later fight such a war. If correct, this would undoubtedly affect one's assessment of all the dangers of deterrence including that stemming from proliferation. But I believe it is incorrect. The truth, in my opinion, is that both of the superpowers believe at least in part in the strategy of Overall Strength. They are acquiring such ominous-looking weaponry as the highly-accurate inter-continental ballistic missile not because they really credit the feasibility of a disabling first strike which would leave the opponent at their mercy but because they are convinced, or partly convinced, that worthwhile political gains can accrue to the opponent from an appreciable edge in such technology. This interpretation fits the evidence at least as well as the argument that the superpowers are squaring up for a nuclear showdown and has the great merit that it does not require us to assume that decision-makers in Washington and Moscow are crazy.

My second reason for dwelling on the dialectic between Atlanticist deterrence and Overall Strength is to ensure that we have a realistic picture of the strategies currently at work in the East-West deterrence system for comparison with the proliferated world. Two points bear emphasis in this connection. Firstly, the strategy of Overall Strength contains within it something very like the traditional, pre-Hiroshima belief that war is an instrument of policy. It does not claim that a nuclear war is winnable but it insists that the military balance has usable political implications and leaves open the question of how far one may expediently move along the spectrum from advantageously impressive military parades to all-out thermonuclear war. This strategy, with its opening towards war, is part of deterrence as it has developed since 1945. Secondly, the strategy of Overall Strength encourages nuclear weapons states to involve themselves in areas of instability and tension. It repudiates the sharp frontiers of competence within which NATO is currently confined and connects superpower insecurity with every political quarrel in the world. This must have some bearing on the nature of the proliferated world, to which I now turn.

II

By far the most important feature of the proliferated world is this: if the bomb continues to spread there is no reason whatever to suppose that it will continue to be confined to political arenas as conducive to the avoidance of general war as those that we reviewed earlier. On the contrary: many states face chronic problems altogether more intractable than those which have faced the five nuclear weapons states in their thinking about nuclear weapons. If the bomb continues to spread it will come into the possession of states whose boundaries are a potent source of conflict, whose populations have not been subject to centuries of nation-building or to the stark lessons in respect for existing frontiers administered to Europe by two world wars.

A second danger in the proliferated world arises from irresponsible states and irresponsible methods. Deterrence requires a certain minimum of rationality or responsibility in those who are to be deterred. Resting as it does on the prospect of massive devastation if certain actions are undertaken, it cannot be expected to work if the opponent values intangibles such as honour more highly than physical survival. If the bomb were to spread to states or terrorist groups to whom survival was not the first priority then deterrence would certainly be imperilled. Perhaps still more unsettling is the possibility of using nuclear weapons in such a way that the target does not know who has attacked him or is misled as to the identity of the attacker. Such a usage would indeed be irresponsible in that the attacker could hope to avoid answering for his attack and might even draw retaliatory fire upon an innocent third party. It is a horrifying prospect but one might well doubt that there are many states so sanguine as to expect to profit from catalytic war.

Both the danger of the bomb spreading to the most conflict-riddled parts of the world and the danger of irresponsible states and methods are very considerable but emphasis exclusively on the latter can be misleading as to the implications of proliferation. For it suggests that deterrence so far has worked well among hard-headed pragmatic states and that all we need to fear is the wild fanatic. It can even be reassuring in that fanatical states and groups have very often shown a remarkable tendency to put survival before all other values. If I am right in thinking that deterrence since 1945 has developed within a relatively congenial political environment then such reassurance is profoundly mistaken, for transfer of the bomb into an adverse environment will take us into the unknown and could well result in the minimal rationality on which deterrence theorists rely being pitted against the forces of history.

A third type of danger in the proliferated world arises from the lack of any guarantee that the process of proliferation will be uniform. To put the point at its most lurid, if two traditional enemies are racing to acquire nuclear weapons and one tests a deliverable device before the other has any retaliatory capability then the state with the temporary advantage may well have a very considerable incentive to strike at once. This would be extremely dangerous for all of us because either the great powers would be drawn into major conflict or the attack would go unpunished and the incentives to use the bomb would be greatly increased, the taboos against use which have prevailed since Nagasaki would be irretrievably broken. The pressures to avert gross imbalances from developing by giving military support to the state which was lagging behind in such a race would be hard to resist but the involvement that this would bring for the great powers would be very dangerous. It would threaten to entangle them ever more deeply in political quarrels over which they might well have no control.

A fourth type of danger concerns the type of deterrence that proliferation may bring. We noted that Western deterrence policy is torn between the relatively unambitious and stable notion of Atlanticist deterrence and the boundlessly ambitious and inherently destabilizing concept of Overall Strength. Both of these have developed in a particular political culture and it would be a mistake to expect that either would be transferred automatically to other possessors of nuclear weapons. But the USSR appears to have believed at all stages in Overall Strength. In the West it is principally civilian strategists who have argued for Atlanticist deterrence and at the moment they seem to have been defeated in Washington. The simple, bluff idea of Overall Strength has a natural attraction for military men throughout the world and it is surely more than probable that the nuclear weapons doctrines of new possessors will approximate more closely to Overall Strength than to Atlanticist deterrence. It is only human to look for usable political gains from the very large commitment of resources required for an indigenous bomb programme. This does not automatically commit all possessors of nuclear weapons to the quest for a war-fighting capability but it does, as we saw, imply a perilous opening towards the thought that war is an effective instrument of policy.

A fifth type of danger in the proliferated world is closely connected with this openness of Overall Strength ideas to the possible utility of war. In the proliferated world it would be at least as important as it is in the East-West deterrence system for the possessors of nuclear weapons to avoid fighting between their own nationals. This is dismaying for a reason that proponents of deterrence never tire of stressing. War, they emphasize, seems to be endemic in international relations. War will keep on breaking out, however unnecessary and ill-advised it appears to outsiders. It is wildly optimistic to hope that complete avoidance of war will be possible in every political context, however different from that which we reviewed in the first part of this essay. The basic political objectives underlying the East-West deterrence system have been conservative ones, e.g. to safeguard Soviet territory by means of a dependable buffer zone and to prevent Russian aggression in Western Europe. In the aftermath of decolonization there are many states whose objectives are far from being conservative. It would be very optimistic to believe that they could all be persuaded to rechannel their energies towards conservatism in military affairs, confining change to quite other dimensions. As an instrument of political change, nuclear weaponry is profoundly dangerous.

III

What are the implications of the five-fold danger of proliferation for our understanding of the nature of deterrence? Let me first draw out what I take to be the direct implications of the argument so far, then discuss the causes of proliferation and what might be done about them.

The contrasts I have drawn between the East-West deterrence system and the proliferated world indicate the necessity to see deterrence against a realistic political background. This requirement might seem self-evident but any reader who samples the technical literature on deterrence, especially the very extensive and influential American literature, will see that it is far from being met by the professionals.[1] The deterrence literature is pervaded by a highly, and I think unrealistically, abstract conception of politics. States are conceived as analogous to economic actors, maximizing their utility where they can, resorting to game-theoretical techniques where they cannot. All states in all political environments are seen in the same terms. The temptation of all politicians to see their own problems as having as much gravity and difficulty as any that can possibly be faced interacts with this abstract conception to ensure that the conflicts that have preoccupied the nuclear weapons states since 1945 are taken as a fair sample of how the model relates to experience. The possibilities of controlled escalation, nuclear bargaining, limited war, etc., are discussed in highly abstract terms fleshed out only by the unexamined data of experience to date. The danger of proliferation that tends to be emphasized is not the real-world likelihood that others will have graver political problems than we have had but the complexities introduced into bargaining processes by the shift from a two-party to an n-party bargaining matrix.[2]

The attempt to describe all possible types of deterrence in a uniform abstract language is profoundly misleading. It overrates the achievements of deterrence to date and underrates the perils to come. The successes of the East-West deterrence system are overplayed by the abstract model, by its commitment to the unexamined assumption that nuclear war is always a real political option – deterrence being credited with the achievement of having persuaded the great powers not to exercise this option. The perils to come are underplayed by the assumption that every kind of political chaos is amenable to analysis in terms of economic man maximizing his utilities or minimizing his maximum disutilities. A very important possibility which is almost completely neglected in the professional literature is this: deterrence to date has largely functioned to formalize and enforce an underlying political consensus on the inviolability of the East-West border that existed in Europe at the end of the Second World War. I do not say that this is the whole truth of the matter. My suggestion is rather that a hypothesis as plausible and telling as this is systematically excluded from consideration by the intellectual framework within which the professional strategists operate.

In this essay I have attempted a very broad-brush treatment of the contrasting backgrounds of deterrence to date and deterrence in the proliferated world. Even if I am largely mistaken or excessively vague as to the details, my argument may nevertheless be correct to claim that we can and must identify the political realities underlying deterrence. The professional literature does not make the attempt.

If the contrast I have drawn is anything like correct, the nature of deterrence cannot be read off from experience to date since for very good political reasons we have seen nothing yet of what deterrence is really like. An ocean-going ship must prove itself in the harshest of storms and the longest of punishing voyages. The ark of deterrence has barely ventured out of its home port so far. This has damaging implications for three very familiar elements in current debate about nuclear weapons. Firstly, we are very often told that deterrence has kept the peace for thirty-odd years. The critic is accused of being reckless in proposing to discard this solid achievement. Part of the answer to this is that experience to date is at best a very limited guide to the real nature of deterrence. Secondly, we are often urged to put our hopes and efforts into multilateral rather than unilateral efforts for peace. In this connection 'multilateral' means arms control. It invokes the highly sophisticated and eloquent body of thought which has developed around the idea that the negotiated control of force levels can be a valuable source of stability and peace. What has to be said about this is that arms controllers never claim to be doing more than to reduce the avoidable costs and risks of deterrence. They are not seeking to remove nuclear weapons from their central place in the security policies of the great powers but to make the world a little safer for deterrence. It is not the professional arms controllers but propagandists who pretend that arms control is addressed to fundamental issues. Whatever the relative merits of multilateral and unilateral strategies of various sorts, arms control does not address the perils that we have been discussing in this essay.

Thirdly, there are some who wish that the critics of deterrence should concentrate not on 'moralizing' but on the simple proposition that there are too many nuclear weapons in the world, and that there is much room for constructive reduction of numbers. This advice is often said to be 'realistic' in that it may commend itself to hard-boiled decision-makers who cannot be expected to respond to 'moralizing'. Whatever the merits of this advice applied to existing nuclear arsenals, it has nothing to say about the perils of proliferation that we have been discussing. Even if the number of nuclear weapons is reduced to the level at which the great powers have only as much as they 'need', the dire spectre of drift towards the proliferated world remains. It is important to be clear about this because there can be misunderstanding about the thrust of the complaints often made about the nuclear weapons states by the have-not countries. Whenever the Non-Proliferation Treaty is mentioned, the complaint is heard that the nuclear weapons states are in breach of their undertaking in the Treaty to negotiate in good faith for the curtailment and reversal of 'vertical proliferation' (growth of nuclear arsenals). This could be read as meaning that what the potential proliferators require of us is that we negotiate in good faith down towards the levels of weaponry that we require. A moment's reflection will make plain, however, that this cannot be so. Whatever the link between existing nuclear stockpiles and proliferation, it can hardly be the unnecessary weapons that worry the potential proliferators.

This brings me to the last question that I shall discuss in this essay. What are the causes of proliferation, and what might be involved in preventing it?[3] The question is as difficult as it is vital. I can do no more than to suggest a personal view. Let us distinguish three types of thesis about why states acquire nuclear weapons. Firstly, there is the thesis that a state proliferates for reasons having to do almost exclusively with its relations to states that already have nuclear weapons. Let us call this the complete linkage thesis. It might be argued that the USSR developed the bomb solely out of fear of the US or that the UK proliferated nuclear weapons solely in order to possess something which the emerging great powers possessed. I speak of complete linkage to suggest that the proliferation is linked exclusively to attitudes to states that already have the bomb. Secondly, there is the thesis that a state proliferates for reasons having almost nothing to do with its relations to states that already have nuclear weapons. Let us call this the no linkage thesis. An example of this thesis would be the argument that Israel has developed nuclear weapons exclusively as an ultimate deterrent against Arab invasion and not at all to deter the USSR or to entangle the US still further in the fate of Israel. The third thesis, which I shall call the partial linkage thesis, is that a state proliferates partly by reason of its relations with the nuclear weapons states, partly for other reasons. Thus one might argue that de Gaulle sought the bomb partly to deny exclusivity to America, Russia and Britain, partly as a focus for recovering a lost sense of national pride.

Is it possible to generalize about which of these theses offers the most persuasive account of future proliferation? I think it is. So long as the East-West deterrence system continues to appear to operate as effectively as it is widely thought to have done since 1945 it is a standing invitation to other states to attempt to join. It is inviting precisely because of its perceived success. Very many other states have experienced, and can be expected to go on experiencing, dire insecurity and disaster whereas the privileged few have enjoyed relative security. The more one emphasizes the success of deterrence in a world of insecurity, the more alluring the deterrence system is bound to appear. Although I have laboured the point that this appearance may well be illusory, the argument I have put is a minority view and the abstract literature of deterrence suggests very strongly that the deterrent is readily exported from one political environment to another.

If the wider world is indeed impressed by the success of deterrence then the partial linkage thesis offers a very persuasive account of future proliferation. For it suggests that states will proliferate partly with an eye to their own unique security problems but partly with an eye to the one great seeming success story in the post-war search for security, namely, the East-West deterrence system. This speculation need not rest on a crude mechanical imitation. One would expect decision-makers to hesitate and adapt if they are attracted by the nuclear option as embodied in the East-West deterrence system. One fact that may well give them pause is that the members of this system are deeply enmeshed with one another in a way that he who desires non-alignment may wish to avoid. If they go deeply into the nature of the East-West system they may well find further grounds for misgiving, as many Western critics have done. But none of this should be allowed to conceal the very simple thought that deterrence makes proliferation more likely the more it is seen to succeed. It is this very simple thought that makes me believe that if we continue as we are, relying on nuclear weapons for our security and reducing risks and costs at the margin by means of arms control, then we are bound to drift inexorably into the proliferated world. Nothing will avert this short of a fundamental alteration of the East-West deterrence system.

I am suggesting that the practical problem which emerges from these reflections on proliferation is to remove nuclear weapons from the central place that they occupy in the security policies of the great powers. Plainly no mere change of technology could bring about the requisite change. A mere substitution of other weaponry for nuclear weapons would, on my argument. create a tendency for that new technology to proliferate, and for nuclear weapons as the ultimate deterrent to proliferate along with it. What is needed is a radical shift in political relationships. It is probably clear from my earlier argument what kind of shift appears to me to be both necessary and desirable. We can and should abandon the destabilizing and dangerously ambitious concept of Overall Strength in favour of a single-minded concentration on Atlanticist deterrence and if we do so then it is arguable that our *military* security needs are modest since the main function of our armed forces is to ratify and confirm a political stalemate whose perpetuation has long been recognized on all sides as being in our mutual interest. The shift that we require is basically one of foreign policy, supported by the insistence that military procurement be confined within the narrow limits set by a modest foreign policy.

Of the many objections that might be urged against this view three are so important as to require some discussion, however brief. Firstly, it might be objected that the desirability of a more peaceful foreign policy is agreed but that the obstacle to it is the Russians, who continue to preach and practise subversive 'wars of national liberation' and to assemble a colossal armoury. A brief reply to this is as follows. The Russians may be wasting their money by devoting such colossal efforts to a dimension of foreign policy – the military dimension – which has brought them such meagre rewards and seems likely to continue to be a source at best of impoverished and unreliable client states. We fail to do justice to the West's capacity for creative political thought if we take as our model for foreign policy the mulish Soviet example. Furthermore, it is likely that a large part of the Soviet militancy of recent years derives from Western hawkishness in foreign policy, Western attempts to assemble anti-Soviet coalitions throughout the world as ingredients in Western security. Beyond these points, the implications of the Russian threat require a careful discussion of what deterrence can and cannot do. I have tried to show elsewhere that such a discussion supports a modest rather than a militant foreign policy.[4]

Secondly, it might be argued that the suggestion that the great powers moderate their military ambitions is naive and irresponsible, a failure to take account of the realities of power. If the point that is being made is that the great powers have always tended towards hubris and a cruelly self-interested reliance on the perceived potential of military force then it can be conceded at once. What needs to be argued is that the hubris documented to such devastating effect by Thucydides is a good idea for us to emulate. Those who continue to insist that the realities of power preclude any radical change of foreign policy must answer two charges: firstly, that the traditional practices of international relations have never been a great success, so that there has always been merit in seeking alternatives to them; secondly, that the existence of nuclear weapons alters our situation radically. I see no sign that the self-styled realists can cope with either of these challenges. Ironically, they are in the vanguard of those who insist on the revolutionary impact of nuclear weapons. What they cannot explain is how this impact can be prevented from requiring revolutionary changes in foreign policy and in our expectations about the potential of military power.

A third objection to my argument's concentration on foreign policy as the key to containing proliferation is that military procurement is to be explained in terms of the military-industrial complex within each of the nuclear weapons states rather than in terms of foreign policy. It seems to me that this argument is wide of the mark despite the very considerable lobbying power of military and industrial interests, especially in the US. A good illustration of the argument's deficiencies is the fact that the military-industrial complex is at such great pains to present its desires in terms of foreign policy objectives. To dismiss this as a mere obscurantism, a necessary obfuscation of underlying socioeconomic realities is to miss the essential point that there must be a political reality at work in the society for the obfuscation to be needed. To be more specific, without the need to convince voters and parliamentarians of the Soviet threat, aeroplane manufacturers would not need to engage in the expensive business of presenting their desires in political terms.

The argument of this essay can be summed up very briefly. Deterrence has not yet shown its true nature in the nuclear age because so far nuclear weapons have been confined to political confrontations which have been relatively amenable to political solution without resort to major war. What deterrence is and what should be done about it are to be gauged not from experience to date but from informed speculation about the proliferated world. The highly abstract model of international relations employed by most strategists, especially in America, is extremely misleading in this regard because it highlights the common features of the East-West deterrence system and the proliferated world whereas it is the differences that need to be emphasized. Without radical changes in international relations the proliferated world is virtually bound to come into being since states acquire weapons partly in response to their own unique perceived security needs but partly also with an eye to the experience of existing nuclear weapons states. The very success of deterrence to date is bound to be a factor making for the deeply subversive proliferation of nuclear weapons. Nothing short of a major shift of foreign policy, with the West taking the initiative, can bring about the kinds of changes in the East-West deterrence system which will remove nuclear weapons from their central and all-too-charismatic role in the one security system which, so far, has been a success since the Second World War.

Notes

1 I have found two books especially helpful in the attempt to make clear to myself the general characteristics of the technical literature. These are Lawrence Freedman's admirable historical survey *The Evolution of Nuclear Strategy* (Macmillan, 1981) and Donald Snow's incisive protest against the *ad hoc* nature of much recent strategic thinking *Nuclear Strategy in a Dynamic World* (University of Alabama Press, 1981).
2 The abstract model is not confined to those, such as Schelling, who are explicitly committed to game theory as a key to strategy. It is equal prominent in, for example, the theoretical writings of Henry Kissinger.
3 The mainstream literature on proliferation is well represented by Leonard Beaton, *Must The Bomb Spread?* (Penguin, 1966), George Quester (ed.), *Nuclear Proliferation* (University of Wisconsin Press, 1981) and Kenneth Waltz, *The Spread of Nuclear Weapons: More May Be Better* (Adelphi Paper 171, IISS, 1981).
4 'Deep Cuts are Morally Imperative' in Geoffrey Goodwin (ed.), *Ethics and Nuclear Deterrence* (Croom Helm, 1982), and 'Containment and the Nuclear Danger' in Richard Harris (ed.), *What Hope in an Armed World?* (Pickering and Inglis, 1982).

Games Theory and the Nuclear Arms Race

Nicholas Measor

I

Games theory is a mathematical theory invented by J. von Neumann and first described at length by him and O. Morgenstern in their classic text 'Theory of Games and Economic Behaviour'.[1] It is designed to enable one rationally to choose the optimum strategy in a game.

Although games theory is a theory about *games*, it is often claimed on its behalf that its implications are considerably more wide-ranging, and that it can be put to work in the context of divers political, economic, and international situations which are supposed to be in some respect analogous to games. The subject of this paper is the question of whether this claim can be made good in the case of nuclear deterrence.

It is frequently thought that if games-theoretic reasoning is applicable in this area it would lead to the conclusion that our nuclear arsenal should be retained. One type of strategy, therefore, which unilateralists adopt against a games-theoretic pro-armament stance is to deny that games theory is applicable to complicated strategic situations. I argue here, on the other hand, that even if one does adopt a games-theoretic approach it will lead to a type of unilateralist conclusion. Those who are agnostic (or even sceptical) about games theory can read what I say as simply an *ad hominem* argument against a certain type of protagonist of nuclear armament, but I think myself that enough of the games theory approach is worthwhile to give my unilateralist argument some strength in its own right.

A preliminary distinction which circumscribes my subject matter is between two-person games and n-person games where $n > 2$. I shall only discuss two-person games, even though the 'game' of international relations involves rather more players than that. Let us think of the arms race as a contest between just two parties − which is not, in any case, a gross misrepresentation. When I talk henceforward of 'unilateral disarmament' I mean one of the two superpowers resigning from the struggle. I shall not take account of the added complexity created by the fact that the United Kingdom participates as a junior partner of one of the main contestants.

The outcomes of the various possible combinations of moves by the players in a two-person game can be represented in a two-dimensional matrix. Consider an adaptation of a well-known childrens' game. Each player starts with an equal number of sweets (the players are A and B). Immediately after the command 'go' (given by the referee) each player must raise his hand either in a shape so as to represent scissors or in a shape to represent paper (Figure 1).

Player B

		Scissors	Paper
		Scissors	Paper
Player A	Scissors	0,0	+15, -15
	Paper	-15,+15	0,0

Figure 1

Here the top right-hand compartment, for example, represents the pay-offs to the players if A does scissors and B does paper. The first number represents the number of sweets lost or won by A, the second the number lost or won by B.

Clearly the only rational move for either player is scissors. If he makes this move the worst that can happen to him is a draw, and he may in theory win fifteen sweets if the other player is sufficiently ill-advised as to try paper. In practice if both players are rational the upshot will be a monotonous game: an endless series of draws with both players repeating scissors.

This is an example of what is known technically as a 'zero-sum' game. It is sufficient for our present purposes if I define a zero-sum game as one in which in each box the pay-offs for the two players in that box sum to zero. In practice this means that such a game is strictly competitive. Since no money or other asset is coming into the reckoning during the game but the players are merely redividing between themselves the assets which they already have, no advantage is to be gained by them forming any agreement between themselves. There is no scope for fruitful 'preplay jockeying'.

Contrast with this the most famous example of a *non* zero-sum game, the so-called 'Prisoners' Dilemma' (attributed to A.W. Tucker) (Figure 2).

B

		Confession	No Confession
	Confession	-2,-2	+15,-15
A			
	No Confession	-15,+15	0,0

Figure 2

This matrix has associated with it a somewhat bizarre anecdote. Two prisoners (here, A and B) have been incarcerated in separate cells, unable to communicate with one another. Both are suspected of a serious crime for which the penalty is fifteen years in prison. In order to obtain a confession the authorities resort to guile. Each prisoner is addressed by his interrogator as follows:

> If you confess and the other prisoner confesses then you will both
> be given a nominal sentence for a minor offence which we would
> be able to get you convicted of — two years in prison would be the
> total you would serve. If neither of you confesses then you will
> both be released without charge. *But* (and this is a big but) if one
> of you confesses and the other does not then the confessor will
> be awarded a free holiday in the Bahamas but the other prisoner
> will be sent to prison for the full term of fifteen years.

In the matrix +15 represents the value of a holiday in the Bahamas, -15 that of fifteen years in jail, 0 release scot-free, and -2 the nominal sentence.

By what process of reasoning should the prisoner decide on his course of action? In fact, if he is reasonably sensible he will argue like this:

Either the other prisoner will confess, or he will not. Let's first suppose that he does. Then if I confess I shall receive a nominal sentence but if I do not then I shall find myself in prison for fifteen years. So I'll be better off confessing. Suppose on the other hand that he keeps quiet. Then if I confess I'll earn myself a fabulous holiday, but if I clam up I'll simply be allowed to return home. So whatever he does I'd be better advised to confess.

The practical import of the reasoning should be clear enough. Both prisoners will reason in this fashion, so both will confess, and they will always finish up in the top left-hand box. But there is often thought to be something paradoxical or absurd about this. For if both had instead not confessed they would have found themselves in the bottom right-hand box, and both would have been better off. From the individual's point of view the reasoning seems to be impeccable, but the result is a kind of collective irrationality which damages the personal interests of both.

A simple solution to the problem seems attractive at first sight. In the example given the prisoners cannot communicate with each other. Change the story, then, so that they can. *Now*, one first wants to say, the sensible thing will be for them to get together and *agree* that both should not confess. Is this not a method of transferring themselves from the top left-hand box where they do not want to be to the bottom right-hand box where they would rather find themselves?

Sadly, however, the advantages of consultation are illusory if both parties are primarily concerned with personal interest. For suppose that they have entered into an undertaking that both will keep quiet. Each prisoner, when his interrogator appears, must make a decision whether or not to keep to the agreement which he has made. But that decision is itself a move in a game, and the matrix for the game is the same as before, except that 'breaking agreement' must be substituted for 'confession' and 'not breaking agreement' for 'not confessing'. So each prisoner will break the agreement he has made in order to minimize the disadvantage if the other breaks the agreement.

What the prisoners need is a method of making their agreement irrevocably binding. It would, for example, be in their interests to find a third party who could police the treaty and wreak some terrible penalty on either of them if he broke his word. The threat of such punishment would be beneficial to each of them, since it would deter him from straying from the 0,0 box in the misconceived hope of finding +15 in the Caribbean.

The possible relevance of the Prisoners' Dilemma to the arms race is clear. Simply replace confession with nuclear armament and non-confession with disarmament. As a result you will have something which looks remarkably familiar, namely two contestants who feel forced to arm themselves even though they admit that they would both be better off if bilateral disarmament could be arranged (Figure 3).

B
(USSR)

		Arm	Disarm
A (US)	Arm	-2,-2	+15,-15
	Disarm	-15,+15	0,0

Figure 3

How are the figures in the arms race matrix calculated? In particular, since the arms race might lead to mutual extermination, why is the disutility associated with joining in the race (upper left box) a modest -2, whereas the disutility associated with being disarmed in the face of an armed foe is -15? Does this valuation imply that it is better to be dead than red?

In fact the difference in the figures relates as much to the probability of various outcomes as to their intrinsic nastiness. The large negative score of -15 for being disarmed in the top right-hand box is based on the thought that in such a situation there is a *high* probability of major political disadvantage ('becoming red'). If the Western Alliance laid down its arms it is *possible* (as idealists point out) that the Soviet Union would do likewise, but I am cynical enough to think that this would be a very unlikely eventuality. It would be much more probable that the party which had kept its nuclear armaments would take advantage of the opportunity to use nuclear blackmail. On the other hand I am assuming in this paper that the party which had given up its arms would be prudent enough to give way if the other side resorted to nuclear blackmail, and thus (contrary to some opinions) that if one side unilaterally disarmed a nuclear holocaust would be unlikely. Such, at any rate, is the basis of the +15, -15 figures.

What of the -2, -2 score in the top left compartment? If nuclear holocaust followed B's strategy in the top left box with the same probability as that with which political conquest follows his strategy in the top right, then the negative scores in the top left would be far higher than -15, provided that one makes the (presumably widespread) assumption that being red is in itself preferable to being dead.

The claim, however, that the arms race instantiates the Prisoners' Dilemma matrix relies on the theory of nuclear deterrence, the theory that the possession by both sides of nuclear armaments makes a nuclear exchange highly unlikely, since each side is frightened off the use of his weapons by the near-certainty of retaliation.

The question of whether nuclear deterrence works will be my major concern in the second half of the pape. But at this juncture I want to make the point that if the theory of nuclear deterrence does work then it will justify assigning small negative scores to the top left even though nuclear extermination is so much worse than political conquest. For the figures are arrived at by means of a function which takes as its arguments both the objectionability rating of the various possible outcomes and their probabilities. In other words, better a very low probability of being dead than a very high probability of being red.

Why is the figure for disarmament in the face of an armed foe -15? There are those who maintain that unilateral disarmament makes a nuclear attack more, rather than less, likely, or at any rate that it does little to increase one's security. If this were true, -15 would be optimistic, perhaps disastrously so. But note that by disarmament I mean laying down one's arms and then adopting an extremely co-operative and ingratiating stance towards one's enemy. It is surely clear that such a 'hearthrug' policy would remove many of the dangers associated with jettisoning nuclear arms but retaining substantial conventional weaponry and the belligerence that goes with it.

The thrust of the argument is that if nuclear deterrence works then we are in a Prisoners' Dilemma matrix. But if we are in a Prisoners' Dilemma matrix then unilateral disarmament makes very little sense at all. What possible reason could there be for abandoning -2 in favour of -15? (I shall be examining one reason — altruism — which might be suggested presently.)

Provided that the scores in the other boxes remain as shown, then the efficacy of deterrence will be a sufficient condition for the matrix to be Prisoners' Dilemma. It might seem natural to take it to be a necessary condition as well. Unilateralists in practice often try to discredit the deterrence theory, and, given this natural assumption, they would in so doing be by implication attacking the Prisoners' Dilemma argument against disarmament.

What of multilateral disarmament? Even if we are in the Prisoners' Dilemma matrix, no one could deny that we would be better off all round if we could get ourselves into the 0,0 box. The practical difficulty is to find a way into it. We saw in the case of the Prisoners' Dilemma itself that a formal agreement between the prisoners not to confess was useless if not backed up by any sanction. A policeman to enforce the agreement might be effective in their case.

It has often been argued that a justification of the state and its judicial apparatus is that it enforces a mutually beneficial agreement between persons who would otherwise be engaged in a costly struggle between one another ('the state of nature'). This Prisoners' Dilemma foundation for political philosophy is particularly associated with Hobbes. But notoriously there is a difficulty in fully applying to international relations the so-called 'domestic analogy' with the internal affairs of the state. In the case of the prisoners a third party might enforce the agreement and make it binding. In the state we have the police and the law-courts. But what can fill their place to enforce a binding agreement between nations? Who can be so starry-eyed as to believe that the United Nations could perform this function?

On the other hand the fact that no obvious solution is available to the problem of multilateral disarmament, to the problem of forming an effective agreement in an atmosphere of mutual distrust, is not a reason for abandoning a search for a solution. If we are in a Prisoners' Dilemma matrix then the importance of multilateral disarmament is emphasized by the fact that unilateral disarmament is no way out of the problem. This is a point to which the leaders of nations would do well to pay heed, since their protestations of adherence to the multilateral ideal are sometimes belied by their actions.

The last topic which I want to examine in this section is the question of altruism. One common reaction to the Prisoners' Dilemma is to assert that the difficulty is caused by the fact that both prisoners (or superpowers) base their reasoning on self-interest. If one party, far from objecting to the other scoring at his expense, actually regarded it as a desirable object to secure a high rather than a low score for his 'opponent', then he would be prepared to refrain from confessing (or prepared to disarm). And if both participants saw things in this way then they might finish up in the bottom right hand box after all.

To some extent the argument which I shall offer in Section II makes this response redundant. For my suggestion there will be that *even if* one bases one's reasoning entirely upon self-interest it can *still* be shown that disarmament is preferable to armament.

At this point, however, I have two negative comments to make on the suggestion that altruism as a policy might extricate us from the impasse. The first is that if one is to argue for a policy of disarmament (whether multilateral or unilateral) one would be well advised to devise something which has a chance of convincing one's fellow citizens. Perhaps sufficiently large numbers of Britons (not to mention Americans and other allied races) are motivated by burning altruistic ideals, or could have those ideals inculcated into them, sufficient numbers, that is, to give the altruistic argument for disarmament a decent chance of success. But I fear that this is not so, and some support for this pessimistic thought is provided by the results of public opinion polls on the subject of unilateralism.

A complication here is that the argument for the possession of nuclear arms is not presented in a way that appeals purely to self-interest either. On the contrary elements will creep into the argument which appear to be (and perhaps are) altruistic: references are made to the welfare of presently subjugated Poles and of future generations of all nationalities who need to have Western democracy preserved for their benefit. Such ingredients cloud the issue. Possibly they show that there are aspects of the debate which transcend the Prisoners' Dilemma framework. Certainly they mean that appeals to altruism by the disarmer are liable to be trumped by further appeals to altruism by his opponent.

The second point which I wish to make about altruism is simply that altruism as a general policy is no more attractive or effective than self-interest. Here we come to a point which philosophically is of really first-rate interest, and owing to shortage of space I shall simply utter some dogma with perfunctory support in argument.

The problem is this: if altruism is adopted as the basis of strategic decisions then other matrices can be devised which present exactly the same kind of problems for the altruist as those which the Prisoners' Dilemma posed for the self-interested.

Figure 4 is an example of an Altruists' Dilemma. If two altruists are playing this game, then each will adopt choice 2 to avoid the risk

B

		1	2
	1	+2,+2	+15,-15
A			
	2	-15,+15	0,0

Figure 4

of the 'opponent' finishing up with -15, and thus they will finish up in the bottom right box. But each would rather be in the top left box, where the other party is better off than in the bottom right.

So the altruist, although he may arrive at a more satisfactory rapprochement in the Prisoners' Dilemma, is liable in the long run to find life no more rewarding an affair than the self-interested does. It might be suggested that the answer lies in some sort of compromise: be an altruist when it leads to the most satisfactory results and self-interested when that pays off better. But the merits of this proposal are chimerical. For the upshot of a strategy adopted in a particular situation can only be judged satisfactory or otherwise against the fixed background of some consistent view about one's goals in life. A policy of oscillating between altruism and self-interest does not constitute such a background but is instead a form of philosophical schizophrenia. Indeed, many of the decisions taken during one's altruistic phases will come to be a source of bitter regret during one's periods of self-interest.

II

In the previous section I argued that if deterrence theory were correct we would be caught in the trap of the Prisoners' Dilemma. Multilateral disarmament would be difficult and unilateral disarmament would be irrational. In what follows I shall try to work out matrices describing rather more complicated sets of choices which are arguably closer to those which we shall soon find ourselves facing. First I am going to consider whether deterrence is likely to work in current conditions and those likely to obtain in the near future. The question to be tackled is not whether to disarm but whether firing our missiles would ever be preferable to not firing them.

In its classic form the theory of nuclear deterrence is based on the concept of mutually assured destruction ('MAD'), the notion, that is, that if either side launches a nuclear attack on the other the party which had been attacked would be able to reciprocate with a devastating onslaught on the cities of the aggressor. This requires the possession by each side of a more or less invulnerable second-strike capability, an ability to respond from 'invulnerable' submarines, aircraft in flight or hardened missile silos.

In my view if MAD exists its presence will serve as an extremely effective nuclear deterrent. To see why this is so consider a somewhat degenerate matrix where the choices of the two players are between firing their rockets with nuclear warheads or not doing so (Figure 5).

USSR

Figure 5

The mammoth negative figures in the top left box reflect the fact that if either party fires, a nuclear exchange ensues resulting in catastrophic losses to both sides. Why are two of the boxes scored out? Nominally, I suppose, if one side fired and the other did not then the firer might hope to gain some advantage (although quite what, if his opponent were a victim of nuclear devastation, is less than clear). But since the whole point of this game is that if one side fires the other side will always retaliate the only rational course for a participant is to discount the top right and bottom left boxes altogether, and assume that firing will always move him into the top left box.

The game is easy to play, since the choice is between firing and earning -500 or not doing so and earning 0. So if MAD, and therefore nuclear deterrence, obtains, the modest negative figures in the top left box of the Prisoners' Dilemma matrix, which obtain when neither side disarms, are perfectly appropriate to the arms race. They should, however, be less advantageous than 0 (say, -2 as above), since the chance of a nuclear exchange starting by accident is never to be discounted, nor should we forget the potentially ruinous cost of the weaponry.

So much for MAD. Let us now consider what matrix is appropriate for a very different kind of strategic situation, namely one where both contestants have what I shall call first-strike capacity (possibly diverging from the standard use of this term by strategists). In my usage of the term a contestant has first-strike capacity when he has the ability to destroy *all* his opponent's weapon delivery systems in a single attack in such a way as to prevent his opponent retaliating with nuclear arms (note that to possess a first-strike capacity in this sense requires one to be able to evade or disable the enemy's early warning system).

Figure 6 is not too far off the mark for the appropriate matrix.

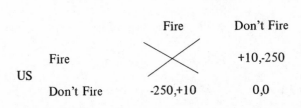

USSR

		Fire	Don't Fire
US	Fire		+10,-250
	Don't Fire	-250,+10	0,0

Figure 6

Here the figures for disutility associated with being fired on may be somewhat arbitrary. I am taking it that having all your rocket silos destroyed by nuclear attack is definitely bad news, since there is radioactive fallout to contend with on top of massive immediate loss of life from other causes, but that it is not as bad as having your cities wiped out as in the MAD scenario. The firer in the top right and bottom left boxes earns +10 because he does not himself become the victim of nuclear attack, having knocked out the enemy's weapons. He does indeed obtain political advantage, but I have reduced this from 15 (as in the Prisoners' Dilemma matrix) to 10 since the conquest of an opponent who has suffered extensive nuclear attack must be less advantageous than the gains to be reaped from defeating him by nuclear blackmail.

Obviously as the matrix stands the rational course (in that situation) is to fire, since if I do not fire I will achieve either 0 or -250, whereas firing will bring in +10.

The top left box is crossed out since the nature of the game is that he who has been fired upon cannot himself fire. This is not strictly speaking correct since both parties might fire simultaneously, with a resulting score of -250, -250. This is perhaps a relatively unlikely event, although it should not be discounted completely if both contestants are following the same course of reasoning at the same time.

These notional figures for the top left box do not, however, provide any further reason for hesitation. Suppose that I am deliberating about whether to fire at a time t. The enemy may or may not fire at t. If he does fire at t my position if I do fire simultaneously is no worse than if I do not fire (-250 in each case). But if he does not fire at t I am much better off if I do fire then. So I should fire – and as soon as possible, since the probability of his firing during the next ten minutes is greater than the probability of his firing during the next five.

Another possible 'game' is one in which, say, the US does have first-strike capacity but the USSR does not. The matrix looks like Figure 7.

USSR

	Fire First	Don't Fire First
US Fire First	✕	+10,-250
Don't Fire First	-500,-500	0,0

Figure 7

The figures in the bottom left box have changed. If the USSR attacks first the US can retaliate in the usual way familiar from MAD, since the USSR, unlike the US, does not have first-strike capacity. I am assuming that a Soviet attack would be on American cities (hence an American figure of -500 rather than -250 in the bottom left box). The available strategies have been changed from firing to firing first and from not firing to not firing first: in the case of the US, firing does not imply firing first. Not firing first *includes* both firing second and not firing at all (although in the case of the Russians, firing second is not a possibility; note also that I have assumed that the Americans, if attacked, would retaliate, so that in the bottom left-hand box the

US not firing first is taken to be the US firing second).

By reasoning which we have already examined the rational course for the US must be to fire as soon as possible in the hope that she will be firing first. The USSR, on the other hand, is faced with a very different problem. If she stays in the game her best hope (and it is a slim one) is that if she does not fire then the Americans may fall victim to some mental aberration and fail to fire either, in which case she will escape with a near-miraculous 0. But in any case she should operate on the policy of maximizing her minimum pay-off, which dictates that she should not fire, thus making her minimum pay-off (or worst possible loss) -250 rather than -500.

The Soviet Union would, however, be much better advised to withdraw from the game represented by this matrix altogether by finding some method of unilateral disarmament and/or surrender. For her minimum pay-off will then be the -15 of the Prisoners' Dilemma (equals political conquest), and this is a great deal better than the virtual certainty of -250.

The moral of the matrices involving first-strike capacity on the part of one or both of the contestants is that such a capability constitutes a nuclear incentive rather than a nuclear deterrent to its possessor, whereas to the player unfortunate enough not to possess it when his opponent does it serves not only as a deterrent but also as a powerful reason for pulling out of the arms race altogether.

If one or both sides has a first-strike capability where does this leave the matrix for armament/disarmament?

Consider first the case where both sides have first-strike capacity. If we assume that both sides are aware of their first-strike capacity, then we can take it for the purposes of the calculation that the chance of the US firing first (and therefore last) is exactly the same as the probability of the USSR doing so. One might be tempted at first, therefore, to construct a matrix like Figure 8.

The figures of -120 are reached by the following reasoning. Where both sides are armed and possess a first-strike capability, I have taken it that the chances of either side firing first are equal to each other (I ignore, for this calculation, the possibility of neither firing or both firing simultaneously). Now if the chances of either of two things happening are equal, one says in probability theory about each of the outcomes that the probability of it happening is 1/2 or 0.5 (in more popular parlance this is often referred to as a '50 per cent chance'). I calculate, therefore, that the utility to a side of being armed is the

USSR

		Arm	Disarm
	Arm	-120,-120	+15,-15
US			
	Disarm	-15,+15	0,0

Figure 8

pay-off for making a first-strike multiplied by 0.5, plus the pay-off for being the victim of a strike multiplied by 0.5. But the pay-offs in question are +10 and -250 respectively (see Figure 5, top right-hand box). So the 'utility' of being armed is $(10 \times 0.5) + (-250 \times 0.5) = (10 \times 0.5) - (250 \times 0.5) = 5 - 125 = -120$.

But there is something seriously misleading about the matrix. It suggests that the rational thing to do in these circumstances (on a policy of maximizing one's minimum pay-off) would be to disarm, and in a sense this is true, but the seemingly pacific nature of this conclusion masks the fact that undertakings to disarm may be either sincere or insincere, and it is yet to be determined whether a sincere undertaking is more or less advantageous than an insincere one.

To convey to one's opponent an intention to disarm and to persuade him of one's sincerity takes a certain period of time. During the period when one was setting one's unilateral disarmament in motion (I'll call this the 'disarmament period') one could instead fire one's weapons — for obvious reasons this can be called a policy of 'insincere disarmament'. Provided that the opponent did not fire during the disarmament period (an important proviso) the resulting pay-off will be +10 instead of the -15 of unilateral disarmament.

At first sight this suggests a straightforward advantage in making an *insincere* promise to disarm. But there are further complications which I have not yet mentioned. For one thing if I sincerely promise to disarm there is a greater than zero probability that the other side will fire on me during the disarmament period (this is so whether or not *he* has undertaken to disarm, since any such undertaking to disarm may be insincere). This shows, incidentally, that my original Figure 8 will not do as it stands, since the disutility of disarming when the other side does not must be worse than -15. Furthermore the advantages of making an insincere promise to disarm are complicated by the fact that there is a greater than zero probability of the other side firing on me during the disarmament period, in which case I will not collect my +10.

To construct a suitable matrix for the decision between sincerely disarming and insincerely disarming is, therefore, not without its complications. More detailed discussion of how the various utilities are arrived at has been relegated to an Appendix. But the conclusion can be summarized in a few words: the matrix for the sincere/insincere disarm game will be Prisoners' Dilemma, provided that (a) the chance of the US firing upon the USSR during the disarmament period is not lower than 1/25 (i.e. a 4 per cent chance), and that (b) the corresponding chance of the USSR firing during that period is not lower than 1/25. But it would be realistic to assume that the probabilities in question would be higher than this – probably much higher.

What this would mean in practice is singularly depressing. When I say that the sincere/insincere matrix would be Prisoners' Dilemma I mean that both sides would be driven by the logic of the game into making an insincere promise and firing within the disarmament period, even though both would be better off making a sincere promise. If both sides had a first-strike capacity, therefore, the chances of nuclear conflict would be high indeed. For either both sides retain their first-strike capacity or at least one of the sides enters into a process of 'disarmament' (whether sincere or insincere). In the first case, as Figure 6 shows us, each side has an incentive to fire. If both sides 'disarm' then, as I have just argued, each side will be driven by Prisoners' Dilemma reasoning into firing within the disarmament period. I have not considered in detail the case where just one side 'disarms', but it should be clear that, by the same reasoning as in the case where both 'disarm', the 'disarmer' will see it to be to his advantage to be insincere.

The same kind of reasoning does not, however, apply in the case where one side has first-strike capacity and the other does not, and the matrix for the arm/disarm game is in that case nothing like the Prisoners' Dilemma. Firing first is not a serious option for the side which does not have first-strike capacity but is threatened by a foe who does (as we've seen – Figure 7, bottom left) – the pay-off is -500. So his only realistic choice is between disarming sincerely and keeping his arms but doing nothing with them. To present the matrix for such a game requires the same kind of probabilistic complication as in the case where both sides have first-strike capability, so this exercise too has been consigned to the Appendix. But it will not come as a great surprise to learn that in the long term it will be more to the advantage of the party who lacks first-strike capacity to disarm than to retain his arms.

I remarked in the first section that if the success of the deterrence theory were a *necessary* condition for the arms race matrix to be Prisoners' Dilemma then the unilateralist who attacked the deterrence theory would be by implication attacking the use of Prisoners' Dilemma reasoning in this context. The recent course of the argument shows that it is not strictly true that the deterrence theory is a necessary condition for the matrix to be Prisoners' Dilemma. It is a necessary condition for the matrix to be Prisoners' Dilemma that the pay-off for (sincerely) disarming should be worse than that for keeping one's arms. *One* situation which can produce such a relative arrangement of pay-offs is where deterrence obtains, but it is not the only such situation, since we also have a worse pay-off for disarmament if the risks of disarmament equal or exceed those associated with keeping one's weapons *and using them*.

The following does seem, however, to be true. The success of the deterrence theory is a condition which must obtain if *both* of the following are to be true: (a) the matrix is Prisoners' Dilemma, (b) the Prisoners' Dilemma reasoning leads one to keep one's arms but *not* use them. So the unilateralist is right to see if he can overturn the deterrence theory, since his main target is the person who maintains that Prisoners' Dilemma reasoning should lead us to keep our arms in order to minimize the danger of them being used.

There are two points remaining which I propose to examine. The first is the question whether either or both sides is at all likely to obtain first-strike capacity, and the second the practical implications of that likelihood.

The first of these issues has been extensively discussed, and there appear to be two main schools of thought. Both agree that the accuracy with which nuclear warheads can be delivered to their targets has increased, and will continue to increase, to a remarkable degree, and both agree that there has been a change in policy from targeting the warheads on cities to aiming them at enemy missile systems (the so-called 'counter-force strategy'). But the two parties disagree on the question of whether the implications of these developments is a move towards first-strike capacity.

The opinion that the increase in accuracy portends the coming of first-strike capacity is eloquently stated in Professor Michael Pentz's

Nicholas Measor

booklet 'Towards the Final Abyss?'.[2] To have first-strike capacity is to have a very high probability of knocking out *all* the enemy's missile firing sites in one strike. Pentz points out that quite a small increase in accuracy can make an enormous qualitative difference in this respect. For example, if there are 1,000 Soviet launching sites (not so far from the truth in fact) then a 0.99 probability for each American missile of destroying the Russian silo it is aimed at will give a very low probability (0.99^{1000}, which is scarcely greater than 0) of knocking out *all* the Soviet sites in one attack. But an increase in accuracy of American missiles such as to give each a 0.99998 probability of knocking out its target will tip the scales dramatically, since the chance of disabling *all* the Russian launching sites will now have increased to something which is scarcely smaller than 1. But the US is striving to produce just such an increase in accuracy in its weapons, and Pentz therefore concludes that it is aiming to have first-strike capability by the end of the decade.

Let us note two points which are produced in response to this.

The first is simply the assertion that the counter-force strategy, and the increase in accuracy which goes with it, is not intended to produce a first-strike capability but is instead designed as part of the deterrent strategy called 'flexible response'. But, whatever the current intentions of, say, the controllers of the Pentagon, once the increased accuracy exists the possibility of using it for first-strike purposes will exist. There is no guarantee at all that future leaders of nations will not come to relish and use it. The technological developments imply progress towards a first-strike policy by implication even if the intentions which accompany them are innocent.

The second response to Pentz's type of argument is to point out that not all Soviet warheads are launched from rocket silos. There can also be movable delivery systems in aircraft and, most significantly, submarines. The US could not realistically suppose itself to be capable of a first strike until it had licked the problem of how to target weapons on these comparatively elusive missile launchers.

Now it is true as far as I know that the US is not currently able to identify the positions of Soviet submarines once they have left port, and it is true that until they are able to do so there will still be a deterrent against an American first strike. But how much comfort should the Soviet Union derive from that fact? It appears to me that Soviet euphoria on this score would be sadly out of place. Even if the US is not currently trying to develop an effective submarine tracking system (which seems unlikely), and even if the US has not yet realized the possible significance of its counter-force strategy, it is surely only a matter of time before it *does* realize the significance and pull out all the stops in the attempt to remove the remaining obstacles to a first-strike capacity.[3]

It is perfectly reasonable, therefore, to see the arms race as now being a race to achieve first-strike capacity.

Let us suppose, then, that it is highly probable that at least one side will eventually achieve first-strike capability. How should we take this into account in planning our (i.e. NATO's) present strategy in the arm/ disarm game?

I take the strategy of arming here to consist not just in possessing arms but in striving to develop them as well. Strictly speaking there are at least three options open, namely (1) keeping one's weapons and not developing them, (2) developing them, and (3) disarming. In practice, however, we can safely ignore the first of these strategies, since not to develop is to invite the other side to acquire first-strike capacity when one does not have it oneself, and if that occurs one will be worse off than if one disarmed now (basically because one then has the risk that the enemy may make a first strike before one has managed to disarm — Figure A3 in the Appendix is the relevant matrix).

Effectively, therefore, the choice is between technological development and disarmament. Now it only makes sense to persist with development of weapons if the worst pay-off, the one which should be avoided by the rational principle that one should maximize one's minimum pay-off, comes from disarming (when the other side is still armed) rather than from meeting armament with armament. If both sides continue to develop their weapons there are three possibilities open: we get first-strike capacity and they do not, we do not and they do, or both do (*ex hypothesi* we are ignoring the possibility that neither will).

In the first eventuality we get a positive pay-off of less than 15 (+15, representing bloodless conquest, is the *best* we can hope for, and this will not be achieved if the other side fails to resign when he observes our superiority). In the second eventuality we get a negative pay-off worse than the present disarmament pay-off (see the last paragraph but one and the part of the Appendix referred to there). In the third case we get a pay-off determined by the probabilistic calculations consigned to the Appendix (Figure A1 is the relevant matrix); it will almost certainly be worse than the present armament pay-off of -2 (Figure 3) — indeed if the probability of the other side attacking us during the disarmament period is around 0.1 or higher then the figure is worse than the present disarmament pay-off of -15.

How, then, is one to construct a matrix for develop/disarm on the basis of these three possible outcomes of development? I am afraid that I do not know. I do not see how one is to compute the probabilities of the various relevant outcomes in even the roughest way. To illustrate this point, let us consider two possible ways of calculating the score for armament (when the other side arms), one of which makes it sensible to arm and the other sensible to disarm.

Suppose first that the probability of my side obtaining first-strike capacity before the other is 0.45 (= 9/20), that the probability of the reverse happening is also 0.45, and that the chance of both obtaining it at once is 0.1.

To all intents and purposes the third eventuality can be ignored, since its contribution to the final figure will be so small. The utility of developing one's weapons, therefore, I shall compute as the score for winning the first-strike race times the probability of this happening, *plus* the score for losing the race times the probability of *that* happening (this sum will in practice, of course, turn into a subtraction since the second figure will be negative).

I remarked before that the *best* which can be hoped for from obtaining first-strike capacity before the opponent is +15 (if he resigns). There is also a chance that he will not resign and that my score will therefore be reduced by such factors as the devastation of parts of the enemy's territory and nuclear fall-out. Let us therefore reduce the score for winning the first-strike race to 13. The chance of me winning this race we have supposed to be 0.45, and 0.45 times 13 is approximately 6.

Let us also assume that if the opponent wins the first-strike race then my side will be sufficiently prudent to surrender and disarm (clearly the pay-off will come out worse if we do not make this assumption). The second component in our calculation is, therefore, the pay-off for disarming when the other side has obtained first-strike capacity multiplied by the probability of him winning the first-strike race. Now I have already explained that to calculate the pay-off for disarmament when the other side can make a first-strike one must know the probability of him attacking during the disarmament period. Let us suppose it to be relatively small, say 0.1. If we feed this probability into the relevant formula (which is in fact $-[(250 \times p2) + 15(1-p2)]$, where p2 is the probability of attack — see the Appendix) the pay-off for disarmament when the other side has first-strike capacity comes out as

-38.5. So the second component in the calculation comes out as -38.5 x 0.45, which is approximately -17.5. So on these assumptions the utility of developing one's arms is the sum of 6 and -17.5 = -11.5. But the score for disarming now is -15, so on these assumptions one would be better advised to develop one's weaponry.

Compare this, however, with the result one obtains if one keeps everything as before except that one allows a probability of attack during the disarmament period of 0.2 instead of 0.1. The positive component in the pay-off remains 6 as before. But the pay-off for disarmament when the other side has first-strike capacity becomes -62, so the negative component in the calculation becomes -62 times 0.45, which is approximately -28. On these new figures, therefore, the score for developing one's weapons becomes 6 - 28, which is substantially less appealing than the disarmament pay-off of -15.

Reflection on the dramatic difference between these two ways of doing the calculation suggests an important moral. If one is to decide the merits of a policy of armament on the basis of a game-theoretic matrix in an age when the advent of first-strike capability is very probably imminent, some way must be found of assigning values to a number of crucial variables. The contrast I drew highlighted the importance of just one of these, the probability of attack during the disarmament period. I would not care to lay a bet on whether the higher or the lower probability of the two mentioned in this context is the more plausible. Do not dismiss the higher figure of 0.2 out of hand, however, for you should remember that it is by no means clear that a future government would in a precipitate manner disarm once it suspected that the other side had first-strike capacity. If it did not then the effective disarmament period might be quite prolonged, and the probability of being attacked consequently higher. Nor is it certain that a government would have speedy intelligence that the enemy had acquired such a capability.

There are, moreover, a number of assumptions relied upon in both the sample calculations which I supplied which might be changed quite radically with a consequent change in the armament pay-off. For example the figure of +13 for the result of achieving first-strike capacity before the other side may be much too high (since a drift of devastating fall-out from enemy territory might be a highly likely result of the use of such capacity) or, alternatively, too low (since perhaps the surrender of the enemy would be almost inevitable under such circumstances). Again, how is one to calculate the chances of

Nicholas Measor

either or both the sides obtaining first-strike capacity? If my side could be seen to be a strong favourite to obtain that capacity first then this would certainly increase the advantages for me (and decrease those for the enemy) of continuing with technological development.

Some of these uncertainties may be simply a product of my ignorance. Perhaps there is somewhere in the Pentagon a Dr Strangelove seated in front of a computer terminal who can supply you on demand with accurate calculations of the probability of the United States obtaining first-strike capacity before the Soviet Union, who can make a truly reliable estimate of the amount of fall-out which would follow on a United States first strike and calculate the probability of that fall-out blowing across the Bering Strait and down the West American seaboard. But this is improbable. There are so many shortcomings in our ability to foretell the future course of events, so many deficiencies in such matters as intelligence gathering and weather forecasting, that to put a confident figure on the relevant probabilities on the basis of the available information is only marginally more sensible than consulting the entrails of goats.

Where, then, does this uncertainty leave us? Some might be tempted to reply that it leaves us with no certain conclusion at all, but they would be wrong. It is true that I cannot say whether we are still in a Prisoners' Dilemma matrix, since I am quite unable to tell what figures should be inserted in the top left box. But it does not follow that there is no rational procedure for making a decision between armament and disarmament. For the choice is between a strategy with a (more or less) known disutility and a strategy whose pay-off *may* be worse than the known disutility or *may* be better. The rational course for an agent faced with such a choice will normally be to choose the known evil rather than embark upon uncharted waters, and it is only when unusual special features obtain that this may cease to be the preferred option.

Consider a little fantasy which by analogy may throw some light on the correct reasoning to adopt. I am forced by a dictator with a warped sense of humour to undergo a curious ordeal. I am faced with two boxes, one of which I must open. If I open the first box a hand, clad in a boxing glove, will emerge on the end of an arm and hit me forcefully in a painful spot (this is a definite consequence of opening the first box). If I open the second box one of two things will happen: either a whirling blade will emerge and cut off both my legs, or I will be presented with a new set of hi-fi equipment. I have absolutely no way of calculating the relative probabilities of these two results of

152

opening the second box. For all I know dismemberment may be far the more, or far the less, probable.

If I found myself in the situation described in this version of the story I should certainly be inclined to open the first rather than the second box, even though the painful consequence is not one that I should relish. The conclusion which I am urging about the arms race is that if you would act like me in the imaginary situation then you should also regard disarmament as a more attractive prospect than joining in the race to first-strike capability. It may help, however, to quell any remaining doubts if I mention two sorts of special circumstances which would be relevant, circumstances which I suggest are not present in the arms race.

There is some resemblance between my fantasy and the puzzle known as 'Newcomb's Problem'.[4] In Newcomb's Problem, however, there is additional evidence which may give support to opening the second box. A near parallel to this in our story would be a regular correlation in the past between opening the second box and doing well. I did admit earlier that if we had good evidence of some kind that we were going to obtain first-strike capability before the other side this might make it relatively sensible to press on. But no evidence of *this* kind exists in the real life situation, no observed correlation between entering the first-strike race and winning it.

Another kind of feature which might be present relates to the preference scale of the dictator's victim. He *might* regard a blow in, say, the groin as worse than the loss of both legs. If so, he would be well advised to open the second box. There is a rough parallel to this in the arms race if a participant regards political conquest as so awful that he thinks that nuclear devastation is no worse. But for those of us who do not share this 'better dead than red' sentiment such considerations should not affect our reasoning.

My concluding claim, therefore, is that in joining in the first-strike race one is buying a pig in a poke, a pig which has an unknown probability of possessing a savage bite. If a method of disarming unilaterally can be discovered this is the more rational option even if it leads to political subjugation.

Appendix

Our first task is to construct a matrix for the strategic decision between sincerely disarming and insincerely disarming (i.e. firing one's weapons during the disarmament period). The left-hand box pay-offs for the US in such a matrix might come out like Figure A1.

USSR

Insincere   Sincere

	Insincere	$10(1\text{-}p1)+(\text{-}250 \times p1)\dots$
US		
	Sincere	$\text{-}[(250 \times p2)+15(1\text{-}p2)]\dots$

Figure A1

Here p1 and p2 are probability variables — their values are fractions between 0 and 1. p2, for example, is the probability of the USSR attacking the US during the disarmament period, 1 - p2 is the probability of this not happening (since the only possibilities are for such an attack to happen and for it not to happen, and the probabilities must add up to 1). Let t be the time at which the US will fire (if not previously fired upon) in pursuance of a policy of insincere disarmament. Then p1 is the probability of the USSR attacking the US before t, and 1 - p1 is the probability of this not happening. Thus the top left figure for the US, for instance, represents the pay-off for the US if she makes a surprise strike during the disarmament period times the probability of that happening *plus* the (negative) pay-off for the US for being attacked before she can attack times the probability of that happening.

Some features of the matrix are worth pointing out. The US figure in the bottom left box is negative whatever value is assigned to p2. Furthermore, although the US figure in the top left box may be either positive or negative (depending on what value is assigned to p1), the US pay-off in the bottom left is always worse than her pay-off in the top left since p2 is bound to be larger than p1 (the strategy of insincere disarmament, remember, is a strategy of firing before the end of the disarmament period, preferably as soon as possible).

Although the top left pay-off *can* be positive, the probability of attack during the disarmament period must be very low for this to be the case. The watershed is a value of p1 between 0.03 and 0.04: if p1 is 0.03 then the pay-off is 10 (1 - 0.03) + (-250 x 0.03) = 9.7 - 7.5, while if p1 is 0.04 then the pay-off is 10 (1 - 0.04) + (-250 x 0.04) = 9.6 - 10.

Two further points: the figures in the bottom right box where both sides disarm are (as usual) 0,0. And the pay-off for a policy of insincere disarmament when the other side is sincerely disarming (e.g. the US top right pay-off) is positive – given that the sincere disarmer is not going to attack, the pay-off to the insincere party is, if Figure 6 is to be believed, +10.

Provided that the value of p1 is 0.04 or greater and the corresponding probability for the USSR top left figure is at least 0.04, then the matrix will have the shape shown in Figure A2.

USSR

		Insincere	Sincere
	Insincere	-A,-B	+C,-D
US			
	Sincere	-E,+C	0,0

Figure A2

where A<E and B<D (i.e. -E for instance, is a worse pay-off than -A). If the value of p1 is the same as the corresponding probability for the USSR, and likewise for p2, then A=B and D=E, with the result that the matrix will be straightforward Prisoners' Dilemma. But even if we do not make this assumption, the reasoning appropriate to the matrix will still be like the Prisoners' Dilemma in that each side will be insincere in order to maximize its minimum pay-off, even though each would have been better off if both had been sincere.

The same reasoning does not, however, apply in the case where one side has first-strike capacity and the other does not, and the matrix for the arm/disarm game is in that case nothing like the Prisoners' Dilemma. For the side which does not have first-strike capacity but is threatened by a foe who does, firing first is (as we've seen) not a serious option, the pay-off being -500. So his strategy alternative to sincerely disarming is keeping his arms but doing nothing with them. Let us assume that it is the USSR which has the first-strike capacity and the US which does not.

Let us say that the disarmament period lasts from now to t, and let us consider the pay-offs over a period from now to t+, where t+ is later than t. Let p3 be the probability of the USSR attacking the US between now and t+, and let p2 be the probability of the USSR attacking the US during the disarmament period. The matrix for the relevant decision will now look like Figure A3.

USSR

		Keep arms	Disarm
	Keep arms	-250xp3	
US	Disarm	-[(250xp2)+15(1-p2)]	

Figure A3

The figure of -250xp3 stands unadorned in the top left box because in the event of the USSR not attacking the US (probability 1 - p3) the pay-off to the US will be 0. The bottom left figure is the same as in Figure A1.

The important point about this matrix is that the later we take t+ to be the higher the value of p3, whereas the bottom left figure remains the same whatever t+ may be. There is a t+ in the future, therefore, such that over the period till that t+ disarmament is the best bet, so in the long run the matrix is not Prisoners' Dilemma.

Notes

1   J. von Neumann and O. Morgenstern, *Theory of Games and Economic Behaviour* (Princeton, 1947).
2   J.D. Bernal Peace Library Pamphlet, 1980.
3   On this, see F. Barnaby, *The Nuclear Arms Race – Control or Catastrophe?*, Proceedings of the British Association for the Advancement of Science 1981 (London, 1982), pp. 33-4.
4   A description and comprehensive bibliography of this puzzle may be found in Ellery Eels, *Rational Decision and Causality* (Cambridge, 1982).

Three Main Fallacies in Discussions of Nuclear Weapons

W.B. Gallie

In this paper I am not concerned with fallacies in the sense traditionally favoured by logicians, namely mistakes in reasoning due to neglect either of basic logical principles or of the deceptive ambiguities of language. The fallacies I want to expose are of a more important and elusive kind. They are the result of assumptions – for the most part unnoticed or never adequately articulated – which underlie our thinking in areas which do not easily admit of formalization. Such an area is mankind's addiction to war, the development of weapons of war, and, more particularly, the necessity or possibility of limiting or totally eliminating war. Notoriously, men's opinions on this last topic vary enormously; but in the present, nuclear, age they fall into three main, sharply conflicting groups – unilateralists, multilateralists, and those who have resigned themselves, often heavy-heartedly, to the necessity of maintaining nuclear arms and even of adding to their number and destructive power. I believe that the arguments usually put forward in favour of each of these positions are seriously flawed by the acceptance of assumptions of which their spokesmen, for various reasons, are barely aware. These assumptions are not the result of mere intellectual laziness or of linguistic inadequacies and confusions. They are, rather, elements of total, if largely submerged, belief-patterns with regard to war and the possibilities of limiting or eliminating it; belief-patterns which are too deep-seated to be easily questioned or criticized, and indeed, with many people, may be too deep-seated to be clearly identified and described. Once unearthed and examined, however, it soon becomes plain that, while containing elements of value, they are in other respects *ad hoc* contrivances patched together by wilful or hopeful thinking or non-thinking which cannot any longer be condoned. I shall not try to spell out the practical political consequences which recognition and correction of each of my three 'fallacies' would involve. I simply present them, and up to a point explain them, as three sources of dangerous weakness in much current political reasoning.

I

The first assumption that I want to question is best introduced in a somewhat roundabout way. What seems to most of its critics to be the chief weakness of the unilateralists' case, namely its relative indifference to the political and technical means of achieving its goal, is thought by most of its advocates to be its peculiar glory — that it is primarily, and indeed in its essentials exclusively, a moral case. Clearly there are grounds here for much radical misunderstanding and fruitless disputation between the two parties. There is one thing, however, which they seem to have in common: the belief that, in any serious political issue, it is possible to pick out and respond to the dominant moral considerations without reference to the political, strategic or technical considerations which help to determine our actions. Of course, the two parties apply this belief in very different ways. Multilateralists, and indeed some reluctant nuclear re-armers, often bow their heads in respect for the *moral* ungainsayability of the unilateralist case, but then proceed to assail unilateralism fiercely for its political naivety and strategic and technical unfeasibility. Frequently, too, they thus end up seeming to overlook the moral case for unilateralism which they had at first acknowledged. Unilateralists, on the other hand, tend to bundle together the whole hideous business of producing or purchasing, deploying, threatening to use or even endeavouring to limit the use of nuclear weapons, and thereby wish them out of existence with a single gesture of moral repudiation. 'The bomb', they repeatedly tell us, is an incomparable evil, in the face of which the primary task is to get the majority of mankind — first in one's own country, ultimately throughout the world — to recognize it for what it is. Only when this is done will it be worthwhile to engage in questions about how to dismantle and dispose of nuclear weapons, how to alter national policies and vital interests which nuclear weapons are supposed to defend, or how to persuade or force recalcitrant governments into making such changes. It is in this sense that unilateralists commonly maintain — or more commonly assume — that their case is a purely moral one.

But in this assumption, I now want to argue, they are mistaken. So far from resting wholly or even predominantly on moral considerations, the unilateralists' case depends upon a belief which, in respect of its practical persuasive functions, is morally neutral or indifferent. This is the belief that mankind is threatened by a disaster of unthinkable magnitude, unless every social and physical process making for it is speedily rejected or put into reverse. This prophesied disaster is seen by most unilateralists as in part the result of various forms of human wickedness, and as such is regarded with moral repulsion. But the distinctive role which the prophesy plays in unilateralist thinking is largely, if not entirely, independent of the moral condemnation that accompanies it. To see that this is so, imagine an as yet inexactly dated prophesy of a cosmic disaster capable of destroying all human life as we know it. Given widespread acceptance of such a prophesy, we can imagine, among the more rational and optimistic reactions, whole societies combining to forestall or mitigate the effects of the expected calamity. And among rational but pessimistic reactions we can imagine some societies preparing themselves with stoical piety and fortitude for the extinction of everything they have held dear. In neither case would there be any suggestion of a moral condemnation of the coming calamity or its causes. And yet belief in its coming would have powerfully affected not only the feelings but the possibilities of thought and action open to those who accepted it. Not only would it have concentrated wonderfully the minds of those who believed it, inducing an unusual consistency to their thinking, it would have given rise to a new general perspective, within which what can be done and what ought to be done would be recognized in much clearer and sharper fashion. In particular the great issues of life and death would have been simplified and clarified around the idea of a single, and rapidly approaching, end. A prophesy of disaster which has this effect is commonly called Apocalyptic. And it seems to me important to see as clearly as possible the persuasive mechanisms by which such prophesies, and the whole style of thinking which surrounds them, succeed in producing their characteristic effects.

The salient features of Apocalyptic thinking are familiar from its major historic instances – the warnings of the Old Testament prophets, the expectations of the early Christian church and of later-millennian Christian sects: to which some would add the hopes of those French revolutionaries who worshipped at the altar of Reason, and of certain early – and indeed certain latter-day – Marxists with their total faith in 'revolutionary practice'. All these, despite their notable differences, have been alike in believing that the crucial turning point in human history was at hand; and that this incomparable change demanded, from all who had the wit to foresee it and hoped to survive it, new ways of thinking and acting – an entirely new moral perspective, uniting and constricting all legitimate human interests, here and now. Thus Apocalyptic thinking curiously combines prophesy of a disaster so nearly complete that beyond it little can be described, with an ethic which, although mainly negative and world-rejecting, has on occasion mightily affected mankind. It is the linkage between these two main limbs of Apocalyptic thought which, in my belief, helps us to understand better what is unmistakenly pertinent and what is painfully wanting in much contemporary unilateralist thinking. But before I demonstrate this point, let me say something about the two main limbs of Apocalyptic thinking themselves.

Firstly, Apocalyptic prophesy is neither a species of, nor a rival to scientific prediction, nor is it even a candidate for scientific respectability. For it is not a theory that can be variously criticized, tested, reformulated, and re-applied to a persistent or recurrent problem. On the contrary it is a peremptory indication; it warns of a particular, unprecedented and – except in one important respect – wholly discontinuous change. An all-dominating empire will perish without a trace. An all-inclusive, authoritative system of religious thought will crumble before the claims of the individual conscience. The capitalist system will collapse under the weight of its most characteristic successes. These claims are not the result of anything that can properly be called, or even usefully be compared with, experimental science. Each of them is the object of a passionate unifying vision, evoked by deep tensions in society and having as its focus a catastrophe which, although imprecisely dated, is promised for the very near future.

It would, therefore, be a complete mistake to demand tests of Apocalyptic truth modelled on those required in experimental science. All great Apocalyptic prophesies are grounded in truth born of quick observation and profound reflection; but these truths are not organized and available for testing as in the sciences, they are expressed through casual illustrations or symbolically, or are felt as subliminal ideas adding mysteriously to the persuasiveness of a very sketchy argument. But the fact that they are presented in ways that would be intolerable in science does not mean that Apocalyptic prophesies are intellectually negligible. Perhaps the best analogue of their intellectual importance is provided by those sudden, unheralded and usually quite unspecific warnings of danger close at hand — danger that may be physical or moral — of which most of us, I imagine, have had experience. (When the danger is physical, the warning is closely akin to that experienced by animals, such as a horse shying; when moral, it is sometimes ascribed to 'conscience'.) Such vague warnings never of themselves provide sufficient grounds for correct action: they have to be filled out, interpreted, rendered more precise and intelligible by questioning and reflection of a more work-a-day, and where possible of a scientific, kind. But this does not alter the fact that, if only in rare situations, and if only as promptings to appropriate actions, they may be indispensable for physical survival or personal integrity. Such warnings dominate, if only briefly, all other considerations. They have a now-or-never quality: they dictate not *what* but that *something* must be done and done quickly. Similarly, although on an immensely enlarged scale, with Apocalyptic prophesies.

The analogy just suggested helps us to appreciate another feature of Apocalyptic prophesies. Unheralded warnings of danger can be regarded as momentary intensifications of a more general awareness which is commonly kept on the very margin of consciousness, namely awareness of the permanent fragility of both physical and moral well-being and security. Similarly, many Apocalyptic prophesies, notably those of the ancient Hebrews, of the first Christians and of the early Marxists, can be considered as projections of more fundamental insights into the fragility of the societies which evoked them. In fact, almost all known civilizations, to judge from their calamitous endings, were targets well suited for Apocalyptic prophesy.

But having said so much in partial exoneration of this kind of thinking, I must add some obvious critical points. Most Apocalyptic prophesies have turned out to be false. Either the calamity did not come, or if it did, it proved to be a recurrent or persistent threat, not a once-for-all affair. Again Apocalyptic prophesy is peculiarly liable to abuse. Fake prophets are not only those who mis-see the future; they include large numbers of ruthless power-addicts and vulgar self-advertisers. Thirdly, and perhaps more importantly, there is a suspicious, because indefinitely extendable, fissure in the seeming unity of most Apocalyptic prophesies. In their most arresting statements they present the coming calamity in quite unconditional terms. *Everything* will be changed: the discontinuity between before and after will be complete. But then a note of conditionality creeps in. On certain conditions and in some form, a 'remnant' will survive: the thread of continuity, no matter how slender, will link the sufferings that went before with the recompense and glory that will come after.

And now a brief general comment on Apocalyptic ethics. I mentioned above that this is predominantly negative and world-rejecting in character, but it is now necessary to add a severer judgment. Granted that the prophesied calamity is likely to concentrate the minds of believers on a few crucially important moral commands, it is just as likely to divert or exclude men's minds from other commands no less important. In particular, it is certain to militate against any free expansion of moral concerns such as often accompanies a vigorous development of social life. For every Apocalyptic ethic is the ethic of a society essentially at a standstill: a society whose major concerns have already been summed up, and as it were wrapped up, in a general belief in imminent disaster. Apocalyptic ethics, therefore, owe their special character to their exclusive focus on the prophesied calamity, the great change, the last day. Hence they are so many variants of the simple command, 'Take no thought for the morrow.' Or, to translate them into Kantian form, their supreme imperative is 'Choose always that path of action which would commend itself to you if this day, indeed this hour, were your last and the world's last.'

We can now consider the logical or quasi-logical links between these two main limbs of Apocalyptic thought. Two have already been indicated. The magnitude of the prophesied calamity wonderfully concentrates attention on its consequences and requirements for conduct. At the same time, the persistent uncertainty of its date stimulates moral alertness in combination with attitudes of world-rejection. These links, however, are psychological rather than logical: they express powerful emotional and practical compulsions. But there is also a more specific and restrictive connection between the nature of the prophesy and the nature of the prescription which it gives rise to. Taken together, they have the effect of convincing believers that there is nothing more that they must find out about the prophesied calamity, and nothing more that they must try out or learn to do, or do better, during the 'run-up period' between the promulgation of the prophesy and its expected realization. The great calamity will put a stop to life and history as we know them: therefore recognition of its imminence puts a stop to all further questioning, to all further search for information, and in particular to self-doubt and criticism of any kind. The spell is wound up: the prophesy is held to be logically complete, sufficient for all serious purposes of thought and action.

This point is so crucial that it is worth reconsidering it from a slightly different angle. In so far as it presents the coming of calamity as the climax of all history, Apocalyptic thinking may be said to have encouraged long-term historical attitudes of mind. But in the short term, especially in the 'run-up period', Apocalyptic thought is markedly anti-historical. How indeed can it recognize and acknowledge that 'history is continuing to happen' under the shadow of a disaster which may strike this very day? And the same holds, *a fortiori*, of whatever future awaits the remnant on the other side of the great calamity. Always an inadequate guide for the future, history becomes worse than useless when faced by the promise of an almost total discontinuity. The result is that the lives of Apocalyptic believers tend to be pursued in relative isolation from most current, seemingly urgent public concerns: and the logical completeness which they impute to the prophetic (and consequently to the ethical) elements in their creed gains support from their relative social isolation.

These intellectually restrictive, indeed inhibitive, effects of Apocalyptic prophesy, taken in conjunction with its refusal to submit to any specific tests of its truth, make it seem worthless to minds imbued with the standards of contemporary science. And the two weaknesses of Apocalyptic thinking may well seem to spring from a single cause. It claims to tell *all*, to be logically complete or unconditional, but only achieves this by refusing to consider the different possible conditions under which it might be fulfilled — or refuted. And it is this which makes it logically vacuous, useless for all inferential purposes, whether in theory or practice. But this accusation could not be brought against Apocalyptic prophesy if we were to assimilate it to those unheralded and ostensibly unexplainable warnings of danger which I mentioned above. As thus interpreted, Apocalyptic prophesies contain no bogus claim to logical completeness and unconditionality: they address us — and sometimes profoundly affect us — through their manifest vagueness and incompleteness. However attractive this more modest interpretation may be, it still leaves us with the task of explaining how vague peremptory warnings of a grave disaster ahead give rise to what is distinctive about Apocalyptic ethics, namely their peculiarly world-rejecting character. I here offer the following suggestion. The peculiar character of every Apocalyptic ethic springs from a condition of mind which is wholly intelligible, although far from logically justified, in view of the horrendous content of the prophesy which precedes it: namely that which inclines us to accept, almost masochistically, the

163

so-called 'worst case' principle.

The worst case principle tells us that, in seeking to counter any danger, we should be prepared for it in the deadliest form that it can take. As ordinarily applied, however, this principle is never thought to provide by itself a sufficient basis for choosing a particular course of action. On the contrary, it is always employed in conjunction with some assessment of the probabilities attaching to a whole range of possible outcomes or solutions of the problem in hand. But for Apocalyptic ethics the worst imaginable case is the one and only case on which all attention must be fixed and by which all plans and styles of action are to be determined. All less bad cases − all possibilities of forestalling or moderating the danger before it reaches its climax − are dismissed as delusive, as if on the principle that only the worst is bad enough for us!

But could anyone ever consistently adopt such a principle of action? For example, imagine a doctor called to examine a seriously poisoned finger or toe, for which a number of diagnoses and treatments are possible. Can one imagine him asserting that the only really safe treatment is the one which would be required if the poison were to spread to the point of extreme danger, amputation? What this example shows us is that in dealing with any serious danger, physical or moral, there is no one manifestation or phase of the danger − whether it be the earliest discernible or the last conceivable before disaster strikes − that decides the course and style of action that one ought to follow. Some deterministic theorists, such as Freudians, favour the former alternative: Apocalyptic moralists favour the latter, as a special form of the worst case principle. But both schools of thought neglect the experimentally directed and self-controlling character of all rational action, which begins by assessing the relevant alternatives and proceeds − even in the full flush of confidence and commitment − by keeping them all, if only marginally, in mind.

How do these criticisms of Apocalyptic thinking help us to understand what is wrong, unconvincing or misleading, in most arguments in favour of unilateral nuclear disarmament? Considered first as prophesy the unilateralist message lies open to a number of criticisms. It does not always make clear where and how it identifies the nuclear menace. Does it lie in the sheer existence of the weapons systems, which if dismantled or destroyed could easily be replaced? or in the targeting plans and trained personnel of the rival nuclear powers? or in their claims that their essential interests can be secured only by the threat, if not the actual use, of nuclear weapons? Again, unilateralist predictions of when, where, how and how suddenly a nuclear disaster is most likely to strike, are no doubt often amateurish. But these criticisms are of a minor, indeed of a trivial character. No intelligent person today has any difficulty in understanding what unilateralists are saying about the probable destruction of whole civilizations, perhaps of whole generations of mankind and of the earth's surface as a habitat for higher forms of life. No one can deny that the risks of the deliberate self-destruction of mankind are incomparably greater now than at any earlier time; while, in comparison with the most powerful of earlier Apocalyptic prophesies, the weight of technical and scientific evidence supporting unilateralist prophesies is now so great, that accusations of exaggeration or fantasy are wholly out of place. The visions of destruction that haunt us − the whiff of impending insanity on the air we breathe −are only too near, only too real.

It is when their prescriptions for action under the shadow of the prophesied calamity are considered that unilateralists lie open to more serious criticism. And, as with other Apocalyptic teachings, the fault here is to rely, for direction and impetus, excessively upon their prophetic base. This is not to say that all unilateralists are simple-minded or fanatical visionaries, for whom the prospect of a nuclear holocaust says everything there is to be said, and indicates everything that ought to be done, in order to forestall the nuclear menace. What we are faced with here is a belief-pattern which continually inclines its adherents to accept assumptions and inferences that stem directly from the prophesied disaster, and to shy away from projects, analyses and arguments that might begin to divert, mitigate or contain the disaster here and now. More simply unilateralist thinking is always focused on *that* day when the truth of its prophesy may indeed be horrifically vindicated, rather than on *this* day when the disaster which so properly obsesses its adherents may, if only in some degree, be forestalled.

The point of this criticism is perhaps best brought out by quoting one of the most telling sentences of unilateralist propaganda that I have ever read: 'Once the transistor crackles out the warning, once we know that there is four minutes left before the sky becomes fire, we shall all, you, me, Mrs Thatcher and the Admiral ... we shall all become totally committed supporters of unilateral nuclear disarmament!'[1] On its own terms this argument is unanswerable. In so far as it forces its opponents to imagine what the consequences of their policies are likely to be, it could not be improved. Yet experience shows that it will fail to touch or turn the thought of its opponents, to get under their guard or open up their defences. To do that, unilateralist thinking must be directed as much upon effective action now as upon prospective irrefutable proof of its own correctness at some terrible future date. And to that end it must learn to work with all available means — argumentative, psychological, economic, industrial, and even in a sanely restricted sense, military — which may begin, and begin quickly, to reverse the current crazy accumulation and proliferation of nuclear weapons.

Without wishing to develop this argument in any detail, let me conclude this part of the paper with the following general reminders. The task upon which unilateralists are engaged is one of persuasion. But to persuade people — and principalities and powers — on any major political issue involves presenting that issue within an enlarged context in which traditional assumptions are shown up for what they are, or have recently become; and it also involves showing that one means business and is prepared to sustain one's efforts for the foreseeable future. It is time, therefore, that unilateralists looked more carefully to their priorities, to the sequence of targets they must aim at, to where their best allies are to be found, and to where and for how long they will have to keep up the pressures. It is time they realized that in political life protest is not enough.

II

If unilateralist thinking is flawed by its Apocalyptic assumptions, so is multilateralist thinking by a tendency of quite opposite character: namely a particular form of 'rationalism' which dates back to the Enlightenment, Kant and Bentham having been its first and most distinguished exponents. Bliss was it in that dawn to be an Enlightener — to point forward to a long bright future when men's conflicts would be resolved by 'truths of reason' which as yet only philosophers could descry. And among truths was one, particularly pertinent to the elimination of war, which I shall call CRTMC, standing for Conflict Resolution Through Mutual Concessions.

In its widest sense, the CRTMC principle says: given a conflict of interests between two parties, such that further intensifications of it are likely to hurt and possibly to ruin them both, it is reasonable for them to look for some area of common interest which they can secure, and with luck enlarge and build on by trading off various balanceable items in their original claims or complaints against each other. Stated thus, as a general principle of prudence, CRTMC comes so close to platitude that it is hard to gainsay it. At the very least it expresses a consideration which is always worth bearing in mind although very easy to forget. It is hardly an inspiring principle, however. Individuals, groups, states or blocks of states that proceed in accordance with it will never obtain complete satisfaction on any disputed issue. The results will always be something of a second-best. On the other hand, those who conform to it can reasonably hope for satisfaction on two scores. If the process of trading-off is carried through successfully, neither side can complain that it has been cheated or brow-beaten — each will have given way on some issues, but their concessions will be approximately equal; and neither side will have submitted its future to the brutal, costly and capricious test of war. On both these counts it is easy to see why CRTMC appealed so strongly to early liberal theorists of international relations. And it is significant that it should have been invoked by economists to control the mutually ruinous effects of tariff wars between rival commercial powers.

No serious thinker, however, has ever maintained that CRTMC by itself provides a sufficient means or recipe for the prevention of wars. It was always understood (most clearly by Kant) that other powerful human interests and passions would have to be enlisted, and that much statesmanlike skill would have to be exercised, if mankind's 'war-making proclivity' was to be overcome. Nevertheless, throughout the history of nineteenth- and twentieth-century peace-seeking, we find thinkers of different tempers relying on CRTMC as the distinctive presupposition of their pacific theories and projects. Although seldom clearly articulated or argued, CRTMC has fulfilled two functions. It has supplied a general framework for thinking about international conflicts, which excludes, totally and on principle, traditional bellicose methods of settling them. And it has suggested other methods of settlement: the use of arbitrators, the establishment of an international court of justice, and eventually the League of Nations. In these ways CRTMC has seemed to provide the crucial *substitute* for war in the endless task of adjusting international relations.

But CRTMC took on a further significance when it was seen not only to promise an escape-route from the age-old causes of war, but to have an equally important bearing on the essential *means* of war, that is armies, fleets, weapons and armaments of all kinds. If rival states could be induced to trade off their petty ambitions for territorial advantage, why should they not be persuaded to trade off comparable items in their permanent arms-bills — for their war-fleets and standing armies in particular? Gradually the truth (first glimpsed by Kant and by Bentham) became clearer: these two applications of CRTMC were complementary. If war ceased to be a means of first resort then there was no call for standing armies or fleets at the ready. But equally, if there were no standing armies or fleets at the ready, there would be, perforce, ever-increasing reliance on other methods of settlement, and a willingness to support new peace-keeping institutions. The convergence of these two lines of thought was effected in the Covenant of the League of Nations, where, for the first time, equal emphasis was laid (a) upon the necessity of 'cooling-off periods', for discussion, arbitration and adjudication of international disputes, and (b) upon the need for general disarmament to ensure that the rivalry and fear fuelled by arms-races should never again hurl great nations upon each other in mutually ruinous wars. To many of the best minds of that age, with the terrible lessons of 1914-18 before them, this combination of ideas seemed to mark the beginning of a new chapter in international relations. But of course they were deceived; as have been all those who in our age have assumed that CRTMC supplies the essential framework for any serious project of multilateral nuclear disarmament.

Why this cruel disappointment? Underlying all the historical complexities is the simple fact that CRTMC has never provided an adequate framework for peace-making in a world of politically independent states. I shall first try to set out the most general and decisive reasons for this, and consider, very briefly, one key episode in the history of multilateral nuclear disarmament during the last three decades: an episode brings out more clearly than any abstract argument can what is wrong — or rather what is fatally missing — in CRTMC when conceived as the framework within which nuclear disarmament must be achieved.

My first general objection to CRTMC is that, from the outset, it was proposed with a small group of elite, liberal-capitalist nations primarily in mind. (Bentham wrote in terms of Britain and France alone, Kant in terms of a handful of Western powers whose contributions he regarded as in effect republican.) Such powers were in a special sense privileged or 'have' powers; they had something which other existing states had not, the means of self-enrichment which did not require territorial aggrandizement through war. This permitted them to forgo all aggressive

168

designs against one another and therefore all armaments specifically designed against one another. But this happy idea left open the question of the relations of these potentially pacific powers to others of a more backward and bellicose character. Here Bentham shut his eyes to the fact that France and Britain owed their commercial supremacy largely to their military strength; while Kant to some extent fudged the issue by conceding that, in certain circumstances, his group of elite nations might have to act as a defensive alliance against its bellicose neighbours.

To generalize from these failings, it would seem that CRTMC, as a proposed new basis for pacific international relations required a homogeneity among political societies which has never existed; and when it recognized their heterogeneity, it became at best a recipe for *half* of a new foreign policy for a small class of economically and politically privileged nations. With one hand — and vis-à-vis each other — Kant's elite nations disarmed; with the other hand, however, — and behind their backs — they remained ready to deal with the barbarians. And this defect in the first, classic, version of CRTMC has not been lessened by the passage of time.

A second objection arises from the fact that even between like-minded liberal states CRTMC rarely works as smoothly as my initial description of it suggested. I allowed that its results would never be wholly satisfactory to either conflicting party. But they may even prove so intolerable as to bring the parties back to the point of war. In an ideally simplified situation, both parties would be comparably, if not identically, placed with respect to the issue that divided them. But a much more likely situation is one in which party A finds it hard to concede on one issue, say the retention of a disputed territory, while party B cannot concede on a different issue, say its monopoly of a certain branch of trade. Trading-off in this kind of situation calls for not only an agreed code of principles, but well-advised judicial machinery and, in extreme cases, effective methods of enforcement. But legal enforcement between independent states means either military sanctions or other sanctions so severe that they may evoke military resistance. This does not mean that the claims of CRTMC are fraudulently circular; even if it should often fail, the attempt to make it work marks a great advance on the acceptance of war as the standard means of settling inter-state disputes. What the present objection teaches us is that in international affairs, as in other human relations, a prolonged period of uncertainty, postponement, frustration and continually mounting anxiety — especially on matters where high hopes of progress and harmony have been entertained — may come to feel as unbearable as the most violently destructive blow-up could possibly be. The belief that equality in concessions provides an *easy* road to international peace is thus not only a cruel but a dangerous delusion.

This second objection has a special bearing on disarmament. If considered in abstraction from other causes of conflict, armaments may seem like a common burden, a persistent world-wide epidemic, weighing down mankind and causing mutual distrust and hatred between nations. Rational projects for the removal of the burden, by equal or proportional cuts in their arms-bills, must therefore commend themselves to all responsible governments. Unfortunately, however, speedy, simultaneous and permanent abolition or reduction of armaments smacks of the miraculous. For disarmament, whether nuclear or conventional, will always and at best be something that has to be sustained, continually reviewed and re-orientated by patient processes of negotiation. For one thing, the vital interests of nations change, and change at different times, thus affecting the kinds of armaments which governments believe they require. Secondly, even in the most civilized international system there will remain, in the minds of citizens and governments alike, a peculiar sensitivity over questions of national security, one that is liable to turn into atavistic suspicion. To leave one's people defenceless is a nightmare fear which no-one wishes his government to be wholly without. But this does not mean that disarmament is a hopeless proposition, nor that defence need take the form of crudely bellicose preparations and posturings.

My third general objection to CRTMC is of a more speculative kind. CRTMC works by appealing to the governments and peoples to forgo and forbear on certain issues, to hold back natural impulses and reactions, to concentrate on concessions, for the sake of distant goals, conceived and articulated in negative terms. Such appeals may be contrasted with others of a supremely positive kind, appeals to individuals and peoples to join in creating or establishing some institution or artefact — be it cause or practice, city, country or cathedral — or in rescuing or securing great works or objects of veneration. Now it seems to me obvious that men and women are capable of much greater efforts and feats of endurance in response to the latter than to the former sort of appeal, which suggests that as long as peace-making and peace-keeping are conceived of in negative terms — so long as they cannot be identified with the creation or securing of values which evoke one's deepest feelings of dedication – they are handicapped, perhaps fatally. CRTMC is certainly an indispensable rule of practice in international dealings; but it is a rule which, like those of checker or umpire, can function only in support of more positively inspiring motives. But where, on the present issue, may these be found?

It might have been expected that, in the nuclear age when warheads are of fissile material and are directed with unimaginable accuracy and penetration, governments and peoples would have felt strongly moved to scale down, equally or proportionately, their weapons of mass destruction. But nothing of the sort has happened. In the endless wrangles over mutual concessions between the nuclear powers, fear, and the certain knowledge of what nuclear war would mean, have had little effect in the face of traditional, suspicious, ideological rivalry and military inertia. As a first step to identifying the missing motives in this agonizing story, it is important to see clearly where and why CRTMC should have proved so ineffective as a framework for disarmament negotiations. And for this purpose I shall consider briefly the one period in the thirty odd years of superpower confrontation when the two giants seemed on the verge of sharing a new vision, and of showing a much needed new basis for intellectual and diplomatic initiative.

The period in question covered the last year of the Kennedy, and the first years of the Johnson administrations in America; its inspiration was the shared experience of the Cuba crisis, and its intellectual vigour was embodied in the US Secretary of Defense, Robert McNamara. During this period American nuclear strategy moved through three stages. First, there was the recognition that 'mutually assured destructive capability' (MAD), if possessed by both superpowers, could provide an ultimate regulator of the kinds and numbers of nuclear weapons required for defence purposes. To be sure, MAD rested on the assumption that each side could achieve nuclear 'invulnerability', in the sense of the survival, after the severest enemy first-strike, of a nuclear force still capable of inflicting intolerable reprisals. But this thought gave rise to the question and the hope: might not science and military technology determine what was the *minimum*, in respect of numbers and types of nuclear weapons, necessary to ensure 'invulnerability' to either side? Here, apparently, was a really promising starting-point for negotiation in terms of CRTMC.

Unfortunately, this approach was never seriously developed between the superpowers. Instead, American strategic thinking was enlarged to include two further approaches, each aimed at lowering the probability of all-out nuclear war. These were (a) counter-force strategy, aimed at the destruction of enemy nuclear forces rather than enemy cities, and (b) 'flexible response', originally conceived as a means of postponing the use of nuclear weapons and thus giving time, while conventional forces were engaged, for diplomatic second thoughts and concessions. However the hopeful, forward-looking possibilities in these strategies were lost in the 'strategic mix' eventually favoured by the Americans, and used by them to justify their subsequent contributions to the nuclear arms race. Was there ever any real chance that the two superpowers, given their ideologies and international outlooks, could have carried through substantial reductions in their nuclear armaments, using standard CRTMC principles? My answer is 'No'. For this would have meant for both of them not only reducing the margin of their 'duopoly' over all other powers, and each abandoning the hope of achieving a definite diplomatic advantage over the other (which neither has ever abandoned), but also accepting a mutually insured nuclear paralysis. By this I mean that they would have had to proceed, in all diplomatic moves and military preparations, as if the weapons which embodied their political, industrial and military superpower-dom, simply did not exist. In the event, of course, both superpowers preferred the risks, the frustrations and the political demoralization which the nuclear arms race entailed to accepting what would have felt like voluntary military mutilation.

What changes in political perceptions and assumptions could conceivably have helped the superpowers to avoid this seemingly fatal impasse? In general terms, the changes would relate not so much to ideas of fair-dealing, open inspection and mutual concessions in nuclear arms reduction, as to a shared sense of common danger, of common responsibility for the future of mankind and of common guilt for the nuclear insanity which threatens to engulf us all. Above all, the greatest change would be for the superpowers to recognize that their respective ideologies are alike impotent from the point of view of removing the nuclear peril . . . . which might seem to demand a miraculous overnight political conversion on either side. But, as discussion of the third fallacy will show, this is where other strategies, other possible levers of political change, become relevant.

III

The third fallacy can be regarded as a special case of the 'realist' approach to international politics, which holds that important issues between nations are always, of necessity, decided by the relative power, and ultimately by the relative military power, of the parties involved. Realism in this sense has grown up in international theory during the last forty years or so, as a natural reaction to facile liberal idealism and the kind of rationalism implicit in CRTMC. It has found favour not only with official spokesmen of the superpowers, but among students of international relations in many countries. Nevertheless, the assumption that only those who wield potentially world-destructive nuclear power can do anything to initiate control over that power is far from self evident. In what follows I propose to examine this assumption from the point of view of Britain's nuclear problems and policies since 1945, and shall try to establish conclusions that are relevant to medium-sized powers and, indirectly, to the superpowers themselves.

Britain today is a minor nuclear power whose declared policy is to turn itself into a much more nearly self-sufficient nuclear power, in order to increase its security and independence while continuing its close nuclear ties with America. Objections to this policy are well known, so a summary of them will suffice. Firstly, the proposed new British deterrent will be no more independent than the old; it will still be part of a package which includes the use, for American nuclear forces, of British land and sea bases, thus making Britain a prime target for nuclear attack in the event of a Soviet-American confrontation. Moreover, Britain's new nuclear missiles, being American-made, will always be liable to fall under American control. Secondly, the new policy will contribute in a politically conspicuous way to the nuclear arms race. It may well encourage other medium-sized industrial powers to go nuclear, or to go more nuclear, in the future – a form of imitation which nuclear re-armers tend to ignore. Thirdly, the overall deterrent policy to which Britain's new nuclear forces will contribute is designed 'for the duration', that is, for as long as the politico-economic as well as the military rivalry of the superpowers continues. Fourthly, Britain could not conceivably use or threaten to use its proposed new nuclear forces against Russia without the assurance of American support – whatever that would imply about the possibility of worldwide nuclear war.

Each of these objections seems to me very persuasive. When employed in political debate, however, they are liable to be countered by an argument which modern governments have learned to use with skill. They tell us that our objections are fair enough when considered

173

as bits of amateur judgment; but unfortunately they rest upon ignorance of certain facts – some of them technical, some diplomatic, some of a terrifying urgency – which it is the duty of government to keep secret. This counter-argument is maddening; in our nightmare world it is usually impossible to refute, yet one may have the strongest reasons for distrusting those who employ it. We could fashion a blunt, two-fold answer: firstly, British nuclear policy has at best limped from poor expedient to poor expedient, secrets or no secrets, and secondly, its manifest inadequacies betray a fallacious assumption which no secret information could warrant. But then the argument develops around a combination of political *hubris* and inertia characteristic of nations which, like ours, are in a period of relative decline. How could any government or succession of governments of *our* country have saddled us with a nuclear policy which leaves us open to such shattering accusations – of abandoning our independence, of speeding up the arms race, of inviting Russian nuclear attack, of spending our money and staking our hopes on a small nuclear force which no government, unless completely demented, would ever threaten to use? Is it possible that we, the British, could have taken such a completely wrong road, could have slid into a defence policy so ill-conceived, so inconsistent, so nearly fraudulent? And is it imaginable that we could completely change our nuclear policy without – to repeat another well-worn governmental adage – seriously upsetting the 'existing delicate nuclear balance'?

In order to deal fairly with this very natural reaction to criticism on the part of nuclear re-armers, we must keep the following point clearly in mind. The nuclear problem has revealed its character and implications only gradually. Those who made the first atom bombs did not appreciate what they were making, and those who ordered their use did not know what forces they were unleashing. New and terrible truths have been forced upon public attention, not only by the findings of scientists, but through the persistent and cumulative failure of negotiators to catch each other's points of view on nuclear issues, or to sustain any flickerings of trust that may have momentarily lighted up their discussions. Moreover, in Britain, initial political reactions to the new weapons were concerned not so much with their horrific destructive potential as with their relevance to Britain's uncertain international position, as very much the third man of the Big Three.

The historical record here is plain. The motives that led the Attlee government to create an independent British nuclear force were firstly, pique with the Americans for having allegedly reneged on wartime promises of continued cooperation in nuclear matters, and secondly, the conviction – shared by distinguished politicians of left and right, although rejected by a few far-sighted scientists – that Britain's future world status depended upon becoming a nuclear power ('joining the club', 'getting a seat at the top table'). In the late 1940s and even throughout the 1950s, British governments may have been justified in maintaining this policy. But by the time of the Cuba crisis two things had become clear: Britain could aspire to nothing better than client status vis-à-vis America in respect of nuclear weapons and their deployment; while the two superpowers, despite their hatred and distrust of each other, were showing a marked preference for dealing with their nuclear differences on their own, without interference or advice from minor third parties.

The result is that for the last decade and more the motives which first prompted Britain to go nuclear have become largely outmoded and purposeless. Latterly, from having been a possible adjunct to American nuclear strength, Britain has become more like a launching pad or offshore service station for American nuclear forces in Europe; while possession of its own now ageing – but not therefore less costly – independent nuclear deterrent has effectively prevented British governments from joining in any way the growing worldwide protest against the crazy 'overkill' capacity of the superpowers' nuclear forces. The proposed new Trident force will not in any way lessen Britain's dependence on America, and exposes as sheer hypocrisy British claims to support multilateral nuclear disarmament. Moreover it is probable that the new plan will split the nation in two: not only between disarmers and re-armers but between different elements in every main dimension of national life – within the churches, the political parties, within educational and scientific establishments, the civil service and the armed services themselves. Before this happens it is surely time that the fundamental assumptions on which British nuclear policies have hitherto rested should be brought out into the open and rigorously questioned.

Why should it be assumed that the two powers which have put most effort and resources into making and improving nuclear weapons, and which have thereby stimulated and sustained their ever-growing rivalry and mutual distrust, should somehow – at some date, by some means, by some stroke of luck or some military invention – be able to overcome the appalling cloud of nuclear destruction which threatens us all? And, more specifically, why should it be assumed that we, the

British, can make our best contribution to our own future safety by keeping as close as possible to one of the giant contestants, nominally adding our nuclear quota to its already excessive strength, as if our readiness to share in the destruction of our chosen Big Brother would help to sanify the attitude of Big Brother on the other side?

The problem of understanding these assumptions is not one of tracing out and testing their finer implications, but simply that of grasping their enormity — the innocent hugeness and naivety of the habit of thought which they disclose. For this purpose, an image or fable is more likely to serve than any battery of queries and criticisms of recent or current British nuclear policy. I therefore suggest the following: imagine a derelict remnant of the human race, cave-dwellers reduced for the most part to stone-age conditions, after a nuclear holocaust. They may well have problems very like our own. The group may be dangerously divided between two rival claimants for leadership, each being a giant of abnormal strength and having in his possession a cache of high explosive devices — say grenades — left over from the industrial age. One all-important truth about the grenades has been passed down to them; they are most effective when released within a confined space, so that the survival of the cave-dwellers is constantly at risk. What, then, should the cave-dwellers do? Wait in hope for the rival giants to see the light, forgo their rivalry, and bury their grenades in 'a place of safety'? Or should they humbly petition the giants to do so? Or, judging the giants to be irreconcilable, should they take their pick between them, and put their relatively slight strength behind the one whom they think more likely to win out and more likely to befriend them if he proves victorious? Or should they look around for more — even if probably dud — grenades to increase their usefulness as allies of the giant of their choice? What these suggestions have in common is this: they all present the problem of the cave dwellers' survival as primarily dependent upon what the giants will do. And, on the face of it, the giants, who rely upon their grenades, have already decided to settle the issue between them by means which threaten the very existence of the group, the giants themselves included.

Suppose, however, that one or more of the cave dwellers come to recognize the intolerableness, and indeed the inherent illogicality, of the situation that faces them so long as the giants' choices of action are assumed to be decisive. There are then two things which they must contrive to do. Firstly, get across to the giants how they — the new resisters — see the situation; namely as one that offers them nothing but the prospect of disaster, and in which therefore they have nothing to lose. But secondly, they must indicate, as tactfully but as firmly as possible, what the giants themselves are now liable to suffer from those they have reduced to this dangerous position. For a number of courses of action may now for the first time seem feasible to the cave-dwellers. For example, they may pack up and go — no matter what dangers and disadvantages that would involve. Or they may withdraw their labour and stop providing the things which the rival giants need most; not only food and drink and material comforts, but amusement and conversation, admiration and trust. All such courses of action might involve great risks, giants being what they are. But to leave the future in the hands of the giants appears to involve not risks, but certainties of ultimate, horrific destruction. In fine, because one party has the power to destroy the other it by no means follows that the former is wholly immune to effective pressure from the latter (cf. Hegel on the master-slave relationship).

This helps us to appreciate the logical character of the resistance that is open to the cave-dwellers in our fable. Whatever forms of action they may decide on, whatever pressures on the giants they judge to be most effective, will presuppose a recognition of something that is there for all to see — the illogicality of the assumption that because the giants possess all-destructive power they alone are in a position to initiate the control and containment of that power. This assumption may have been natural (the cave-dwellers may have depended on the great strength of the giants for a long time) but at a certain point it becomes clear that 'letting the giants decide' spells ruin for all, giants included. The illogicality of the situation now becomes intolerable; and, while the search for a feasible alternative may be anxious and difficult, no alternative could possibly be worse. The result is an upheaval in the thinking, and indeed in the world, of the cave-dwellers, such as is bound to involve bitter disagreement and distrust, and sheer non-comprehending confrontation between different points of view. What seemed unalterable is now seen as disposable; what was unthinkable cries out to be thought through. This is very much the position we find in our current nuclear debates.

Because of this, it seems to me most unlikely that any individual or group will ever experience a simple and direct conversion from being a re-armer to being a disarmer, or *vice versa*. Significant changes in individual and group attitudes will begin only when the background against which standard positions are taken up is itself seen to have changed, and, more particularly, when the roles which each superpower assigns to itself and to its rival can no longer be accepted without question. At the moment, each superpower presents itself as the only possible defender of mankind against its opponent, which it of course presents as a deceiver, a tyrant, and the destined destroyer of the world. But already able critics, of very different backgrounds and persuasions, have begun to show us why this picture must be rejected. They have suggested that each superpower is becoming increasingly the prisoner of its own military machinery and its own propaganda, and indeed that the elements in both giant bureaucracies recognize the need for a permanent opponent, in order to keep their own ploys and plans in steadily accelerating motion.

What then, should we expect if the background of our nuclear debates were widely recognized to be very different from what we have been led to believe; and if, indeed, the superpowers came to be generally regarded, not as the only potential saviours of mankind, but as self-imprisoned giants who need to be rescued from themselves? There should then be, immediately, more hope and more political vitality, but also more bewilderment, more confusion and self-doubt, more bitterly divisive debates cutting across familiar ideologies, faiths and frontiers. There would be immense and daunting intellectual tasks to tackle. But what sane person will expect any escape-route from our world of stifling nuclear dogmatism, defeatism and prospective damnation to be easy?

Note

1   Oliver Postgate, *Thinking it through: the Plain Man's Guide to the Bomb*, The Menard Press, 1982, p. 31.

Index

'absolute war', 50-2
Acheson, D., 26
Afghanistan, invasion of, 33, 45, 115
agreements, 108-9
alliances, 99-104
'alternative defences', 65-70
Altruists' Dilemma, 138-40
ambivalence, 26
Apocalyptic fallacy, 17, 158-66
appeasement, 32
Arab-Israeli war, 87-9
Argentina, see Falklands War
armies: conscripted, 58-61, 76-7; dual function of, 29-30
arms: competition, 49; control, 7, 49, 126-7; arms race and games theory, 132-56
Atlanticist deterrence strategy, 117-24, 129
Attlee, C., 174

Bairnsfather, B., 21
Beirut, 46
Bentham, J., 166, 168-9
Berlin, 113-14
Bevin, E., 83
blackmail, see nuclear blackmail
Blake, N., 1
Blechman, B.M., 88, 111
bluffing, 108
Booth, K., 9, 13-14, 41, 79-82
Brandt, W., 114
Brezhnev, L., 43, 88
Britain, 3-4, 9, 173-5; and Clause-witzian reform, 50-7; conventional forces, 102; and CRTMC, 168-9; and East-West deterrence system, 112; and Falklands, 22, 33, 60, 96; independent nuclear deterrent, 41, 71, 97-100; and NATO, 99; as non-nuclear member of NATO, 11, 14, 65-6, 70-1, 75-6, 102; and nuclear black-mail, 84; peace movement, 54-5; strategy, need for change, 46-50; as target in war, 51-2, 67, 76; unilateralism in, 41-83; and US, 173, 175
Brodie, B., 54, 81
Bundy, McG., 45, 100

Callaghan, J., 10-12, 18
Carter, J., 47
Carver, Field Marshal Lord, 1-2, 17, 22, 41, 56, 81
catalytic rationale, 56
causes: of proliferation, 127-8; of war, 45-6
China and East-West deterrence system, 115-16
Christianity, 39, 161
'city busting', 21
Clausewitz, K. von, 13, 50-7, 80
Clausewitzian reform and uni-lateralism, 41-83
coercion, 14-15, 85-6, 92-3, 96
Cold Wars, 44, 58, 71

communication, 23-6
community, membership of same,
    23-5, 28
complacency, 22
concessions, 96, 166-72
'confidence', false, 48
Conflict Resolution Through
    Mutual Concessions, 166-72
confusions, past, 20-2
conscription, 58-61, 76-7
containment, 117-18
controversial games, avoiding,
    19-20
conventional forces: in Britain,
    102; cost of, 82; defence in
    depth, 104-5; development of
    and prospects for, 14, 61-5, 75;
    in NATO, need to improve,
    14, 57-65, 78, 82-3, 99, 102,
    109; *see also* non-nuclear costs:
costs: of empire, 72; of war, 3;
    of weapons, 56, 75, 82
counter deterrents, 4, 8, 172;
    see also missiles
credibility, 24
CRTMC, *see* Conflict Resolution
    etc.
cruise missiles, 11, 71, 74-5, 84
Cuba, 115, 171

dangers: of proliferated world,
    122-4; warnings of, 161;
    see also risks
de Gaulle, C., 116, 127
defence in depth, 104-5
defensive, trend towards, 61-5
'demonstration' missile, 47
detente, 31, 44
deterrence: concept of, 12-13;
    fallacies, 157-78; games theory
    and nuclear arms race, 132-56;
    nuclear blackmail, 84-111;
    proliferation, 112-31; provoca-
    tion and Martian temperament,
    19-40; sceptical look at nuclear
    debate, 1-18; unilateralism,
    41-83
disarmament: and 'Prisoners'

Dilemma', 145-55; talks, 48-9
division of Europe, 113-14, 125
duties, 2

East-West deterrence system,
    15-16, 112-16; and China,
    115-16; and Europe, 112-14;
    and proliferated world, dif-
    ferences, 117-22, 124-31;
    seen as success, 125-6, 128;
    and Third World, 114-15
economic: concept of politics,
    125; hardship, 42-3; problems,
    113
Eden, A., 87-9
effectiveness, problem of, 20
Egypt, 87-9
elite nations and CRTMC, 168-9
empire, costs of, 72
endemic nature of war, 124
enemy, meaning of, 32-3
equal nations, 25
escalation, 34, 58-61, 63
ethics, Apocalyptic, 162-3
Europe, 31-3, 36, 60, 73; and
    CRTMC, 168-9; division of,
    113-14, 125; Eastern, 43,
    45, 81, 113-14; East-West
    deterrence system, 112-14;
    flexible response in, 34; uni-
    lateralism in, 62; *see also*
    Britain; NATO; Warsaw Pact
ex-nuclear countries, 108
'expedients, strategy of', 58-61
expertise, 6
extended deterrents, 99-104

Falklands War, 22, 33, 60, 96
fallacies in discussions of nuclear
    weapons, 8, 16, 157-78;
    Apocalyptic, 158-66; CRTMC,
    166-72; realism, 172-8
fear, 35-6, 43; *see also* risks
fellowship, 23-5
Ferdinand, Archduke, 45-6
'Finlandization', 68
first strike capacity, 8, 142-53
fleets, nuclear, 4, 118-19

'flexible escalation', 63
'flexible response', 9, 21, 56,
  61-3, 172; and deterrence,
  34-5, 118-20; and NATO,
  9, 61-3; political purpose of,
  119-21; and 'Prisoners'
  Dilemma', 148-9
Foch, F., 54
France, 31, 36; conscripts in,
  60; and CRTMC, 168-9; and
  East-West deterrence system,
  112-13; and NATO, 70

Gallie, W.B., 16-17, 157
games, controversial, avoiding,
  19-20
games theory and nuclear arms
  race, 16, 132-56
Garnett, J., 63, 79-80, 82
Germany, 32-3, 65, 73; and East-
  West deterrence system, 113;
  and NATO, 47, 58, 100; and
  unilateralism, 62
global imperialism, 33-4
Gray, C., 53, 81
guerilla warfare, 66, 107
Gulf War, 45

Hackett, General Sir J., 54, 81
Haig, A., 47
hard unilateralism, 57-61
hardware comparisons, 29, 34
Hart, D.M., 88, 111
Healey, D., 63
Hegel, G.W.F., 177
Hobbes, T., 138
hostile, meaning of, 33
Hungary, 114
Hunt, K., 82
hypocrisy, 15, 59, 81

idealism, 8; *see also* morality
Iklé, F.C., 55, 81, 100, 111
illogicalities, 1-2
imperialism, global, 33-4
independent nuclear force, 41, 71,
  97-100
industrial interests, 130

insincere disarmament, 145-6,
  154-5
instability, 28, 43, 113, 122-3
interests, 2
intervention, 43
intransigence, 35-6
invasions, 33, 35-6, 45; *see also*
  war
irrationality, collective, 135, 140
irresponsibility, 122-3
isolationism of US, fear of, 119
Italy, 32, 113

Japan, 32, 68-70, 87, 90-1
Johnson, L.B., 171
justice, 30-2

Kant, I., 162, 166-9
Kennan, G., 22, 118
Kennedy, J.F., 115, 171
Kissinger, H., 80, 87-8, 100, 131
Korean War, 37

language, threatening, 27-8
Latin America, 43, 81
League of Nations, 167-8
Lenin, V.I., 38
Lewis, F., 88
'liberation, national, wars of',
  129
'limited' nuclear options, 53
linkage theses of causes of proliferation, 127-8
'Lisbon goals', 62

McMahan, J., 14-15, 83-4
McNamara, R., 62-3, 171
MAD, *see* 'mutually assured des-
  truction'
Martian hypothesis, 37-9
Martin, L., 20, 26, 32, 37-40
Marx, K. and Marxism, 39, 159,
  161
Measor, N., 7, 16-17, 132
Midgley, M., 12-13, 17, 19
misinterpretation of threats,
  28-9
missiles, 4, 8, 11, 47, 56, 64,

71, 74-7, 84, 175
modernization of nuclear
weapons, 75-6
Moltke, H. von, 61
Monroe Doctrine, 43
morality, 3, 10, 56-7, 126, 158-9,
166
Morgenstern, O., 132, 156
motivation, 22-3, 30
Multi-Lateral Force, 76
multilateralism, 16, 138, 140,
158; and arms control, 126-7;
little hope for success, 47-9
Mutual Force Reductions, 48
'mutually assured destruction',
20-1, 141-3, 171
MX missile, 8

Nasser, G.A., 33
national service, 58-61; 76-7
nationalism, new, 42
NATO: and Atlanticist deterrence, 118-24; and Britain, 99;
and Britain as non-nuclear
member, 11, 14, 65-6, 70-1,
75-6, 102; conventional forces,
need to improve, 14, 57-65,
78, 82-3, 99, 102, 109; and
flexible response, 9, 61-3; and
France, 70; and Germany, 47,
58, 100; non-nuclear, 14, 71-6;
and nuclear blackmail, 67-8;
nuclear deterrents in, 4, 8, 11,
46-7, 56, 62-4, 71, 74-7, 84,
109, 175; and 'Prisoners'
Dilemma', 149; and Soviet
Union, 4, 101-2; and Third
World, 120-1; and US, 12,
58-9, 67, 71-2, 75, 99-103
Nazi Germany, 32-3
negotiation, 11
Neumann, J. von, 132, 156
'Newcomb's Problem', 153
Nixon, R., 88
Non-Proliferation Treaty, 127
non-nuclear: countries, nuclear
blackmail of, 94-109, 111;
defence, problems of, 70-4;

NATO, 14, 71-6; *see also* conventional forces
'non-provocative' posture, 67,
83
non-violent resistance, 66
North Atlantic Treaty Organization, *see* NATO
North-South relations, 43; *see also*
Third World
Nott, J., 84, 88, 100
nuclear blackmail, 14-15, 84-111;
notion of, 84-97; prevention
of, 93, 97-109
nuclear debate, sceptical look at,
1-18
nuclear deterrence, *see* deterrence
'nuclear umbrella', 100

order, breakdown of, 43
Overall Strength Strategy, 117-24,
129

paradoxes, 1-2
parity, 29-30
Paskins, B., 9, 15, 34-5, 40, 112
past confusions, 20-2
patriotism, 22
peace movement, 54-5
peacetime, nuclear blackmail in,
93-7
penal deterrence, 23-4, 30-1
Pentz, M., 147-8
Pershing IIs, 4, 11, 74-5, 84
Poland, 45, 81
Polaris, 76
Pole, K., 1
political: instability, 43, 113,
122-3; parties, 9, 65; penalties
of nuclear attack, 95, 104;
problems of unilateralism,
74-5; purpose of flexible
response, 119-21; relationships, need for change, 129;
situations, interpretation of, 2
politics: economic concept of,
125; and war, unity of, 50-2,
55, 80
Postgate, O., 178

Powell, E., 41
prediction of war, 46
prevention of nuclear blackmail, 93, 97-109
'Prisoners' Dilemma', 134-53
'proliferated world', 112, 122-4; different from East-West system, 117-22, 124-31
proliferation and nature of deterrence, 112-31; East-West deterrence, 112-16; differences between East-West deterrence and proliferated world, 117-22, 124-31; proliferated world, 112, 122-4
provocation and deterrence, 19-40
psychology of deterrence and provocation, 22-3
punishment, 23, 30-1

Rapaport, A., 78, 80
rationality, 8
Reagan, R., 3, 10, 47, 49, 71, 81-2
realists, 6-8, 44, 80, 126, 130
Realpolitik, 50
rejection, 23
resources, non-renewable, competition over, 42
retaliation, 86
retribution, 30-2
risks of war, 10, 42-6, 51-2, 67, 72-4, 76, 103-4; *see also* dangers
ritual threats, 26-8
Rogers, General B., 63, 82-3
Rostow, E., 82, 84

Sadat, A., 88
SALT II, 48-9
sceptical look at nuclear debate, 1-18
Schlesinger, J., 53
Schlieffen, General von, 73
second-strike capability, 118-19
secrecy, myth of, 5
self-interest, 138-40
sincere disarmament, 145-6, 154-5

social cohesion, 113-14
Soviet Union, 11, 14; and Afghanistan, 33, 36, 45, 115; and Arab-Israeli war, 88-9; attack by, risks of, 72-4; and China, 115-16; counter deterrents, 4, 8; deterrence strategies, 118-19, 123; doctrinal uncertainty, 47; and East-West deterrence system, 112-13; invasions of, 35-6; as Martians, 37; and NATO, 4, 101-2; and nuclear blackmail, 93-4; political insecurity, 42; and 'Prisoners' Dilemma, 136, 142-8, 152, 154-5; sanctions against, 81; and unilateralism, 9-10; wars, 36, 38, 129
space-based weapons, 84
speech, threatening, 27-8
Spender, S., 43
SS20s, 11
Stalin, 39
START, *see* Strategic Arms etc.
steps towards unilateralism, 75-7
Strategic Arms Reduction Talks, 49
strategic option, unilateralism as, 41-2, 50-7
strategy differences between deterrence systems, 13-14, 117-24
submarines, 118-19
Suez incident, 33
surrender, 85-6, 107
Sweden, 71
Switzerland, 38
symbolic use of threats, 26-8

taboo against nuclear war, erosion of, 43, 53, 79
tanks, 64
Taylor, A.J.P., 45, 79
territorial defence, 66, 107
Thatcher, M., 3, 10
Third World: and East-West deterrence system, 16, 114-15;

and NATO, 120-1
Third World War: scenarios, winning, 54
Thompson, E.P., 58, 81
threats, 13, 26-9
Thucydides, 129
Tomahawk, 4
treaties, 108-9
Trident, 4, 8, 56, 74, 76-7, 84, 175
'trigger rationale', 56
Trotsky, L., 41
Tucker, A.W., 134
Turkey, 81
turn-taking, 26
two-person game, 132

unilateralism, 3, 9-11; and Apocalyptic fallacy, 16-17, 158, 164-6; and Britain in NATO, 11, 14, 65-6, 70-1, 75-6, 102; and Clausewitzian reform, 41-83; hard, 57-61; and 'Prisoners' Dilemma', 137, 140; *see also* morality
United Nations Special Session on Disarmament, 48
United States: allies, 34; and Arab-Israeli war, 87-9; and Britain, 173, 175; and China, 115-16; and CRMTC, 171; deterrence strategies, 112, 118-19, 123; flexible response, 35; ideological dogmatism, 42; isolationism, fear of, 119; and Japan, 32, 68-70, 87, 90-1; leadership, 47; and NATO, 12, 58-9, 67, 71-2, 75, 99-103; and nuclear blackmail, 84,

87-9, 93-4; and 'Prisoners' Dilemma', 136, 142-8, 152, 154-5; sanctions on USSR, 81; and Vietnam, 29, 37, 49, 54, 115
UNSSOD, *see* United Nations etc.
USSR, *see* Soviet Union
utility of war, 124

'victory', as meaningless idea, 52-4
Vietnam War, 29, 37, 45, 49, 115

Walzer, M., 41, 78, 81
war: 'absolute', 50-2; Arab-Israeli, 87-9; Britain as target in, 51-2, 67, 76; Cold, 44, 58, 71; Falklands, 22, 33, 60, 96; Gulf, 45; Korean, 37; and politics, unity of, 50-2, 55, 80; prediction of, 46; risks of, 10, 42-6, 51-2, 67, 72-4, 76, 103-4; and Soviet Union, 36, 38, 129; and Third World, 45-6, 54; Vietnam, 29, 37, 45, 49, 115; *see also* invasions
warnings of danger, 161
Warnke, P., 71
Warsaw Pact countries, 8, 64, 72-3, 83, 101, 109; *see also* Europe, Eastern
weapons, *see* missiles
Weinberger, C., 47, 71, 84, 88, 93-4, 110-11
Weiszacker, C.-F. von, 79
Wells, H.G., 37
Williams, F.K., 37, 40
world empire idea, 33

'zero-sum' game, 133-4